Eleven Steps to Building a Profitable Accounting Practice

Eleven Steps to Building a Profitable Accounting Practice

Norman S. Rachlin, CPA

with

Laura Cerwinske

SHEPARD'S/McGRAW-HILL
P.O. Box 1235
Colorado Springs, Colorado 80901

McGRAW-HILL BOOK COMPANY

New York • St. Louis • San Francisco • Colorado Springs
Auckland • Bogotá • Hamburg • Johannesburg • London
Madrid • Mexico • Montreal • New Delhi • Panama • Paris
São Paulo • Singapore • Sydney • Tokyo • Toronto

Library of Congress Cataloging in Publication Data

Rachlin, Norman S.
  Eleven steps to building a profitable accounting practice.

  Includes index.
  1. Accounting firms. I. Cerwinske, Laura.
II. Title.
HF5627.R3 1983   657'.068   82-10106
ISBN 0-07-051103-9

  2 3 4 5 6 7 8 9 0   KGPKGP   8 9 8 7 6

ISBN 0-07-051103-9

The editors for this book were Bonnie K. Binkert and Esther Gelatt, the
designer was Jules Perlmutter, and the production supervisor was Thomas G.
Kowalczyk. It was set in Melior by University Graphics, Inc. Printed and
bound by The Kingsport Press.

I can dedicate my first book to only one person—my wife. She not only made this possible, but also made possible all the joys and pleasures of my life. To Reva, for her patience, understanding, and continuing love.

Contents

Preface

The time has come to change the image of the accountant! Traditionally, the accountant has been viewed as an introverted scorekeeper, making endless historical entries to record the accomplishments of other people. Because of the phenomenal proliferation of financial and tax laws and regulations over a number of years, the need for effective accounting services has been expanding faster than the supply. Public accounting has become more attractive today as a lucrative and professionally rewarding career in increasing demand.

The reticent kind of personality traditionally associated with the accountant, which is often associated with a short-sighted perspective on acquiring new clientele (other than the types already serviced), is not viable for the new dynamics of the profession. This attitude inhibits many an accounting practitioner from accomplishing—or even envisioning—the potential successes available.

Now the time has come for you, as a progressive accountant, to make *yourself* your most important client! The time has come for the public accountant to see far beyond the next trial balance and into a world of unlimited potential, if he is ready to dedicate the time and effort to realize that potential. The time has come to stop thinking in terms of debits equaling credits and to start thinking bigger thoughts. The theme of this book is to accept thinking big in a profession traditionally dedicated to minutiae. "Big" means a goal of more than one million dollars in annual billings per year.

This message is addressed to both women and men in the profession. Today more and more women are entering the field with great success. The goal of a big accounting practice is today as viable for "her" as it is for "him." In the following discussions, therefore, please be aware that though the masculine pronoun may be used to avoid the awkwardness of a repeated "he or she" and "himself or herself," reference to both men and women is to be inferred. And it is meant to indicate that either are capable of achieving the goals set forth.

The steps in building a big accounting practice are in planning, in creating a strong organization, and in creating an imaginative practice development program. By developing self-enthusiasm, a practitioner can learn to be more comfortable in relationships with clients and to improve in selling himself to prospective clients. He can learn how to stimulate motivation in other members of his organization. And by developing imaginative, far-reaching, yet practical goals, he will be able to lift himself beyond the day-to-day routine of meeting deadlines, posting books, and preparing tax forms to the realization of the rewards of building a larger clientele and, of course, the ultimate profits associated with a larger practice.

These are not idle challenges. The author started his own practice 25 years ago with a firm consisting of only himself and his wife. Ten years ago, the firm included seven people. Today there are nearly 100.

This book is not meant to be a promise of instant success to the reader. It is a guide to assist you on a long, difficult journey designed by one who has already traveled the road. As the author often quotes to his partners at times when they are feeling frustrated with the day-to-day problems of servicing clients and operating the practice, "Look, if this were easy, everybody would do it."

The message to his partners and to you is that if building that big accounting practice were a simple matter, then most public accountants in this country would be accomplishing it. But because it requires unique skills, applied in a dedicated fashion, it is a goal reachable only by a select few. Therefore, as in any risk-reward situation, the rewards for accomplishments should be great. And, in fact, they are great—in terms of both compensation and feelings of personal worth and gratification.

Indeed, building that big accounting practice is not an easily attainable goal. But you may be one of those who can accomplish it. The first step toward your big practice requires some introspection and dedication. Without a willingness to really study yourself and without the perseverance to put into action what you learn, the insights this book offers will be of little value. The title of the book may be very stimulating, and the prospects of having such a practice might be an exciting objective, but before you start counting the gross revenues, realize that you would not even have picked up this book if something inside you were not crying (whether meekly or loudly) for change. That change has to begin within yourself.

To apply an appropriate metaphor, you must first look in the mirror and take a detailed "balance sheet" of your own assets and liabilities before you can begin to accurately analyze the current condition and future prospects for you and for your firm. Looking in the mirror might sound like the simplest action in the world, but how many of us have ever taken the time and self-discipline to do just that in a serious way?

Have you ever read or heard stories about people in responsible, high-paying positions who suddenly give it all up and pursue an altogether different course in their lives, like the president of a large chain of retail stores who resigned his job, surrendering a high-paying, prestigious position to pursue a new career as a professor in a small college town? Now there is an individual who probably looked in the mirror.

Certainly our own revelations need not bring about changes as radical as that. And even more certainly, it is not the intention of this book to cause you to abandon your practice for more exotic pursuits. But the story does illustrate the power of inner revelation.

Knowing yourself will give you the knowledge necessary to deal with everything around you. Your own motivation will stimulate action in others. Your changing awareness about yourself will have incredibly far-reaching effects, in more directions than you had ever considered, and your self-enthusiasm will be a foundation for building a large practice.

For example, one of the significant periods in the history of my own firm came about with our first planning session (a full chapter is devoted to planning sessions later). At that initial session we *collectively* looked into the mirror as an entity and said to ourselves, "What kind of firm do we want to be? Who are we now? Where are we going?" In the process of considering these questions, it became apparent to us that one of the partners did not share the same ambitions as all the others. Except for him, every partner wanted a firm which was growing and dynamic, one which could increase by four times its size within five years, expand its services and horizons, one which would reach out into new areas of practice (both geographically and technically). All but the one partner were interested in a very enthusiastic growth approach. He was content with the practice just as it was and was happy doing the things he had always done before: visiting the same clients, bringing order to their books and records, striking a trial balance, reconciling the bank statements, producing regular financial statements and tax returns on a timely basis. Since he was concerned about producing a quality product, he would not trust anyone but himself to get these things done properly. He was resistant to change, reluctant to use staff members, and closed to any new ideas concerning the handling of clients and development of new clients.

Because his philosophy was so contrary to that of all the other partners, it was obvious that ultimately his withdrawal from the firm would be necessary. The general feeling was that not only would the firm profit by being relieved of his resistance, but that he himself would be happier pursuing a personal career more suited to his own style. Unfortunately, the encounter and separation were difficult for this partner to deal with since, at the time, he barely recognized his inner objectives. The pain of this separation could have been avoided if only he had known himself well enough to understand what his personal capabilities and directions were all about. He could have recognized that not all of us are alike, not all of our interests are the same. He could have seen that we can be happiest doing what is most comfortable for ourselves, in a manner that is most suited to ourselves. Fortunately, he subsequently found satisfaction in a smaller firm, and he remains on good terms with our firm today.

There is nothing in the world wrong with having a one-, two-, or three-person practice, so long as it is the kind of practice you will enjoy conducting (and it will bring you an adequate living). After all, not too many people in practice have the executive capabilities necessary to serve as managing partner of one of the "big eight" firms. Or, even on a less impressive scale, there are not many people who can develop and manage a large local practice that runs well over the million-dollar mark.

But one of those people may well be you! As a first step in determining this for yourself, you may want to look into yourself now and start to discover who you really are. There are a number of exercises at the end of the book in Appendix A devoted to the nature of self-exploration.

Other materials in the Appendix include forms and procedures from successful local practices which may be adapted for use in building your practice. Practices, like individuals, may have a number of traits in common, yet each one is unique; therefore, in using materials of others, make sure they are modified to the structure and operations of your practice.

At the end of some of the chapters are appropriate case studies relevant to the topic. Some of them are from the author's experience, others are from the experiences of other practitioners, and only a few are fictional. In all case studies the names are fictitious. You are challenged to develop your approach to the problems presented in the case studies to test your skill in management, a critical ingredient to the practice-building process. The case studies are reviewed, though they typically have no real "solution." But notice how important to each one are the aspects of planning and organizational structure.

Each chapter, or step, in this book is a separate building block designed to reveal to you a specific aspect of both personnel and business development, beginning with the most fundamental. Therefore, each chapter is of itself a whole and complete exploration, which, in its process, prepares you for the progression to the next chapter. You may build on these blocks as far as you feel they are applicable to you. And if you eventually choose to go no further than this introduction and Appendix A, your investment in this book may well have paid off from the important self-realization it can generate, revealing to you more realistic goals. Because this book is based on the author's 25 years of experience in the building of a multimillion-dollar practice, however, its ultimate intent is to stimulate and guide those readers who share the capabilities and desires for the same goal—building a big practice in public accounting.

Norman S. Rachlin, CPA

Acknowledgments

I acknowledge with great appreciation the permission granted by various publishers to use in this book adaptations of material which has appeared in other media, especially:

The Journal of Accountancy (AICPA)
Practitioners' Forum, Journal of Accountancy
The Practical Accountant
The Practicing CPA (AICPA)
Continuing Professional Education Programs (AICPA)

Their friendship, guidance, and encouragement have been a great source of motivation. I thank them all.

Building the Structure

Five major changes in the last decade have had their effects on the accounting profession: greater attention to the quality of life; evolution of the "me" generation; rapid changes in the economy; the age of consumerism; and acceleration of rules and regulations. These changes are among a number of factors prompting CPAs to come increasingly to the realization that they are not only practicing a profession but they are also operating businesses in a very competitive environment. In order to provide quality professional service to clients at a profit to the firm, it is essential that the CPA operates the business in an efficient and effective manner. It has become a fact of contemporary professional life that the public accountant's own business requires more and more time and attention, and that this attention must be given not at the expense of clients but for their benefit as well as for the CPA's.

Surveys of local firms have indicated that among the most serious problems facing them are: (1) insufficient attention to their own practices, (2) lack of management skills, (3) lack of planning, (4) loss of clients, (5) inadequate fee structure, (6) ineffective staff recruitment and training, (7) lack of specialization, and (8) insufficient consideration of their firms' perpetuation. This book addresses these issues and provides—through personal experiences, case histories, examples, and forms—positive actions for your consideration in responding to these challenges.

This opening chapter begins the process by dealing with the basic factors of structuring your firm: defining your service, developing effective controls and forms, billing the client and collecting your fees, and, finally, learning how to become your own best client.

Defining Your Services

One key to distinguishing your practice from the ordinary category into which most people place the local accountant or tax preparer is not only to provide needed services efficiently but also to communicate effectively. The CPA who wants to build a substantial practice should provide services in a professional manner, be distinctive in performance and execution, and do something special for clients in addition to the routine compilation of financial statements, preparation of tax returns, and posting of books, which virtually every other CPA can do. Your ability to do a better job at the basic services is not necessarily a crucial factor in attracting or retaining clients since, for the most part, neither the client nor the public has any real way to judge your work. But your ability to offer distinctive services and *more* services to your clients, your willingness to expand your practice around those extra services and to communicate the value of your services (both the regular and the special), could make a difference in the size and quality of clientele you will attract.

Specialists in public accounting, just as in medicine, tend to command higher fees than general practitioners. Fortunately, there are probably more avenues for specialization open to accountants today than at any other time in the history of the profession. Today practitioners can offer their skills as business, management, and financial advisers. They can also make tax planning a primary rather than a subsidiary service, especially for businesses whose complex strategies (franchising, acquisitions, plant expansion, foreign operations, and new markets) require continuing consultation. Even though your firm may provide business and tax planning services, ask yourself if the firm initiates these services or if, more often than not, they are only initiated at the client's request. If vigorous promotion of your services is not part of your regular activities, then you are overlooking a valuable resource for your firm's development.

A common avenue in developing specialization is the cultivation of particular industries. If you have a few important clients in a certain field, you can begin your growth toward specialization naturally by expanding your knowledge and expertise in that field. Make a conscious effort to understand their nonaccounting problems as well as their unique accounting ones, learn their terminology, absorb the economic implications of the industry, and discover what makes it different from other businesses. Steep yourself in the available knowledge of that field, read everything you can of significance on its related subjects, and develop an original point of view which you can publish or express publicly. Though CPAs are not at present permitted to advertise specialties, you can promote yourself by speaking before interested groups and making your name synonymous with authority on the subject of the selected industry. Once you are known as the firm which is best informed about a particular industry, you will be among the first to be considered by others in that field who need assistance. For example, a firm in a small northern city became known as a specialist in hospital auditing and systems. Eventually this firm developed a multimillion dollar practice serving hospital clients all over the country.

There is nothing to prevent you from developing recognition in more than one field. One partner can hardly keep informed of the continuous developments in more than one or two dynamic fields; however, other partners can contribute to the firm's reputation of specializing, by expanding their knowledge of other industries and disciplines.

One flourishing area in which accounting firms can extend an important capability to their clients (and to professionals who may, in turn, become clients) is that of computer services. A CPA firm with a reasonably sophisticated computer facility can market its capability to provide monthly financial statements, depreciation schedules, amortization schedules, accounts receivable and accounts payable, financial forecasting, estate tax planning, tax projections, business projections, and payrolls with attendant payroll tax reporting.

There is good software available today for the production of individual income tax returns, and more and more firms are beginning to process 1040s internally. Experience indicates that internal processing costs far less than using a commercial tax service, with better turnaround time and more effective control of return processing. (We once had a package of twelve tax returns addressed to a tax preparation service end up in the Atlanta dead letter office at the height of tax season.)

General Ledger Services

General ledger services along with compiled financial statements can continue to be an increasing part of a small business department. The product can be made as simple or as complex as the client's business may require. Of course, the accountant (you) should be instrumental in the design of the reports and in supervising how the system is installed and implemented. This includes giving a clear definition of the functions of the client's personnel and the accountant's.

To illustrate the unique services theory of practice development, let me explain how you might take those extra steps with your general ledger services. First comes the packaging. Each client who is on a monthly reporting service can be furnished with a special three-ring binder. (The binder should be delivered and its uses explained by a partner.) The binder's spine, the part that people see when it is on the shelf, could have your firm name imprinted on it in rather large letters. The cover of the binder could read: A-MAP—Active Management Aids for Profit. The A-MAP concept, emphasizing the *active* use of the monthly reports, could be demonstrated on the top page in the binder (Exhibit 1-1). You can then include twelve divider tabs, one for each month of the client's fiscal year, so that the client can readily file and find reports. Each fiscal year a new binder can be provided in a personal visit to the client.

Don't stop with the packaging. As stated in the binder's preamble, A-MAP means that the monthly reports are not created merely for placement in a file or binder. They are meant to be *active* tools of management for the client and the accountant to use together in the analysis of the client's business with

A-MAP

ACTIVE **M**ANAGEMENT **A**IDS FOR **P**ROFIT:

The Human Equation in Compiling Financial Reports

There is a story about a man who fell overboard a short distance from shore. When he was finally rescued, he was found floundering about nearly a mile out to sea. "I was so busy trying to stay afloat," he explained, "that I just didn't pay attention to which way I was swimming."

Keeping afloat is urgent, but knowing our direction is also important.

That is what *A-MAP* is all about. It is designed to help you see where you have been so that you can chart your future course in a profitable direction.

Here is how *A-MAP* works:

1. We provide this binder and divider tabs for keeping your compiled financial information in an orderly permanent fashion. These are commonly referred to as your "books and records".

2. Your books and records substantiate both your income tax returns and financial statement reporting, if applicable.

3. More importantly, they dynamically report on the operations of YOUR business. If reviewed properly, they tell you not only where you have been, but why. From that comes the active planning to make your future reports more profitable than the past. Indeed, this becomes *A-MAP* for profits.

4. We also peruse your compiled information, and, in fact, maintain a duplicate set. (Ours is a working set, yours are the "official books and records"). In this way, we can work together in many areas, if you desire — budgeting, forecasting, charting sales or income trends, reviewing gross profit or expense ratios, income tax planning, estate planning, projecting capital and financial requirements, cost studies, and preparing the necessary reporting for your implementation.

5. This financial information about your company is compiled in our offices using our own computer equipment. This assures security, confidentiality, and facilitates updating of information. It also permits us to provide special applications and expanded services in an expeditious manner.

   (We would be pleased to give you a tour of our computer facilities at our Coral Gables office).

We welcome the opportunity to review these records with you or to answer any questions that you might have in regard to them.

We urge that these records not be relegated to the archives, but be used as an **A**CTIVE **M**ANAGEMENT **A**ID FOR **P**ROFIT!

Together we can work to make these records *A-MAP* for profit.

a goal of improving profits. I'm sure that most practitioners would endorse this goal, much as most Americans endorse the flag, motherhood, and apple pie. But while it sounds commendable—how can it be reached? Or does it become merely lip service? The work should not stop with the completion of the monthly report. Not only should the figures be subject to key number analysis, but you should be concerned also with the follow-up of whatever is of concern to the client. A standardized analysis form (Exhibit 1-2) can be completed by the staff person on the engagement, reviewed by a supervisor, and followed up by a partner.

This is just one way that computer services can become an important part of your practice and its growth. The requirements on business to maintain records are certainly not diminishing. We can anticipate that records will continue to be handled by computers at an increasing rate. This presents one great opportunity for accountants who are alert and able to provide needed computer services to their present and future clients.

Identifying the Market

Consider for a moment the number of businesses which have a need—and recognize it—for a business adviser, a tax planner, a budgeting expert, a computer service bureau. Retailers, wholesalers, manufacturers, and service companies all need one or a combination of these services. And who is in a better position to provide the services than the professional who knows the company's business and also has the knowledge and experience in the needed consulting areas—the CPA.

Do not expect, however, that the very largest public corporations or the small-minded business operators will be a viable part of your market. The giant corporations usually have their own in-house support and turn to national firms because their business is national or international in scope. The smaller business owner who is only concerned with how much must be spent for your service is probably not open to normal risk taking and thus can achieve only the most limited measure of success, none of which would be willingly attributed to you. Go for that almost unlimited market between these two extremes and present yourself with the approach that you are there not only to function in the standard capacity of preparing statements and tax returns, but that you can offer a great deal more which could prove valuable to the client's business and family.

Scheduling a Year-Round Workload

Many local practitioners tend to have an excessive workload in the months of January through April and in the other eight months not enough of a workload to keep personnel productive at a high level.

SERVICE ANALYSIS

It is important to compile financial information accurately. However, any competent accountant, bookkeeper or other financial person can do just that. What distinguishes you as a professional, and we as a firm, is the <u>constructive purpose</u> made of that financial data. How can it be used to HELP the client - spotting trends, reducing costs, tax planning, estate planning, making his business more profitable? We (you as a professional, we as a firm) are measured daily in the market place by how well we service our clients.

This SERVICE ANALYSIS is designed with that philosophy in mind. It is not meant as a compilation exercise to be buried in the client's file. It is a means to help us to help our clients in providing the highest form of professional service.

PART	TYPE OF SERVICE	TO BE COMPILED BY
I.	General	Staff Person
II.	Statistical	Staff Person
III.	Narrative	Staff Person
IV.	Review	Supervisor
V.	Action	P.I.C.

PART I. GENERAL SERVICE

(THIS PORTION CAN BE PHOTOCOPIED EACH MONTH, OR CARRIED FORWARD)

CLIENT_____Number_____

EDP No._____ **Year End**_____

TYPE OF BUSINESS_____SIC NO._____

Following are key financial items from most recently completed fiscal year:

BALANCE SHEET		STATEMENT OF OPERATIONS	
CURRENT ASSETS	$_____	SALES (INCOME)	$_____
CURRENT LIABILITIES	$_____	GROSS PROFIT	_____ %
TOTAL ASSETS	$_____	TAXABLE INCOME	$_____
TOTAL LIABILITIES	$_____	OFFICERS (OWNERS) COMP.	$_____
NET WORTH	$_____	PENSION AND/OR PROFIT SHARING PLAN CONTRIB.	$_____
OTHER KEY ITEMS:		OTHER KEY ITEMS:	
_____	_____	_____	_____
_____	_____	_____	_____

For the month and _____ months ending _____

	CURRENT YEAR		PRIOR YEAR	
	MONTH	YTD	MONTH	YTD
Statement of Operations				
Sales/Income	$	$	$	$
Gross Profit %	%	%	%	%
Net Earnings/(Loss)				
Operating Expense				
☐ Includes Below ☐ Excludes Below Officers/Owners Comp.				
Pension and/or P.S. Plan Contrib.				
Other Key Items:				
_____				
_____				
Balance Sheet:				
Current Assets		$		$
Current Liabilities				
Net Worth				
Other Key Items:				
_____				
_____				

	YES	NO*	N/A
Have all Year-End Schedules been update?	☐	☐	☐
Will all tax returns be prepared on a timely basis?	☐	☐	☐

1) Income (Federal and State) _____   2) Intangible _____
   Date Completed   Date Completed

3) Tangible _____   4) Annual Report _____
   Date Completed   Date Completed

5) Other _____
   Date Completed

Have all Payroll Tax Deposits been made on a timely basis?	☐	☐	☐
Have all Income Tax Deposits been made on a Timely Basis?	☐	☐	☐

(*If NO, explain)

7

PART III. NARRATIVE SERVICE

A. I noted the following extraordinary expenses, statistics, or problem areas:

_____

_____

_____

B. I had the following discussions and/or recommendations with client:

_____

_____

_____

C. The client appears concerned about:_____

_____

_____

D. Problems I am having on this engagement:_____

_____

_____

E. I suggest P.I.C. contact client regarding:_____

_____

_____

F. Other comments or suggestions (Such as: additional services, referrals, plan-

ning meetings, etc.):_____

_____

_____

_____

_____

_____   _____
            PREPARER   DATE

PART IV. REVIEW SERVICES
(Check applicable boxes)

[ ]   Reviewed Financial Information

[ ]   Reviewed Service Analysis Sheet

[ ]   Discussed with preparer

[ ]   Other Discussions or action taken: _____
_____
_____

[ ]   My Recommendations: _____
_____
_____

_____   _____
REVIEWER   DATE

PART V. ACTION SERVICES

P.I.C. to indicate positive actions taken: _____
_____
_____
_____
_____
_____
_____
_____
_____
_____
_____

_____   _____
PIC   DATE

This extreme workload variation can lead to other problems within a firm, such as poor scheduling of engagements, erratic production, late delivery of reports, and an excessive number of tax return extensions. By affecting client service and resulting in staff turnover, poor planning to handle workload variation may lead to a firm's eventual decline. A year-round practice development program, directed at leveling off the workload (at a high level, of course), can help avoid problems. The goal of such a program is to make those other eight months more productive (and more profitable) and enable the firm to obtain and retain qualified personnel.

Instead of fighting the calendar, you should use it to advantage by means of the following actions: List all services which your firm has available during those other eight months and communicate this information to your clients. This information is communicated through firm newsletters, seminars, direct mail pieces, and other methods described in STEP 5 on practice development. Involve your professional staff in the implementation of these services. A typical list might include tax planning services such as retirement plans, income allocations, tax shelters, reorganizations, liquidations, exchange of property, 1244 stock, Subchapter-S corporation, medical reimbursement, incorporating a business, income averaging, loss carrybacks, and depreciation methods.

In the estate planning area the list might include estate tax projections, trusts, gifts, probate and administration expenses, assistance in will preparation and estate planning questionnaires. As to financial planning, services might cover budgets, projections, bank loans, other borrowings, stock sales, investments, refinancing, and personal financial statements. In the business counseling area, coverage might include short- and long-range plans, buy-sell agreements, recapitalization, change of fiscal year, insurance programs, accounting manuals, recordkeeping systems, assistance in litigation mergers and acquisitions, and addition of partners, stockholders, or other investors.

This is meant only as a guide. Each firm, of course, could develop its own list suited to the abilities and background of personnel and to individual capabilities.

Organizing Your Practice

There is no one-size-fits-all blueprint for the organizational structure of an accounting practice. Every organization is as unique as the individuals within it, and what makes one organization work effectively may not be appropriate for another. There are, however, certain characteristics common to all accounting practices. Specifically, every firm should have one responsible leader (managing partner) and at least three professional departments: accounting and auditing, tax, and managing consulting services.

Your firm should have an organizational chart and assigned responsibilities (Appendix C). A committee form of management can be adopted by a large firm as a viable means of participation in management.

Each committee can consist of three or more members, including partners, principals, managers, and supervisors. The managing partner serves ex officio on all committees. One member is appointed as the chairperson. In many firms the managing partner is automatically chairperson of the steering (executive) committee. In other firms the managing partner may serve as a voting or nonvoting member of such a committee.

The committees are not intended to usurp the authority of the partners, but through their effective functioning they can decide routine matters and make recommendations to the partners without all partners having to be involved in all matters.

As your practice grows larger, you may develop the increasingly uncomfortable feeling that you no longer know everything that is going on in the firm. And you may find yourself faced with deep fears of contingent liability and exposure lurking in every dark corner. This is the downside risk of growing large, for with prestige and additional income come these additional problems. The only way to eliminate risks totally is to do nothing. Unfortunately, that prospect is neither pleasurable nor profitable.

Instigation of controls in your practice should begin when your firm is small. It is much easier to do it then, and the controls will be more easily absorbed through practice. They become a foundation upon which the firm grows. A numbering system for clients, time-keeping records, billing procedures, file composition and controls, standardization of workpapers and reports, and engagement letters are but a few kinds of controls that should be developed early in the firm's history.

In Appendix D some of the procedures and control forms (other than tax department forms and practice development material, covered in separate chapters) are presented for consideration. They have been tested and found to serve the goals of a well-managed practice, minimizing mistakes and decreasing the risk of exposure.

Measuring Your Practice

Take a look at your own practice and perhaps gain some insight into the effectiveness of your structure. Complete the exercise in Exhibit 1-3 about your firm for the year that has most recently ended.

Does this very general evaluation reveal that your fee structure is adequate to provide appropriately for the incomes expected by you, your partners, and your staff as well as for the proper maintenance (and projected expansion) of your firm? (Covered in STEP 2.) Does it indicate you are on the right track to reaching your goals? (Covered in STEP 10.) These statistics should be measured and plotted on an annual basis to chart the firm's growth and improve-

EXHIBIT 1-3. **Management Statistics**

1. Standard fees per person	$_____
2. Standard fees per professional staff (including partners)	_____
3. Standard fees per administrative person	_____
4. Standard fees per partner	_____
5. Net fees per person	_____
6. Standard fees per chargeable hour—professional personnel	_____
7. Standard fees per chargeable hour—professional plus administrative personnel	_____
8. Net fees per chargeable hour—professional staff (effective billing rate)	_____
9. Net income per partner (prior to deducting partners' salaries)	_____
10. Salaries—professional (including partners) per chargeable hour	_____
11. Salaries—total (including administrative) per chargeable hour	_____
12. Operating expenses per chargeable hour	_____
13. Net income per chargeable hour	_____
14. Permanent capital—partners (total) to net income (prior to partners' salaries)	_____ to 1
15. Number of days of billed and unbilled receivables outstanding in relation to standard fees	_____ days

ment—or failure to achieve them. What's a good score? *A good score would be how well you did against your plan and your budget for the year.* If you wish to measure your results against others, consult Section 5, "Management Data," of the *Management of an Accounting Practice Handbook,* American Institute of Certified Public Accountants (AICPA), 1981.

Other standards against which you might wish to measure your practice were offered at a recent practice seminar. The speaker stated that a survey of firms in a national association tried to distinguish between the most successful and the least successful firms since, from outward appearances, they all seemed to be the same or similar. The distinguishing characteristics are shown in Table 1-1.

With these criteria we might summarize the formula for success as: Invest in more and better people (who put in more chargeable hours) per partner.

TABLE 1-1. **Distinguishing Characteristics of Least and Most Successful Firms**

	10 Percent Least Successful	10 Percent Most Successful
1. Gross fees per partner	$115,000	$183,000
2. Average net income per partner	$ 36,000	$ 81,000
3. Persons per partner	2.9	4.4
4. Average chargeable hours per person*	1,267	1,453
5. Recruiting costs		Much higher

*Persons: all members of firm (partners and professional and administrative people).

Being Your Own Best Client

Probably the most important single rule I can give you is: Be your own best client. Let me illustrate with the sad story of Rosalinda "Rosie" Diaz.

When Rosie first established her practice, she was an eager and unflagging go-getter. The momentum of starting up and generating business carried her with reasonable success through the first three years. But by the fifth anniversary of the firm, both her energy and the growth rate of the practice had tapered off. Seeing clients, executing their work, and keeping reasonably informed about the administration of the firm took up almost 14 hours of every working day. She never attended professional meetings anymore, and except for an occasional lunch with her attorney, she never got to spend time with other members of the professional community.

Finally Rosie realized that she had lost control of her practice, that in fact it was running her, she was not running it. She immediately registered for an upcoming practice management program. She sat through every workshop and lecture relevant to her practice, took copious notes, underlined key ideas on page after page of her reference material, and returned home feeling inspired. All weekend long she dreamed about the changes she was going to implement and the new growth potential they would generate. Monday morning she brought all the seminar material to her office, carefully arranged it on the shelves above her desk, and proceeded to jump frantically into the day's schedule. Two years later, Rosie collapsed from exhaustion due to overwork and her firm, whose volume had already shrunk measurably, was bought out by a local competitor. Where did she go wrong?

Rosie's problem was an obvious and, unfortunately, all too common one. Though she was wise enough to have realized that she needed help in gaining control over her business, she neglected to put into practice what she should have learned from her lectures, references, and detailed notes. All of Rosie's carefully gathered materials sat untouched on the shelf above her desk from the very day she arranged them there. And because she never followed through, her practice continued to grow increasingly out of her control. Though Rosie was ready to work herself into a state of exhaustion and jeopardize everything she had built, she was not ready to make herself her own best client and take to heart the kind of guidance she so studiously gave out to those who came to her for professional service.

Had Rosie also made the effort to evaluate her working habits from time to time, as with the exercises in Appendix A, she would have become aware of those aspects of her own personal life style which were restraining her from fulfilling her potential. She would have realized that she needed to set priorities, delegate more of the responsibilities which she seemed to feel only she could administer, and establish target dates for projects, so that plans would not get pushed by the wayside because of perpetual deadlines. By being so tied down with uncontrollable time, she could not properly supervise her staff, and by being preoccupied with "all the things that had to get done," she failed to expose herself to situations which could have produced new clients or which would have kept her informed of new developments in accounting, business areas, and clients' industries.

Being your own most important client is, in essence, the philosophical foundation around which your firm's structure must be developed. Operating your practice as a business, defining your services, developing specializations and conscientiously communicating them to your clients, billing adequately and promptly (STEP 2), and being knowledgeable about the potential as well as the drawbacks of acquisitions and mergers (STEP 9) will give your practice a healthy and firm structure upon which it can grow.

Treating yourself as your own best client is not a selfish concept. Far from it! In being your own best client you will end up with the best-trained staff, the most capable technicians, and the best products, all to the effect of quality service provided to your clients on a timely basis. Next time somebody asks you who your most important client is, answer, "I am."

Building the Fees

Because the foundation of the accounting profession is advising business, it is inexcusable for a good accountant to be a bad business person. Intrinsic to being a good business person is the control of the financial integrity of the practice through its cash flow, generated by an effective system for determining, billing and collecting fees. Since there are many methods, from divine inspiration to strict formulas, for developing these aspects of the fee system, it is your responsibility to decide what is both adequate and appropriate for your practice to charge and for your clients to be charged.

There are many variables involved in the fee setting process, such as the various services you perform, the type of client, the type of engagement, the time spent on the job, the skill and experience of the staff required, the timing of the work, and the sophistication of the equipment required. Also to be considered are the ability of the client to pay, the customary level of fees for a particular service, the urgency of the job, applicable legal factors, whether the client is established or casual, and whether or not you are operating on a contingent or fixed fee basis. The fees you charge should also reflect what it costs you to maintain a respectable office with modern equipment and an up-to-date library, to compensate a high-caliber staff for whom you will provide continuing professional education, and what it will take to provide you with a suitable standard of living, ample leisure, retirement security, and time to participate in professional societies and community activities. *You will find that your own valuation of your worth has a strong effect upon the client's opinion of your worth.* If your firm is primarily engaged in professional service at a truly professional level, you have a right to expect professional fees. If your firm is a bookkeeping service and your demeanor is that of an unimpressive clerk, that too could have an impact on the setting and acceptance of your fees.

If you think that putting together consolidated financial statements for a U.S. conglomerate with foreign subsidiaries, including conversion to U.S. dollars and excluding minority interests, is a difficult task, just wait until you start doing your first billings to clients. It is indeed a difficult task because you want to be fair to the client, to be able to retain the client, and to readily collect the fee; yet you also want to make sure that you are adequately compensated for your professional services. This is a delicate act of balancing several objectives. Perhaps the most successful practitioners are those who are able to obtain the highest compensation for themselves while convincing the client that full value has been received. This, of course, involves the rendering of valuable professional services and the client's realizing that is what was received.

Your billing policies should provide a net income equal to:

1. A realistic salary, equivalent perhaps to that required to hire someone to perform the practitioner's duties.
2. A return on the capital investment comparable to that which could be achieved if the money was otherwise invested.
3. A proprietary share—a reasonable amount which can be considered as the return to the principal for accepting the responsibility for conducting the practice. This represents the true profit of the accounting practice itself, for the other portions of the total net income generally can be realized without establishing or maintaining the practice.

A step-by-step formula which illustrates how billing rates can be appropriately calculated for a sole practitioner, particularly one who is first starting out in practice, is shown in Exhibit 2-1.

Billing Rates for the Experienced Practitioner

Robert Jackson (a fictitious name) and I were junior accountants together. We both left the firm at about the same time to begin our own practices in different parts of the country. We hadn't seen each other for nearly twenty years when, upon being invited to present a seminar in his city, we had the occasion to enjoy a reunion.

After dinner and much good conversation, Mrs. Jackson mentioned how hard Bob worked and asked me if most of the successful CPAs I knew worked as hard as her husband. He brought work home five nights a week, always worked a full Saturday, and took time off only on Sundays. *All* the partners in the firm worked equally hard, and she felt public accounting was a terribly demanding profession.

The next day I visited Bob's office. He had an impressive practice, one of the leading independent firms in the city with a long, respectable history and an impressive roster of long-term clients. I noticed that their workpapers, standards, and finished products—while a bit old-fashioned—were of outstanding quality. When Bob and I got around to discussing fees, he very proudly explained his firm's system to me. "It's so easy to calculate," he said.

EXHIBIT 2-1.   **Billing Rates for a New Practice (Sole Practitioner)**

Steps	Example of Calculations		Your Own Calculations
1. Total projected office expenses for one year (rent, salaries, other overhead)	$20,000	$	
2. Personal net income goal (realistic annual salary)	40,000		
3. Return on capital investment in furnishings, supplies, equipment, deposits, working capital; $10,000, interest factor 20 percent	2,000		
4. "Proprietor's profit," say 50 percent of personal income goal. (This is a totally *arbitrary* determination.)	20,000		
Total	$82,000		
5. Divide by .90 (90 percent effective collections) = projected gross	$91,111	$	
6. Divide by estimated billable hours for one year	1,700 hours		hours
Hourly billing rate	$53.29	$	
Hourly billing rate (rounded)	$53.00, $54.00, or $55.00	$	

"All you do is move the decimal point." His formula was based on dividing a staff person's compensation by 2,000 hours and multiplying the answer by 2. For example, if a staff person were paid $18,000 per year, his hourly rate would be $18 ($18,000 ÷ 2,000 × 2 = $18). Simple, I thought. But that was the very reason Bob and his partners were overworking! They had to compensate with more and more hours for the deficiency in their billing rates. By more progressive standards, that same staff person could have been billed at $32 per hour instead of $18 if calculated as follows:

1. Divide $18,000 by 1,700 hours = $10.59
2. Multiply by 3 = $31.77
3. Round to $32 per hour

There is quite a difference between $18 and $32 per hour charged for the same work by the same person. Certainly, local market conditions unique to any area have a bearing on the hourly rates which Bob's firm could charge. But it was shocking to me that a CPA firm which deals in financial concepts regularly, and is a *counselor* to business in these subjects, could be so casual about its own business that it would adopt a billing rate formula primarily for ease of calculation.

Of course, I have heard equally surprising answers when I ask practitioners all over the country how they determine their billing rates. They have responded: "Whatever I can get." "I think $35 is pretty good." "I think it's what my old firm used to charge." "Low enough not to lose any of my clients. They're too hard to come by." These answers are infuriating. For a CPA to neglect the use of his own professional talents in the management of his own practice is as inexcusable as the dentist who lets his teeth rot. It contradicts the fundamental principle that your own practice is your most important client.

A Cost Accounting Billing Strategy

The following three-step procedure in calculating billing rates is not proposed as a standard for the profession. Rather, it is an attempt to apply one's own accounting skills to public practice. And perhaps to provoke you to reevaluate your own billing policies.

The elements for setting a selling price in a typical cost accounting manner are: materials, labor, overhead, and profit. Since we have virtually no materials, let us consider labor, overhead, and profit.

1. Labor: My friend Bob divided annual compensation by 2,000 hours. Some firms divide by 2,080 hours (52 weeks at 40 hours per week). Neither of these is truly effective! Staff compensation is but one element of cost (labor) in determining selling price (billing rate). You can only recover your cost from units which are sold—that is, hours which are billed. Therefore, the annual compensation of the staff person can only be recovered from the chargeable hours which are billed (sold) to clients. Experience has shown that a typical staff person will average about 1,700 billable hours per year. Therefore, if we bill 1,700 hours of time and the billing rate includes $10.59 for the staff person's compensation (as in our prior example), we would recover the $18,000 salary cost. (Some firms add payroll taxes, insurance, and other fringe benefits to compensation before dividing. In this example, those costs are included in the overhead, item 2).
2. Overhead: Determine your overhead costs for the year (rent, insurance, administrative payroll, telephone, payroll taxes, paper supplies, computer costs, etc.). In this example, we assume that overhead *equals* the total annual professional staff payroll. Therefore, if 1 hour's labor costs $10.59, overhead cost should also be $10.59, or a ratio of 1 to 1.
3. Profit: This is an arbitrary decision to be made by a firm. In this example it is determined to make a 33⅓ percent profit on the sales price for products produced by staff members. (Some firms may be satisfied with 20 or 25 percent, others may seek as much as 40 or 45 percent. A good goal is 33⅓ percent, which appears to be competitive with the profit of other quality firms furnishing similar services.) To get a 33⅓ percent profit you would

have to add 50 percent to your total cost. Therefore, if labor and overhead are the only two costs, and they are equal to each other, to get your selling price you would add an equal amount for profit ($10.59 + $10.59 at 50 percent = $10.59).

To summarize the cost accounting example and the multiplication by 3:

Elements of Selling Price	Amount	Factor	Percent	At 1,700 Billing Hours (Sales)
Labor cost	$10.59	1	33⅓	$18,000
Overhead cost	10.59	1	33⅓	18,000
Profit	10.59	1	33⅓	18,000
Billing rate	$31.77	3	100	$54,000
Rounded to	$32.00			

This particular employee, realizing 1,700 chargeable hours, should thus produce $54,000 of gross billings for the firm, of which $18,000 covers his salary, $18,000 is contributed to firm overhead, and $18,000 is added to firm income.

Extending this concept, the firm should expect its gross revenue to equal three times its professional staff payroll *plus* the billings generated by the partners. The staff generated payroll should absorb the firm's overhead. Therefore, the firm's net income (before any compensation for partners) should be an amount equal to total professional staff compensation plus the amount billed by partners, as shown in Exhibit 2-2.

The illustration indicates a profit of over 55 percent. That is exceptional for a firm with more than a few partners. In fact, the larger a firm grows, the lower the percentage. (Recent annual reports of national firms indicate about 35 percent net.) However, as the percentage may decline, the *total dollars*

EXHIBIT 2-2. Profit and Loss Statement for the Year Ending December 31, 19XX

Gross revenue	
Billed for staff professionals' time	$600,000
Billed for partners' time	300,000
Total gross revenue	$900,000
Operating expenses	
Staff compensation (⅓ of $600,000)	$200,000
Overhead, all other expenses (equal to staff compensation)	200,000
Total operating expenses	400,000
Net income (before partners' compensation)	$500,000
This is equal to:	
Staff compensation	$200,000
Billing for partners' time	300,000
Total net income	$500,000

should be increasing, as should a most important statistic—average net earnings per partner (net income divided by number of partners).

All these steps are intended to maximize the firm's income, keeping in mind that these are the goals and, as goals, they should be set high but should also be realistic. Some of the elements which can keep you from realizing the goal are markdowns, excessive bad debts, poor scheduling, loss of clients, and increased overhead expenses. And those are all reflections of the firm's management.

One other interesting note about the "times 3" formula. As payroll is increased through raises (for whatever reasons), the resulting billing rate after multiplying by 3 should accommodate your related increases in overhead expenses. Billing rates should be adjusted whenever there are increases in staff compensation.

ROUNDING UP

In a billing strategy, it is suggested to round up to at least the next whole dollar. In our example, the calculation was rounded up from $31.77 to $32, but even if the figure had been $31.27, it should still have been rounded up to $32. Some firms round up to the nearest $5, which would have made the billing rate $35. How, or whether, you round up your own billing rate is a matter of firm policy. *The primary factor to always keep in mind is that while you are practicing a profession, you are also operating a business.*

The two exercises shown in Exhibits 2-3 and 2-4 will give you an opportunity to interpret billing rates with regard to the discussions in this chapter.

There is no single correct answer to Exercise 2 (Exhibit 2-4). It merely draws your attention to the many elements which must be considered in the delicate art of billing.

Do you bill less for a first time engagement?
Do you bill for typing time?
Do you bill for copies?
Do you round off a bill?
Do you use a billing draft? (Exhibit D-5)

The only "right" answers, of course, are those appropriate to the style of practice which the partners have adopted for the firm.

A firm's policies regarding fees evolves as a synthesis of most of its experience and of some or all of the factors which have been presented here. That policy should express the basic considerations of establishing a viable fee structure. A firm's fee policy may be stated as follows:

A Fee Policy

A number of factors are taken into account in establishing an equitable fee— equitable to the client as well as to the professional. These factors include

EXHIBIT 2-3a   Exercise 1: Billing Rates and Effect on Gross Profit

The following approach to calculating billing rates uses professional personnel salary cost as a base. With this method you can, using various multipliers, project its effect on gross billing and gross profit. Calculate the following, assuming: *An annual salary of $20,000 and annual billable hours of 1,700.*

	1. Annual Salary	2. + (Hours)	3. × Multiplier	4. Hourly Rate	5. Potential Annual Billing	6. Contribution to Firm's Gross Profit
A.	20,000	2,080	2	$ _____	$ _____	$ _____
B.	20,000	2,080	2½	_____	_____	_____
C.	20,000	2,080	3	_____	_____	_____
D.	20,000	2,080	3½	_____	_____	_____
E.	20,000	1,700	2	_____	_____	_____
F.	20,000	1,700	2½	_____	_____	_____
G.	20,000	1,700	3	_____	_____	_____
H.	20,000	1,700	3½	_____	_____	_____
I.	20,000		(a)	_____	_____	_____
J.	20,000		(b)	_____	_____	_____
K.	20,000		(c)	_____	_____	_____

Column 3: for items I, J, K use these formulas:
    (a) 2 percent of monthly salary, per hour
    (b) .0015 of annual salary, per hour
    (c) A daily rate of 1 percent of annual salary cost ($200 per day ÷ 8 hours)
Column 5: column 4 multiplied by 1,700 (annual billable hours assumed above)
Column 6: column 5 less column 1

EXHIBIT 2-3b   Solution to Exercise 1

	4. Hourly Rate	5. Potential Annual Billing	6. Contribution to Firm's Gross Profit
A.	19.23	$32,692	$12,692
B.	24.04	40,865	20,865
C.	28.85	49,038	29,038
D.	33.65	57,212	37,212
E.	23.53	40,000	20,000
F.	29.41	50,000	30,000
G.	35.29	60,000	40,000
H.	41.18	70,000	50,000
I.	33.33	56,667	36,667
J.	30.00	51,000	31,000
K.	25.00	42,500	22,500

the time involved, the degree of responsibility, the skill of the practitioner, the difficulty of the assignment, and the results accomplished. Of all the standards, time has been the most easy to measure and the most commonly used.

We, therefore, would consider a time basis as the minimum determining standard for fees. The hourly fee rates are established effective January 1, 19XX.

EXHIBIT 2-4   **Exercise 2: Billing an Engagement**

You have been engaged by a new client, a small manufacturing concern, to prepare a reviewed financial statement and federal income tax return for the corporation's fiscal year. The client has a bookkeeper who enters the journals, prepares payroll tax reports, and reconciles the bank statements. The fee arrangement, according to the engagement letter, is "at standard hourly rates." How would you calculate the bill for this engagement?

Service	By	Hours	Hourly Rate	Amount
Posting general ledger and trial balance	Junior staff person	8	$ _____	$ _____
Adjusting entries and statement preparation	You	10	_____	
Tax return preparation	Senior staff person	4	_____	_____
Review of tax return	You	2	_____	_____
Typing, proofing, photocopying, and binding	Statistical typist	6	_____	_____
Photocopies (50)	Copy machine	XX	XX _____	_____
Delivery and explanation of report and return	You	2	_____	_____
Total				_____
Rounded off				_____

OTHER CONSIDERATIONS

1. In the case of estate tax returns and income tax returns, the fee can be based on a percentage of the gross estate or of the tax savings effected.
2. In the case of acquisitions, mergers, business combinations, and special engagements, the fee may be set as a fixed amount prior to accepting the engagement.
3. In addition to hourly rates specified, *minimum* fee standards are to be maintained due to the amount of overhead costs inherent in *all* matters processed through the office.
4. Fee policies for individual income tax returns are to be established prior to the beginning of each tax season.
5. Retainer fees are required in advance where substantial new services are anticipated.
6. Where fees become unreasonably delinquent the right is reserved to suspend service.

It is important that the client be fully aware of the fee basis before any job begins, and that he be kept apprised of the accumulated fees as a job progresses. Billing should be done on a regular basis. Should circumstances warrant, time record information may be made available for discussion with a client.

A classic story, which illustrates the importance of the value of services, is told of a surgeon who, after rendering a $5,000 bill for an operation which took one hour, received a call from the irate patient protesting the "exorbitant" fee. The patient demanded an itemized bill. The following bill was promptly sent to the patient:

Time spent in operating room	$ 200
Visits to hospital	400
Knowing where to cut	4,400
Total	$5,000

Having measured the many factors involved in determining appropriate fees, it is then essential to formalize the three basic steps remaining in a billing system: (1) confirming the client's agreement, (2) billing the client, and (3) collecting the fee.

Setting the Fee

Effective communication with a client *before* an engagement is undertaken reduces the chance of the client's being surprised or unhappy with the size of the fee when the job is completed. Often clients are unaware of the amount of time, skills, or processes involved in accomplishing their engagement. By taking the time to help them *understand* quality and scope of services, you should be able to convince them that they are receiving anticipated professional service for their money. After your discussion, advise your client that you will be sending an engagement letter which details your services and related cost. This is the best way to avoid misunderstanding and prevent problems of dissatisfaction at the end of a job.

Engagement letters are critical documents in forestalling (or preventing) subsequent controversies, including unwanted legal actions (see STEP 8). They are not only recommended, they are encouraged. A booklet by the AICPA, "Sample Engagement Letters for An Accounting Practice," 1974, will provide you with numerous examples of letters on the various types of services your firm may provide.

Guidelines on Billing

Even the process of billing can be an opportunity for communicating your professionalism to the client. By sending an *itemized* statement of services, you are not only substantiating your fees, you are also informing the client of what has been accomplished.

Two types of billing are generally used. In a retainer billing system, which is usually for predetermined fixed fees, the accountant bills the client a fixed amount at regular intervals. The other method is to base bills on rates per hour of service. This system frequently includes progress billings, in which the client is billed periodically for the work done to date. Regardless of the system, by being sure your statements are sent promptly and with regularity you reinforce the client's perception of the professionalism with which you operate. A firm can use both methods, adopting the method to the specific needs of each client.

Here are some hints on billing:

1. Make sure the client's name is properly spelled, the address is accurate, and the invoice is professional in appearance.
2. Mail an original and a copy of the invoice so that the copy can be returned with the payment for identification.
3. Enclose a self-addressed postage-paid envelope. It is a small cost to advance for accelerating cash flow.
4. Bill regularly, at least once a month.
5. Develop standard billing descriptions, using code numbers for each item. This speeds up the billing process and standardizes firm billing for statistical purposes.
6. Accumulate all potential billing at standard billing rates and monitor regularly each billing person's actual billing against the standard.
7. Get the bills out as soon after the end of each month as is possible.
8. Distribute monthly billing statistics of the entire firm to each partner.
9. If you rarely receive a complaint about bills, you may not be billing enough. The market should be tested.

Collecting Your Fees

Because you have greater access to your client's records than almost any other creditor, you are in an excellent and knowledgeable position to evaluate the client's financial status. The new client's credit standing and integrity are important considerations which will enable you to minimize uncollectable accounts. A prior agreement on the time as well as the amount of payment is helpful in keeping your collectables current.

In spite of all these precautions, accounts still become past due. It is a constant task of monitoring, for it is all too easy for a client to put the accountant's bill at the bottom of the pile. It is up to you to keep that from happening! Set a firm standard for receivables you are willing to carry. Since you're not a bank, perhaps the limit of your receivables and work in process should be 25 percent of annual billings. Here are some important considerations which can be of help in collecting receivables:

1. Collections are the direct responsibility of each partner. Statistics must be provided monthly. Statistics of collections and past due balances are an influence on a partner's annual compensation.
2. A series of automatic collection letters and phone calls should be established. The first call should be from your office manager or bookkeeper to

the client's bookkeeper to verify mutual balances, provide missing invoices, and determine potential collection problems.

3. Each partner must respond monthly in writing as to action taken on past due accounts.

4. Detailed monthly statements of account should be sent to clients.

5. Service is suspended when a client becomes delinquent.

6. Delinquent clients are encouraged to provide promissory notes. These notes can then be discounted with your bank. It provides you with cash flow and leaves the client to deal with a banker, not you, as collector. It removes you from the "bad guy" role. The client is more concerned about his credit standing with a banker than with his CPA.

7. Many of these actions occur *after* the fact. When a client looks financially shaky, consider obtaining a personal guarantee and a retainer before work commences.

8. Consider using a Profitability Impact Report, Exhibit D-15. It works this way: After the receptionist completes a daily location report (which states where everyone is working and for which client), a copy goes to the internal accounting department. If there is no engagement letter, or the balance is past due, the report goes to the partner with a copy to the managing partner. The partner is required to respond within 24 hours. This program is designed to catch a problem before it develops into a major collection matter.

Building a Partnership

In order to operate a large public accounting practice, it is vital to recognize that such a business cannot be handled by one person alone. Numerous time constraints, productivity limitations, skill limitations, and other factors preclude one individual from conducting this type of a heavy dollar business on a solo basis.

This, then, leads us into a series of situations and evaluations that bring us to a major decision point: Are you willing and able to share your practice? While you may have all of the attributes necessary for conducting a big dollar practice, you may not necessarily be able to accomplish this in concert with other professionals who will be functioning with you on a peer level and whose input will be significant. Operating as a sole practitioner, in complete control of a practice and accountable to no one, is a comfortable position for some people. However, it can also be limiting to the growth and development of a practice. In order to develop into an expansive practice, that autonomy and sole discretionary control must be sublimated to the goals, directions, and operations of a *firm*. The firm then becomes a new entity, one which is not a reflection of any one individual, but rather a composite of features of many individuals. That composite, it is hoped, will result in a blending of the best qualities of all those who contribute.

The concepts of compromise and of subjugating individual interests to the interests of the firm may not be wholly accepted until the practitioner realizes and appreciates that a success *as part of the organization* can far exceed one's individual success. This may be a difficult issue for many aspiring firm members, for the trade-offs involved create important individual decisions involving career choices.

The Delicate Nature of the Partner Relationship

These points can be illustrated by an event that occurred within my own firm. The event concerned a junior partner whom I shall call Domenick

Lombardi. Dom was about 32 years old when this happened and had been a partner in the firm for almost four years. Because of the firm's rapid growth and his ideal position with regard to his age, Dom's future seemed to be flourishing in the field he had chosen and entered immediately upon graduating from college.

In his eagerness to perform well and demonstrate his enthusiasm when he was first made a partner, Dom had tried to involve himself in every aspect of the firm. The dilution of his energies and attention because of this self-proclaimed crusade caused the inevitable failure of many projects. Eventually, Dom realized the futility of this attitude and directed himself toward his specialization and the supervision of a manageable number of the firm's clients. In time he became extremely productive and was billing out a highly acceptable level of business each month. At the time of this story, his earnings were in excess of $60,000 and Dominick seemed to be developing smoothly as a self-confident and effective practice partner.

This story begins on a Monday morning when I, as managing partner, approach my office with a rather forced smile on my face, knowing that when the morning ends I will have been unable to check off any of the items on my "to do" list for the day (since I will probably have had at least three critical events to deal with before lunch). As I reach my office, I pass Dom Lombardi, who greets me with his standard expression, "What's going on?" This particular expression of Dom's has troubled me for the past four years since I interpret it to imply: "Tell me everything that's happening in the firm—everything you plan to do and what you think I should be doing." Before I can even calculate a response, Dom adds, "I'd like to see you for a few minutes this morning." Now any managing partner with experience knows that this request from someone can portend one of four things:

1. The person is leaving the firm.
2. The person wants a raise or will leave the firm.
3. The person is complaining about another person and will leave the firm if something is not done.
4. There is a rumor that someone will be leaving the firm for personal reasons.

When the request comes from a partner, it is safe to assume that the partner is about to say:

1. "I am working harder than the tax partner and therefore I deserve more compensation."
2. "I am more valuable to the firm than the audit partner and therefore I deserve more compensation."
3. "I bill out more business than the MAS partner and therefore I deserve more compensation."

But when I sat down with Dom Lombardi, what he had to say stunned me. He simply stated that he was giving the firm the official 60-day notice that he was leaving. What surprised me so greatly was that Dom seemed to have matured into a solid—and apparently satisfied—partner. He had put a lot of misdirection behind him and was operating most effectively and productively. When I inquired why, and what he planned to do, he replied that he was simply tired of public accounting and was going into business with a client of the firm. This particular client was a small manufacturing company which did fairly well but had always been handicapped by undercapitalization. Dom said he would have a small equity in the business and expected to be happy with his work there.

I knew that Dom would probably accept a substantial cut in salary to take this job, and that its routine responsibilities would ultimately bore him, so I probed further to learn about his reasons for leaving the firm. At length he revealed that he was "tired of being treated like a second-class citizen in the firm," that he was exasperated by what he perceived to be a small clique of senior partners who ran the firm and who, he felt, knew everything that was going on to the exclusion of others, specifically himself. He felt also that this clique paid no attention to him and to the other young partners.

The revelation of Dominick's feelings came to me, and to several other partners to whom I related his intention of leaving the firm, as a bitter shock. I expressed to him my regret that he had not seen fit to express his feelings *before* reaching his final decision and said that it seemed a shame to sacrifice a career of ten years, one which appeared to have all the elements of success, in exchange for the more mundane pursuit of operating a small factory. But, nevertheless, I wished him well in his new career.

At a special meeting of all the partners later that week, I invited Dom to state the reasons for his dissatisfaction and departure. At this point, the next surprise rolled in. Almost half of the partners (in general, those with the smallest equity interest in the firm) joined in support of Dom's remarks. They, too, felt they were being excluded from important matters, that they were treated more like outsiders than partners, and that a small clique of senior partners ran the firm.

The implications of Dom's rejection of the firm, concurred with by so many other partners, was extremely intimidating to the senior partners. They felt a sacred covenant was being broken. And, furthermore, they were being forced to look into the mirror to take account of their own attitudes. They also genuinely regretted losing Dom because they found him a particularly likeable individual who had worked hard to make a substantial contribution to the firm. My own feeling was that—despite my considerable regard for him and his work—his uncertainty and inability to understand his own life or appreciate his career made me doubt his effectiveness in handling clients and in representing the firm. I thought that if he was not able to appreciate the potential which the firm offered him personally, or to be enthusiastic about being a part of the firm, he did not in truth belong with us.

One of the senior partners made an effort to point out to Dom and the other younger partners that every partnership was an open forum in which each person was supposed to feel free to discuss anything. Even though everyone was indeed listened to, it was impossible to act in every direction each individual suggested. He also pointed out that the size of the partnership (12 members) made it unwieldy for every partner to be involved in all matters relating to the firm and for that reason a steering committee had been established to facilitate the decision-making process. Unfortunately, these words did little to mollify Dom and his junior-partner colleagues. Finally, one of the "second-class citizen" partners rose and said, "I move we ask Dom to stay with the firm!" My dilemma, as managing partner, was whether to adhere to my instincts and demonstrate what would be considered "strength of leadership" by opposing the motion, or to risk expressing compassion (which is often interpreted by others as weakness) and support the motion. I chose to move for solidarity and suggested that we not put the motion to vote, but instead unanimously ask Dominick to remain with the firm. Dom was overwhelmed and fumbled for words. "I don't know what to say—this is so unexpected. Let me think it over," he asked, "and I'll let you know."

There followed a week of tension and anxiety in which the other partners bombarded me daily with questions as to Dom's decision. At the end of the week, he approached me with his familiar, "Hey, what's going on?" and eventually got to his point. "I've thought it over," he said, "and I appreciate the gesture on the part of the firm, but I've made up my mind to definitely leave."

A second special meeting of the partners was called for later that week to work out the details of the transition to cover the withdrawal of Dominick Lombardi, that is, the reassignment of responsibilities, amounts and terms of payouts, and so forth, with the intention of working through a rough situation as smoothly as possible. Minutes before the meeting was to convene, Dom walked into my office. "I've talked this over with my wife once more," he explained, "and we've realized that this is more than just a firm to us. When the partners are really operating together, there is such a family feeling of unity that I just can't leave. We've decided that I should definitely stay with the firm."

Apparently, through the trauma of an impending "divorce" from the position he had struggled so hard to achieve, Dom had been forced to reevaluate himself and his own perception of the value of his work. Likewise, the firm was compelled to recognize the great need for regular vehicles of communication. This confrontation with Dominick Lombardi instigated the implementation in our firm of regular accountability sessions for the purposes of consistent communications and regular attention to many of the details of the firm's operation. It also made quite clear that the developing role of younger members must be rewarded verbally as well as financially as they make greater contributions to the firm. In general, they must know that they have the potential to grow, that their contributions are being recognized, and that there are additional opportunities for them within the firm. They must be given sufficient incentives to want to continue.

In Dom's case, including him in more of the decision-making processes and keeping him better informed of firm activities supplied much of the reassurance and attention he had needed. His insecurities about not being kept abreast of affairs eventually dissolved and, to my great relief, he no longer felt he had to greet me with "What's going on?" As a matter of fact, Dominick has turned out to be a vital member of the organization, one whose contributions have consistently grown.

Accountability Sessions

On a bimonthly basis, the managing partner and the deputy managing partner meet with each of the partners for an accountability session, lasting anywhere from 30 to 90 minutes. (The managing partner is also "accountable." His session is conducted by the deputy managing partner.) The accountability session first includes a review of receivables that are over 90 days old, billing markdowns, variations from goals set for chargeable hours and total billing, and deviations from firm policies. Responses are then recorded and followed up in subsequent months.

While the primary focus of the accountability session is statistical in nature—receivables, billing, chargeable hours (Appendix E)—there is always time left for a more personal exchange. During one part of the session partners are encouraged to discuss what's bothering them about the firm, personal problems or whatever comes to mind. It is probably the most important part of the session because it affords each partner the opportunity to address a problem before it festers and grows out of proportion. The session is also an opportunity to reaffirm that the partners are indeed united in their goals and aspirations for the firm.

It is extremely important that these sessions do not deteriorate into unconstructive criticism of the partner for failing to do more, bill more, and obtain more new clients. Reinforcement must be made in positive directions, and negative aspects must be addressed with constructive direction for improvement.

All the forms, responses, related memos, and supporting statistical information are retained in a notebook for each partner. An accumulation of 12 monthly sessions like this gives the managing partner significant information on which to base compensation adjustments.

Annual Evaluations

Besides the monthly reviews which accountability sessions provide, annual evaluations are also vitally important. Each year, before the time for making compensation recommendations, the partners are asked to evaluate themselves and each other. An evaluation form (Exhibit E-2) is completed by each partner on himself and each of the other partners. The forms are summarized, and a copy of the summary is made available to each partner. The managing partner reviews the summary with each partner and they discuss a constructive program responding to any deficiencies noted. The summary and the responses become a part of the partner's notebook, as do the forms from the accountability sessions. The managing partner does not escape review. His summary is evaluated with him by the deputy managing partner and a senior partner. Because principals and managers represent potential partners of the firm, they participate in both the accountability sessions and the annual evaluations.

Subjective Checks and Balances

On the level of subjective evaluation, the partners are observed at the semi-monthly partners' meetings and at the annual planning session. In addition, copies of all partners' correspondence and memos go to the managing partner. Copies of all financial reports are also made available to him. Information on clients gained or lost by each partner comes to his attention. Regardless of which partner generated the business, the managing partner sends a letter of welcome to all new clients encouraging direct contact if in any way the firm should not fulfill the client's expectations. In the case of multioffice firms, these procedures would apply to partners in all the offices, and the managing partner would be expected to visit them on a periodic basis.

Principals and New Partners

It is extremely important for your firm's future that specific procedures be established for the admission of new partners. Partnership is a logical and necessary goal for all star performers on the staff, and it also fulfills a need for you, that of assuring the continuity of your practice so that at some future date you can retire and enjoy the benefits of the practice which you have spent your career in developing. This advice must be tempered with a heavy word of caution, however: While there is the need for the continuing influx of dynamic new people on the partnership level, there is the concomitant danger of committing partnership to aspiring staff members prematurely. This can be as detrimental to the practice as an effective new partner would be beneficial.

One means of precluding the premature admission of partners is by creating a new staff level within the organization—that of principal. The responsibilities of the principal are firmwide (as they are for partners), rather than departmental (as they are on the manager level). Partners delegate functions of a varied scope to principals, such as acting as the partner-in-charge (PIC) for some clients, billing, serving on special task forces, participating in management, and attending some partners' meetings. Like a partner, a principal is also expected to be active in practice development and community and professional activities, such as speaking and writing, and to serve as both a spokesperson for the firm and a model for the professional staff. Attaining the position of principal does not mean a divesture of former responsibilities as a manager in a particular department. Rather, it is an extension of that role, as it expands the scope and depth of involvement into the other areas of the firm's practice.

Probably the most difficult assignment for new principals is making the transition from performing as professional accountants to assuming the posture of concern for the management aspects of the practice. This learning process takes place as principals assume some of their new responsibilities and as they attend partners' meetings and participate with partners on special assignments.

As with any new learning experience, some people learn faster than others and some (for one reason or another) do not graduate. While there is an anticipated progression from principal to partner, there is no guarantee that all principals will make the transition. This is not to demean the importance or contribution of principals who do not become partners, for there is always a need in the firm for the particular skills and talents which bring people to a certain level.

When a member of the firm is promoted to principal, it is extremely important to hold discussions with him or her as to what is expected of a person as a principal in the firm. There are many issues to be addressed, such as the nature of new and old responsibilities, chargeable hours, practice development, supervision of employees, involvement in management, and so forth. And a clear path must be set forth explaining what should be accomplished in order to make the "magic step" from principal to partner. It is equally important to conduct discussions about the possibility that the person who has reached the principalship level may never become a partner but, perhaps by looking into his or her own mirror, might actually be satisfied in the role of a career principal, sharing the growth of the practice and being well rewarded financially without the stresses and burdens of partnership.

Two Classes of Partners

As a further precautionary stage, you may elect to establish two classes of partners within a practice—one, an equity status, the other, a nonequity status. You might also decide that every new partner should be a nonequity partner for a minimum of two years. This junior partner is guaranteed his or her income during these years in contrast to the equity partners, whose ultimate profits are somewhat contingent on the financial results of the firm. In this way, it remains easier to evaluate the junior partner during his initial years of participation in the partnership before a full commitment of entering into the firm is completed by his acquiring a proprietary interest. Listing all the partners alphabetically on the firm's letterhead avoids distinguishing equity partners from nonequity partners. That distinction is known only among the partners themselves and to no one outside of the partnership ranks.

Partners' Compensation

Participation in many practice management seminars on state, regional, and national levels has proved to be very rewarding and has guided my approach to the development and management of a firm. But no matter what topic is being presented at such seminars, the questions inevitably turn to partners' compensation.

Much has been written regarding salary levels of staff personnel. There are even annual statistics published about specific dollars for defined professional levels. The forgotten professionals, in terms of compensation, however, appear to be the partners of the CPA firm (or shareholders of a professional association)—forgotten not only in terms of potential salary increments but also in terms of systems or methods which recognize a partner's contribution to the firm in different areas and how these various contributions affect the partner's compensation.

Under most traditional methods, there appears to be little or no opportunity for a partner to improve his or her compensation status in the firm regardless of the achievements made by the partner in relation to others in the firm. Usually the partners share the profits based on each one's percentage of the firm, with appropriate drawing accounts against the percentage. Frequently, and particularly in smaller firms, the percentage will be equal for all the partners.

There are a few variations on this basic theme. Sometimes there will be fixed "salaries" paid to partners, with the balance of profits over and above the salaries divided in the partnership equity ratio (again, perhaps equally). Some versions of this method tend to be interesting because the amounts designated as salaries may or may not be equal, and the amounts may or may not (usually do not) bear a relationship to the percentage of equity on which the remaining profits are divided.

Other compensation methods are often equally limiting to a partner's prospect of improving his individual compensation. For example, a partner who owns 10 percent of the firm will continue to get 10 percent of the net income even if he or she assumes more responsibilities, has more responsibilities, has more chargeable hours, and brings in more new clients. Conversely, the senior partner, who may be doing less and less in these areas, will continue to collect 50 percent of the net income. This means that even if growth is attributed to younger partners, the older partner will get the lion's share (50 percent) of that growth.

However, in looking at the future of any firm, including the retirement aspirations of the senior partners, attention must also be given to the aspirations of the younger members. They must have the potential to grow, they must be aware that there are additional opportunities for them within the firm, and they must be given sufficient incentives to continue with the firm.

The developing role of the younger members must be rewarded both verbally and financially as they make greater contributions to the firm. These contributions come about in several ways:

· As younger partners mature, they contribute more to the firm in practice development. This happens because their peers have matured to positions of importance and because clients have gained more confidence in the younger partners.
· They have probably assumed more management responsibilities in the firm.
· They may have acquired specialities that are more in demand.
· Their technical skills have improved.
· They have improved the firm's reputation and helped themselves through participation in professional associations.

All of the above are accomplished in varying degrees at varying times in the careers of young partners.

Methods which a firm may use to face these evolutionary changes include:

· A multitier profit-distribution system
· Monthly accountability sessions
· Annual evaluations

These methods are designed to achieve self-improvement, constructive career direction (consistent with the firm's goals), a measurement of performance against standards, partner motivation, an awareness of the value of professional associations, and compensatory adjustments as justified by performance. Some of these thoughts may be of value in the plans of your firm.

Multitier Profit Distribution

In development of a compensation method, four elements can be considered in determining distribution of income to partners. Each of the elements is designed to recognize distinctive types of contributions which a partner makes to the firm.

SALARY (TIER I)

First, a partner should receive at regular intervals (such as semimonthly) a salary that is adequate for daily living expenses. In determining this amount, take into consideration what might be earned elsewhere, what was earned as a principal prior to becoming a partner, and what the prior year's contribution was to the firm. The salary should not be a static amount but should be reviewed on an annual basis to resolve inequities. At the beginning of each fiscal year the managing partner submits a salary schedule to the partners. The schedule can be changed only by a vote of more than 50 percent of the partners (in number and in points). The schedule also includes compensation recommendations for newly admitted partners. A minimum salary standard, which exceeds the highest salary amount paid to a professional staff member, is established for partners.

EQUITY (TIER II)

Payment of partners' salaries is a top priority; the first distribution of firm income should be based on labor. The second distribution of income should be based on capital, or a partner's equity in the firm. Under this system, equity in the firm (normally represented by percentages, units, or points) should be compensated in total dollars equal to the amount distributed for salaries, making capital equal in importance to labor. Although these "capital" dollars are the same total as the "labor" dollars, they are not allocated to the partners on the same basis.

Equity in a firm develops through a partner's contribution of capital (which has enabled the firm to carry its receivables and other assets). Capital units may also result from certain intangibles, such as the development of clientele and years of dedicated and effective service to the firm.

Equity points develop historically from these different sources and can be changed on an annual review basis by a recommendation from the managing partner with approval of 75 percent of the partners, in number and in points. Points may be added to a partner or partners, but normally none are taken away. New points cannot be added during a year unless the firm has enjoyed a proportionate increase in gross annual volume.

SPECIAL ALLOCATION (TIER III)

Compensation should be provided to partners for special efforts or special contributions to the firm which are over and above those normally expected of a partner. For example, what does a firm do when a new junior partner works diligently in practice development, while still effectively carrying his load of client responsibility, and succeeds in attracting $100,000 of new business to the firm? Now that's a contribution which could hardly be overlooked by the other partners! There should be some special allocation method to recognize such special achievements. This method, though not commonly used, should be an available option in the determination of a partner's total compensation. Tier III recommendations are made annually by the managing partner in the same manner as tier I recommendations.

Tier III is also valuable to accommodate mergers (STEP 9). The profit allocations of the merged firm usually do not fit an existing tier system. Therefore, after accounting for salaries (tier I) and points (tier II), an allocation in tier III provides for the necessary adjustment to enable incoming partners to participate equitably in profits within the firm's structure.

EQUALITY (TIER IV)

It is undoubtedly the desire of younger partners ultimately to share profits on an equal basis with their seniors. While the senior partners of the firm may wish to ignore this desire of youth (and hope that, if ignored, it will go away), it is certainly a sufficiently strong enough element to merit consideration in the partners' compensation package. It is concluded that, after a partner's basic needs have been satisfied through salary, the capital of the firm has been equally compensated (usually to the benefit of the older partners) and special considerations have been given to contributions to the firm, any amounts remaining should be divided up in recognition that all of the partners have worked equally hard to achieve favorable results for the practice. Therefore, the fourth element in the multitier plan is a consideration for an equal share of profits from the date of becoming partner. This means that a new partner shares equally with the other partners in any profit increase *after* he or she becomes a partner. For example, assume that the net earnings for 1980 were $200,000. On January 1, 19X1, a new partner is added, and she becomes the tenth partner. If the net earnings for 19X1 are $225,000, the new partner would be allocated $2,500 in tier IV (10 percent of $25,000). Suppose on January 1, 19X2, another partner is added, and the net income for 19X2 is $258,000. In tier IV the new 19X2 partner would get $2,500, as before, plus $3,000 ($\frac{1}{11}$ of $33,000, the increase in 19X2); the new 19X2 partner would only get $3,000 in tier IV as his equal share of the increased profits.

ALLOCATION OF NET EARNINGS FOR THE YEAR

• If the firm does not earn the established salaries (tier I), then each partner's salary is reduced in the same proportion (not necessarily the same dollar amounts but by the same percentage).
• The next amount of net earnings (above the salary) is allocated based on partners' points (units, shares, etc.). Such allocation, in total dollars, does not exceed the total dollars paid out in salaries (tier I).
• Net earnings for the year in excess of the salaries (tier I) plus a like amount allocated on account of points (tier II), and after any special allocations (tier III), shall be allocated to the partners equally from the date that each became a partner (tier IV).

CASH BASIS VERSUS ACCRUAL BASIS

The calculation of a partner's income is based on the accrual method of accounting. A natural question about this method is, "But how much money will one get in cash?" While the accrual method of accounting is the more accurate measure of a firm's earnings (and a proper basis for allocation of income), this question is more indicative of the real world: "How much does it mean to me as money in my pocket?" The resolution between the theoretical (accrual basis) and the real (cash basis) can be resolved by the following method.

The salary distribution (tier I) is a first priority payment, made on a semimonthly basis, and each payment to a given partner is identical in both cash and accrual computations. This payment represents both the partner's cash in hand and the minimum to be distributed to a partner via the firm's yearly net income. (A rare exception occurs when net annual income of the firm is not as much as the total salaries committed to the partners. In that event, the salary distribution to the partners is reduced pro rata based on projected salaries for the year. Any such distribution deficiency is *not* carried over into a subsequent period.)

Earnings allocated to a partner based on tiers II, III, and IV are credited, on the accrual basis, at the end of the fiscal year to an "undistributed earnings account." A firm then considers a profit distribution to the partners four times during the year, coinciding with the due dates for federal income tax estimated payments. This profit distribution is always in addition to what the partners have drawn as salaries and is determined after computing all liabilities and a safe cash reserve. (In our firm the amount available is determined by the managing partner.) This amount is then distributed in proportion to each partner's account balance in the undistributed earnings accounts. For example, if the firm has determined that there is $10,000 available to distribute, and a particular partner's undistributed earnings account amounted to 25 percent of the total of all the balances in that account, he or she would be issued a check for $2,500. Such payment would then be charged against his or her undistributed earnings account.

At the end of the fiscal year any amount remaining in a partner's undistributed earnings account (which means that the firm did not generate enough cash flow to distribute all the profits from the preceding year) is then closed out to the partner's capital account.

Basis for Compensation Changes

The responsibility placed on the managing partner to prepare the partners' salary schedules and make recommendations for additional points or bonuses is indeed a heavy one. However, these decisions should not be made capriciously or arbitrarily, but should be based on the results of both subjective and objective criteria. The managing partner can be assisted by the deputy managing partner in all the evaluation procedures.

On the subjective level, the partners are observed at the semimonthly partners' meetings and at the annual planning session. In addition, copies of all partners' correspondence and memos go to the managing partner. Copies of all financial reports are also made available to him. Information on clients gained or lost, by partner, comes to his attention.

The objective criteria used for recommending changes in the compensation package for a partner are accountability sessions and annual evaluations, including all of the statistical information developed for the accountability meetings.

A compensation program should satisfy the expectations of the senior partners of the firm (who probably founded the practice and enabled others to become partners) as well as consider the hopes and ambitions of the younger partners on whom the senior members must rely for the continuity of the practice. It is time that we look at new approaches in trying to achieve the delicate balance of consideration to all with the detriment to none.

Case Studies in Partnership Problems

The following case studies relate to partnership situations. They are designed to provoke your thinking about the many facets of the relationships between partners, and what you might have done under similar circumstances. Remember the discussion at the beginning of the chapter concerning the trade-offs made in order to build a large practice.

Case 1
FROM THE BACK OF THE CHECKBOOK

The office manager of your Northside office has just called you in a state of great agitation. Excitedly, she asks if she can meet with you privately, away from the office, to discuss an urgent matter. You arrange to meet her for lunch; before you can even look at the menu, she hands you something that is altogether startling—four canceled checks from the Northside office's current monthly bank statement which are made payable to the partner in charge of that office, Rolf Swenson. Each check is in the amount of his regular draw, which is supposed to be made on a semimonthly basis. Two of the checks are of a much higher numerical sequence than the others and apparently have come from the back of an unused checkbook.

As you try to absorb the meaning of this and adjust to its shock, the office manager adds a few other facts. She tells you that Rolf has "borrowed up" all of the money in the petty cash box and, on top of this, is borrowing money from staff members who feel pressured to make the advances because of his position. She tells you that she has been getting calls from stores and various people throughout the community regarding past due bills and checks which Rolf has bounced. An extremely conscientious person, the office manager is deeply disturbed because she had looked upon Rolf with a great deal of respect. You are equally upset because he was a young protégé of yours and you had guided him through the ranks of the firm. In fact, you were his number one "sponsor" in bringing him into the partnership, and it was you who encouraged the other partners to accept him as the managing partner of the Northside office.

You finally ask the office manager if she has any suppositions about why this is happening. Reluctantly, she admits that she suspects that Rolf has become heavily involved in gambling. As the managing partner, it is up to you to handle this deplorable situation.

Discussion

In all likelihood, this is a partner who has worked hard for a number of years in the firm's practice, making this situation all the more difficult. To compound this, Rolf is apparently well liked. Upon being interviewed, he will undoubtedly deny strongly any gambling problem which will mean that you will have to make an extra effort to get to the heart of the problem and to offer as much constructive assistance as possible. If the gambling hypothesis is not accurate and Rolf has merely overextended himself in the purchase of a new home or car or other major investment, you might consider going with him to your local banker and working out a program to borrow adequate funds that will put him in a sound current position with a reasonable plan of repayment to the bank. The bank may require the firm to guarantee the note, in which case his partnership equity should be pledged as collateral to secure the firm. However, should the conditions described in the case persist, then, as managing partner, you have no alternative but to recommend his involuntary dismissal from the firm. Ideally, your partnership agreement will have adequately prescribed methods and penalties to the departing partner whereby this can be accommodated within the partnership structure.

Case 2
IT'S PARTNERSHIP TIME

Mary Alice Brown started with your firm as a junior accountant nine years ago. She has come up through the ranks of the firm as senior, supervisor, and manager; for the last two years she has been a principal of the firm. Along with her ever-increasing titles and responsibilities have come commensurate increases in her compensation, and Mary Alice is now one of the highest-paid staff people in the firm.

About a month ago, Mary came to you, as the managing partner, to review her history with the firm and stated quite strongly that she wished to be considered for admittance to the partnership. At the next partners' meeting, you presented her application for partnership along with all of her employment history and statistics. Unfortunately, upon review, the statistics appeared to be poor. They revealed that Mary's chargeable hours had been dropping and were now about 40 percent of her total time. While she supervises about $200,000 worth of client billing, most of the billing is below standards, averaging about 80 percent of standard. The accounts receivable for which she is responsible represent about 50 percent of her annual billing responsibility. She has brought several small clients into the firm over the past year, with a total combined billing of about $5,000.

The partners reviewed all the information and discussed Mary's application. They concluded that while she has performed well enough through the ranks, she is showing no special performance or "spark" in any area which would compel the partners to admit her to partnership. In fact, not even the partners who work very closely with her showed enthusiasm about making her a partner. Thus, it was decided to retain Mary as a principal, give her a generous increase in salary, and discuss with her the elements that would be necessary for becoming a partner.

After the meeting, you call Mary Alice Brown into your office and explain to her the results of the partners' meeting. She appears stunned and replies, "I don't understand this. I have done everything I was asked to do at every level in this firm and now that I'm ready to become a partner, you change the rules on me. This isn't fair. If I can't become a partner right now, I'm going to leave the firm." How would you respond to Mary Alice Brown?

Discussion

The problem between the firm and Mary Alice Brown seems to involve different perceptions of what it means to be a partner. Mary apparently regards partnership as something *due* a person, as in a civil service situation, where, after putting in so many years of adequate service, an employee is automatically and regularly promoted until she reaches the top. From the firm's standpoint, a partner is a person who has extraordinary capabilities in the profession and has demonstrated outstanding proficiency in one or more areas. In particular, one of the standards is the ability to handle clients in an effective manner (or failing that, to be a superbly outstanding technician). Mary, unfortunately, had neither of these pluses which, from the firm's point of view, makes the difference between an employee and a partner. Partner is another word for entrepreneur, and a partner should certainly have the entrepreneurial drive and skills which are common to the successful clients of the firm.

Unfortunately for both Mary and the firm, this distinction was not made apparent until the time she was being considered for partnership. Mary should have been made acquainted with those standards which the firm requires for partnership at the time she was made a principal or when she became a manager. Had she been aware of the standards, she might still not have made it to partnership, but at least, for the benefit of all involved, she would have been better understood and would have recognized the reasons for her failure to achieve that position. In the development of a firm, it is unfortunate that communications seem to diminish at the higher levels. Too much is often taken for granted or assumed, while it is apparent that even at the highest levels, communication and understanding are vitally important.

Case 3
THE FEES THAT WERE NOT

One of the firm managers has requested a private meeting with you at which he wants to discuss an audit engagement that he is presently supervising for Ari Musof, a partner in the firm. The manager is having a difficult problem with the firm's independence in connection with the audit. It appears that, from the firm's accounts receivable records, the client still owes a significant balance due from the audit of the previous year. However, when the manager checked this out with the client's records, their records indicated that they were all paid up and, therefore, there should be no independence problem.

In trying to reconcile the firm records with the client records, the manager has discovered that the client has in their possession a credit memo from the firm in the amount of $5,000 and that a recent invoice from the firm in the amount of $10,000 has not been recorded on the client's books. The bookkeeper for the client stated that such an invoice had not been received by them.

To make matters worse, the manager shows you a copy of the routing slip of last year's tax return for the client corporation in which all of the sign-off indications that were supposed to be made by the manager of the tax department appear to have the manager's name forged in the handwriting of Ari Musof, the partner.

You thank the manager for giving you this information and for his interest and concern, not only about the audit but also about the integrity of the firm. Immediately you call in Ari. He readily admits to you that he personally typed the credit memo of $5,000 and gave it to the client, without putting it through the records of the firm. As for the bill of $10,000 that was not entered by the client, he also admits that he has not yet delivered it. When you ask why this happened, Ari replies that he was having a difficult time with the client and felt this was the only way he could retain the client. The credit memo had to stand, but he is sure that the client will pay the bill, once he mails or delivers it to them.

Ari Musof also admits to signing the tax manager's name on the routing slip for the tax return, but brushes this off by noting that the tax manager had cleared up all of the review notes relating to the tax return. Ari explains that he signed the tax manager's name to expedite completion of the return so that it could be delivered to the client on a timely basis.

You take in this information while subconsciously reviewing Ari's background: He has only joined the firm within the last few years, bringing in a significant amount of clients and client billings. He has been one of the best practice developers the firm has ever had. However, the accounts receivable on the clients he is responsible for represent about 75 percent of his gross annual billings. He consistently bills at about 100 percent of standard, and has an admirable record of chargeable hours. Now you must decide what to do about this situation.

Discussion

This is one case which should warrant immediate dismissal from the partnership. It is difficult to find any reasonable condition which would exonerate conduct of this nature. In the worst of circumstances, the covert credit memo could have been a cover-up for Ari Musof to have received some amount of cash and/or merchandise from the client, meaning he would have been cheating directly on his partners. In the most conscionable of circumstances, the credit may have been issued to save the client. But Ari Musof should not have taken it upon himself to save a client for the firm in such a manner, that is, without the knowledge and consent of the other partners; he should have at least notified and sought the consent of the managing partner. There is obviously a severe shortcoming in his capabilities in acting as a partner, both toward the client and toward his other partners. On the most generous level, the managing partner might consider suggesting to Ari Musof that he seek professional therapy to discover what might cause his type of conduct and, once knowing, to eventually overcome it.

Case **4**
THE CASE OF THE MISSING PARTNER

It is Saturday morning. Three members of the staff have gathered in the staff room to meet with a manager to wind up an audit report on a job which has to be delivered Tuesday morning. They are allowing for time on Monday to do the typing and processing. Terence John Wellington III, the tax partner, has promised to meet with them to conclude some final questions about a complex tax provision on the report. They have been waiting an hour and a half, and he still has not arrived. No one has received a call from him, nor have they been able to reach him. The manager finally calls you to ask if you have any ideas as to how Terry Wellington can be contacted. You, in turn, call the MAS partner, who, you remember, often plays golf with Terry on Saturday mornings. The management advisory service partner (MAS) sounds disturbed by your call and promises to call you back shortly.

Within an hour, the MAS partner calls you with unpleasant news that he is not pleased to relate. He informs you that he has located Terry at the apartment of a "friend." The friend happens to be one of the firm secretaries. She is not married; Terry is. In fact, it seems Terry has rented an apartment for the secretary not far from the office and has been spending a great deal of his time there. Further investigation reveals that days she has taken off from work coincide with fraudulent entries on Terry's time sheet. You recall that six months ago you had a lengthy discussion with Terry Wellington about billings to clients based on his time sheet, which contained many entries that proved to be fraudulent. The results were substantial markdowns from billings and substantial write-offs of accounts receivable on many of the clients he was responsible for handling.

Terry Wellington has been with the firm about five years and is unanimously considered by all the partners to be one of the most brilliant and creative tax people in the professional community. Until the time you first discovered the problem with the time sheets and the fraudulent entries, you had been extremely pleased and grateful that he was a member of the firm. Based on these facts and circumstances, what do you do?

Discussion

It is obvious that the managing partner has to discuss this situation with the firm's tax partner. It is also obvious that a partner's personal life should not be the firm's concern unless that personal life begins to interfere with his practice life, to the detriment either of the firm's profits or its reputation. The confrontation between the managing partner and Terence Wellington is indeed a difficult one. If the conduct of the particular day and the falsifying of time records are a continued pattern of behavior, the managing partner should in no uncertain terms "lay down the law" to Terry and let him know that this conduct is totally unacceptable because of its effect on the partnership. If, in all other areas, he has, indeed, made a contribution to the firm, then once the ground rules have been established, he should be given an opportunity to conform to the policy set forth or know for certain that if he does not he is to be removed from the firm.

Case 5
MORE FOR ME, LESS FOR YOU

Denise Delgado was just admitted to partnership by vote of the partners. As managing partner, it is your distinct pleasure and honor to call her into the office to tell her of this decision. Along with giving her the good news, you advise her about what her partnership draw will be for the coming fiscal year and you hand her a copy of the partnership agreement and the compensation schedule for all of the partners. She is quite pleased at having been made a partner, and the meeting ends with a friendly handshake.

About a month later, Denise comes into your office with a troubled look on her face. You ask what is bothering her and she explains: "I have been reviewing the partnership papers you gave me and I don't feel my compensation is sufficient." You ask her why she feels this way, and she claims that because of her chargeable hours and the number of clients she handles for the firm, she should be entitled to more money than has been awarded her. You respond by telling her that she is getting 20 percent more than her highest earnings as an employee prior to partnership and that, furthermore, based on the firm's projections for the coming year, there does not appear to be any source of funds with which to increase her compensation, even if it were deemed that her performance warranted it.

Denise responds by saying that there is one way to do it—by establishing a maximum income for partners. The maximum she has in mind would deduct from the four top partners a sufficient sum, she explains, to be reallocated to the newer partners so that they could have a significant increase and thus be raised to a new minimum standard of income.

You must decide how to answer this new, young partner who feels that the older partners are earning an excessive amount of money, part of which she wants to have reallocated to younger partners like herself.

Discussion

A constant source of amazement is the frequency with which new partners, after a few months as partners, seem to feel they know exactly how to run the firm, how to make it expand, and how to increase their own personal incomes. The case of Denise is a difficult one because she had not yet reached maturity in handling the complexity of partnership information which was thrust upon her at the time she became a partner. A better approach to the induction of new partners has been discussed in this chapter in the section concerning "Two Classes of Partner." In the first two years under this system, Denise would not be an equity partner but rather would be receiving a guaranteed annual draw. This would allow for a period of transition between being an employee and becoming a partner in the true sense. During these two years, Denise could absorb and become aware of the complexities and nuances which make up a partnership. She would learn that the firm operated very effectively and very profitably without her as a partner, and that the income earned by the senior partners was also earned without her contribution as a partner. She would also begin to appreciate that her income is substantially increased over that of the employee level, and that she receives many other benefits which do not accrue to employees of the firm. And, finally, perhaps, she would also see that it was through the long, hard, continued efforts of the partners who preceded her that the partnership achieved its present state in which it was able to consider inducting someone like herself. This is a case of learning, maturing, and understanding for Denise; the firm should not become belligerent over her observations, since at her particular stage of development these observations may appear to her to be logical questions of the system. If she is potentially a valuable partner, it is up to the firm to provide the necessary education to influence her attitudes.

Case **6**
THE CASE OF THE LOAN ARRANGER

The firm bookkeeper has just received a call from the bank concerning a $5,000 check from the Adventure Development Corporation that has just bounced for the second time. In checking the cash receipts for the last several weeks, he claims the cash receipt records do not indicate that $5,000 had been received from the client, who has owed the firm a significant balance for over a year. When the bookkeeper asks the bank to recheck their records, the person at the bank, who has become particularly friendly with the bookkeeper, confides that the check had not been deposited in the company's account, but rather in the account of one of the partners, and had bounced twice in his personal account. The bookkeeper comes to you for counsel.

The partner in question, Marvin Goldberg, has the worst record in the firm on compliance with firm rules, regulations, and standards; he is also one of the worst collectors of accounts receivable. But none of this compares to the news you have just been given about a client's check going into his personal account.

You tell the bookkeeper you will handle the situation and immediately call Marvin Goldberg into your office. Marvin's answer to you is, "Oh, it's not really a problem. The client was running short of funds and needed $5,000 to cover his payroll so I loaned him the money. The bounced check was his repayment to me." What is your response? What action should be taken?

Discussion

This case study offers two possibilities. One is that the partner has diverted fees which are due the firm into his own pocket. If this is the case, there is no other course of action but to move for his immediate dismissal from the firm, with possible legal action if the funds are not returned. On the other hand, there may be some truth to the set of circumstances Marvin depicted, in which Marvin felt very close to the client who is going through an extremely difficult period and considered that lending the client money would enable the client to get back on his feet financially and to function profitably again for both himself and the firm. If that is the case, there would appear to be no need to call for dismissal of the partner. Instead there should be sufficient discussion with Marvin so that he understands the eventualities of lending money to a client: first, that one could lose independence in terms of a client relationship, with all the attendant implications of financial reporting, and second, that it is not healthy for the accountant-client relationship itself to be put in such a position. If Marvin can recognize this and resolve to follow company policy in the future, he should be able to continue as a partner in the firm.

Case 7
A LACK OF QUALITY

You have just returned from vacation and find on your desk a week-old letter from the AICPA review team which recently completed the first peer review of your firm. The letter reports that the team found so many deficiencies in your organization that your firm is receiving a modified report, and it is likely that there will also be some sanctions against the firm. To make your day complete, one of the partners, whom you suspect of being lax in the area of quality control (which may, in fact, be a reason for several of the review team's qualifications), has been pressuring you for an increase in her draw. You also find among your pile of old mail her request for approval of a three-week vacation, starting tomorrow, even though she has just returned from a one-week out-of-town seminar.

Discussion

Since this is a more complex situation in which both a very concrete issue directed toward the firm and a problem with a particular personality are involved, it is necessary for you as managing partner to sort out priorities: with one sword, you can only slay one dragon at a time. Addressing the question of the peer review first, you must realize that the poor result is in most ways due to your own lack of participation and planning. In your position of responsibility, you should have been available during the entire review process. But long before the review, you should have insisted upon compliance with procedures for firm inspection and should have monitored those results carefully before you even scheduled the review.

Your only alternative now is to wait for the sanctions and then follow up with a response stating what positive actions the firm will take in the future as a result of the peer review, which, as you will explain, you now look upon as a constructive learning experience for the firm. Do, in fact, take immediate steps to get your own house in order, especially in terms of quality control, and schedule another peer review as soon as this is accomplished.

Turning next to the problem of the partner who has been remiss in her responsibilities, it is time you sat down and had a long talk with her. As a matter of fact, part of your management technique should be regular accountability meetings with partners, so that small problems and frustrations are both vented and resolved before they reach the crisis stage.

As part of management planning, standards should have been established so that this partner (or any partner) would understand and accept her particular draw and her particular vacation allowance. However, in the present case, it is evident you need to have a long conversation with the partner, pointing out that she apparently is not carrying her share of partnership responsibility, that her self-interest seems to be taking precedence over her firm obligations, and that therefore, especially until improvements have been visibly made in her department, her requests regarding draw and vacation should be denied. You can explain to her that her draw will be increased when she has met the firm standards and that her vacation will be postponed until she has contributed more effectively to the firm. Perhaps she can even head up or be part of the inspection team for quality control in preparation for the next peer review.

Summary of Case Studies

These case studies may sound amazing, alarming, perhaps even shocking to you. But they are actually not far removed from my own personal experiences or from stories related to me by close friends who are also managing partners of large local firms. In addition to testing your capabilities at the highest levels of management, these stories point out the fact that, even after being voted into partnership, a person should still not be left unaccountable, allowed to operate in a professional vacuum. Unfortunately, granting the title of partner to an employee does not change the nature or character of the individual. Just as employees have to be told what is expected of them, so do professionals at the partnership level. The same kind of monitoring, evaluation, and even checking up, if that be the case, is as necessary on the partnership level as it is on the employee level. It is a sad commentary, but nonetheless true.

My first serious thoughts about partnership relationships were prompted by a discussion leader at the first practice management seminar I ever attended. This instructor, a man who appreciates humor, introduced the section on partnerships and partnership agreements with the statement, "A partnership is just like a marriage." Then he paused and added, "only without sex."

Several months later I was called upon to fill in for this same instructor at a different, and very remote, location. Thinking I would be well served by following his example, when I came to the part of the seminar about partnerships, I introduced the subject by repeating his dictum, "A partnership is just like a marriage ... only without sex." The response was a few smirks, smiles, and titters, until from the back of the room a voice called out, "You don't know my partners!"

The truth is, there is a strong analogy between partnerships and marriage. Both are voluntary joinings of parties in which the parties expect to benefit more by being together than they were able to separately. Just like a marriage the arrangement must go through a period of transition, adjustment, compromise, and understanding. I can merely draw upon my own marital experience of 35 years and point to the factors which result in success. They are love and respect for one another, coupled with patience and the ability to communicate honestly. If love, respect, patience, and open communication cannot be accomplished among partners as part of the necessary fulfillment of each one's goals, and in conjunction with the partnership objectives, then the partnership relationship, like a poor marriage, should be dissolved. And divorce in partnership is just as painful as divorce in marriage. It is hoped that the parties will eventually end up in different kinds of relationships that more suitably reflect their unique personalities and respective needs which, apparently, could not be fulfilled in the existing relationship.

Conclusion

At a planning session early in the history of our firm, the discussion began to turn negative, and accusatory tones developed in the partners' conversations. Finally, one of the partners who had had his fill of what was happening stood up and said, "Now let's hold it a minute. Don't you all realize that *as a group,* we can accomplish anything!"

This partner was right. We had veered off the track and forgotten the lesson of this metaphor: While individual twigs can be broken easily, when bound together, they are strong and cannot be broken. In this binding is the strength and promise of practicing as a partnership. Each person makes a unique contribution toward the strength of the group, not in competition with the others but *in concert* with the partners.

A solid partnership which draws its strength from the mutual respect, varied capabilities, and open interchange among its members can provide a foundation of immeasurable durability for a growing, success-oriented firm. By knowing the elements of establishing a viable partnership and then managing that partnership with the kind of understanding that has been attained through a diligent effort to understand yourself, you will have developed for yourself the foundation for managing your firm. This, then, leads us to the next step in our large practice goal, which is the process for building your staff.

STEP 4

Building the Staff

Two veteran practitioners chanced to meet at a state CPA convention. After exchanging the usual amenities, one happened to remark: "I just can't understand these new juniors. Even though they're technically competent, they have such wild demands. They expect a 40-hour week all year round, including tax season, and two-week vacations, and they sure do want big salaries!"

"I know what you mean," his friend replied. "It's sure not like the old days when we knew that many times we had to work 60 to 80 hours a week. And no overtime pay either. Why these kids want to be seniors in less than two years, and then start talking about being partners!"

Shaking his head dismally, the first one agreed, "I just don't know what the profession is coming to."

Indeed, young accountants today do want to become seniors in two years. And if they have the technical and managerial talents, they certainly want to become partners in the firm. One question you must be able to answer, then, is how can your public accounting firm accommodate and satisfy the ambitions of its professional staff, knowing full well that every member of the staff cannot become a partner? And when, in fact, is a new staff member ready to become a senior? How will you satisfy the professionals' needs for achievement and how will you keep capable people continuously interested in staying with your firm and not seeking alternative opportunities elsewhere? These are questions which must be answered by every accounting firm—from the one-employee firm to the giant nationals, and particularly by those of us who are now well into discussing our big volume practice. The answer to these vital questions lies in your developing an effective staff motivation program for a large, successful practice.

Prompted by vast changes in our social environment, the need for staff programming has become far more widely recognized throughout the profession in the last decade. Nevertheless, much effort remains to be made toward its implementation, especially in regard to human relationships (partners to staff), motivation (appreciation of work performed), and demotivation (company policy). For as the changes in our social environment have taken place, so have changes in our professional environment. Primary among the noted social changes are:

1. Quality of life. There is a greater-than-ever recognition of the importance of other aspects in life besides that of the career. The joys and pleasures of life are here to be enjoyed today, not at some vague future date that may never arrive. Why aspire to become a partner if it means working exceptionally long, hard hours?

2. "Me" generation. The importance of "doing my own thing" was heralded by an entire generation. Although the attitude appeared to be practical for many young people, it was only because of the previous generation's devotion to the work ethic and family responsibility that the "me" generation's freedom was made possible. The change in perspective nevertheless had a profound effect on attitudes toward working.

3. The economy. "Future shock" of rapidly increasing and decreasing prime rates, recessions, and double-digit inflation is here. Saving for the future may seem foolish when we can pay today's debts in tomorrow's cheaper currency.

4. Consumerism. In addition to protecting the environment, the age of consumerism has fostered more public disclosures by private industry and more price competition. This had led to the virtual abdication or abolishment of most rules of professionalism relating to encroachment, solicitation, and advertising.

5. Rules and regulations. As the promotional prohibitions of practice have been dissipating, the technical rules have been proliferating. The Financial Accounting Standards Board (FASB), Securities and Exchange Commission (SEC), and AICPA have been inundating practitioners with rules and regulations at an accelerating rate.

Along with these changes, both stiff competition with other firms for competent personnel and the staff people aspiring to become partners in numbers that are disproportionate to available partnership openings remain universal concerns. One way of addressing these changes is to build a staff program founded on career progression, recruiting, employee benefit programs, review programs, RAP sessions, communications, and "a little bit more." Let us examine each element in some detail.

Career Progression

By developing staff level guidelines—and with them an understanding of the general body of knowledge and the chargeable time guidelines—a firm will be able to direct its professionals toward career positions most compatible with the goals they have or will develop. Of course, choosing the most fitting direction and traveling it with relative ease are up to each individual, so long as the individual's goals are consistent with those of the firm. People should be able to advance at their own level of professional skill, and promotions should not come automatically with the passage of time but rather when they are earned.

STAFF LEVEL GUIDELINES

In developing a firm's guidelines it is important to consider that not every professional desires the responsibilities that come with being a partner, and therefore the ambitions of many persons may be fulfilled by becoming skilled professionals at certain levels in particular areas of practice. Personnel should also be advised that moving from one level to a higher one is not intended as an abrupt transition from one type of responsibility to another. A staff member will still be handling some of the previously assigned responsibilities along with functions in the new position. Additionally, as a person progresses, challenges come from some of the aspects of the next higher career level.

While it should be a firm's desire to advance people from within the firm, there may be occasions (through merger or specialized needs) when personnel may join from outside at higher levels. These atypical situations should occur with the best interests of the firm and its clients in mind and should provide ultimate growth opportunities for the professionals involved.

Professional levels within the firm should be designated along with estimated time ranges for each level, as shown in Table 4-1. The time ranges are not fixed, and are meant only to indicate a general pattern of development. An outstanding person can better the minimum time ranges (see Figure 4-1). Sometimes, staff people at associate and senior levels have gone beyond the time maximums, only to achieve accelerated progress at the higher staff levels. There are exceptions, and a firm should welcome exceptional people.

GENERAL BODY OF KNOWLEDGE FOR ALL STAFF LEVELS

Rather than be repeated at the various staff levels, there are many items with which *all* members of the firm should be familiar. Knowledge of these mat-

TABLE 4-1. **Estimated Time Ranges for the Professional Levels (In Years)**

Level	Minimum	Maximum
Associate	1	2
Senior	1	2
In-charge senior	2	3
Supervisor	2	4
Manager	2	4
Principal	2	Open

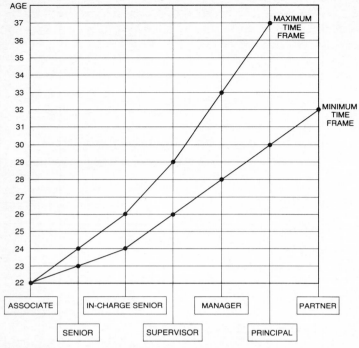

Figure 4-1. Time range of staff levels

ters and their effective implementation are important considerations for promotion to any staff level.

Philosophy

1. We are here, as a firm, to be of service to clients. Never let the form or formality of doing something ever take precedence over this fundamental attitude.
2. One of our most important assets is the reputation of the firm. You are a critical part of the continuity of that reputation.
3. By considering ourselves as "our most important client" we are able to achieve 1 and 2.
4. All clients of the firm are referred to as *our* clients, never "my clients."

Professional

1. The rules and regulations of the AICPA, State Institute of Certified Public Accountants, and State Board of Accountancy
2. The importance of *independence*

3. The importance of *integrity*
4. A professional inquisitiveness and a healthy skepticism
5. An understanding of materiality

Firm

1. Accounting and auditing manual and/or your departmental manual
2. Quality control document
3. Personnel and administrative manual
4. Structure (organization) of the firm
5. Services of the firm
6. Firm brochure
7. Client newsletter

General

1. A sense of urgency in completing assigned tasks
2. The importance of the final product, as to:
   a. Timeliness
   b. Quality
3. The *confidential* nature of the material we deal with

Personal

1. Pride in one's self and one's work. Autograph your work with excellence.
2. Professional bearing and appearance. Look professional and act professional, and you'll be treated as a professional! This includes not only your person, but also your work area.
3. A well-rounded individual will make a contribution to the community as well as to the profession.
4. Career development involves two aspects:
   a. Technical attainment
   b. Client retention and development

GUIDELINES FOR CHARGEABLE TIME

Time guidelines deal with such mundane, but economically important, topics as total annual hours, total chargeable hours, and an ATC (annual time commitment) concept. Standards of chargeable hours should be established as a guideline for all personnel so that there is a common understanding of how the responsibilities and workload may be handled to accomplish two common goals:

1. Timely service to clients
2. Sharing of responsibilities throughout the firm

A utilization schedule should be based on the number of total hours (8 hours times the number of weekdays) during a firm's fiscal year. In most years the standard hours of a year will be 2,080, which is calculated at 52 weeks times 40 hours per week. However, there are certain years, depending on how the fiscal year ends on the calendar, in which one or two more work days fall within the year. For example, in a fiscal year ended April 30, 1980 there were 2,096 hours in the period.

The annual standard hours (2,080, 2,088, or 2,096) can coincide with an annual time commitment (ATC) concept. The total hours include credit for vacation time, holidays, continuing professional education (CPE) programs, authorized leave time, and the like. Each of the authorized nonwork days is an automatic credit of 8 hours.

Under this concept, for each regular pay period the staff professional is paid the same standard check; no pluses for overtime, and no minuses for absences. At the end of the fiscal year (April 30) the total hours credited are compared to the ATC standard hours. For the hours in excess of the ATC, the staff professional has three options available:

1. A lump-sum cash payment calculated at the current hourly compensation rate. (Or at overtime rates, if so qualified.)
2. Compensatory time off during the new fiscal year.
3. A combination of 1 and 2.

The term "chargeable hours" is meant to include all time on the time sheet (Exhibit D-3) which bears a client number designation. Chargeable and non-chargeable hours are to be accounted for on the time sheets.

It is recommended that each individual maintain continuing statistics on personal utilization. Utilization information is part of each professional's personnel records and should be included in the periodic review cycle. Table 4-2 shows a suggested utilization schedule.

Recruiting

Because of a low national economic period in the mid-1970s, accounting firms hired very few entry-level people. As a result, a shortage in senior level staff people came about several years later. This situation was not unlike a college with a poor enrollment in its freshmen class having a small graduating class four years later. One way which proved fruitful in addressing this situation for accounting firms was much the way colleges have approached it—by recruiting.

Determine how many graduates you would hire according to your current needs and projected growth. Establish standards, such as grade point average and starting salaries, and select several universities for recruiting. The partner designated to head up the recruiting program should visit the campuses along with a staff person who had graduated from the respective schools. You will probably receive an outstanding reception.

TABLE 4-2. **Suggested Utilization Schedule**

	Average Annual Total Hours*	Average Annual Chargeable Hours	Average Chargeable Percentage (to Total)	Required Percentage to Standard†
Partners	2,500	1,400	55	67
Principals	2,500	1,700	68	81
Managers	2,400	1,800	75	86
Supervisors	2,300	2,000	87	95
In-charge seniors	2,300	1,900	83	91
Staff—seniors and associates‡	2,300	1,900	83	91
Paraprofessionals	2,300	2,000	87	95
Tax department	2,400	2,000	83	95

*Annual total hours include vacation, continuing professional education (CPE), leave time, holidays, and the like.

†It is anticipated that the percentages will be higher during January, February, March, and April, when the standard work week increases to 50 hours. The number of work days may vary for a fiscal year, with slight modification to the percentages.

‡During first 90 days of probation and training, requirements of associates are modified.

Students are usually curious and anxious to discover the opportunities local CPA firms offer and, particularly, what the differences are between local and national firms. Discuss these differences, not in terms of one being better than the other but rather in terms of suitability for individual needs.

At each recruiting visit invite a number of graduates to visit your offices. Give them a tour of your facility, introduce them to members of different departments, and invite your visitors to lunch with a junior member of the firm. Each person who meets with the recruits should complete a brief checklist of impressions to be forwarded to the partner in charge. After completion of the hiring cycle, questionnaires can be mailed to each of the recruits, soliciting their impressions about the firm and its recruiting program. These procedures should provide a good basis and fertile field for selecting the entry-level people needed.

The first week of the graduates' employment should be devoted to an orientation program in which they are familiarized with firm procedures and technical materials. Special efforts should be made to help them cross the bridge from the academic world to the "real world" of public practice. During the first six months of employment, all entry level people can be assigned to the small business department, where they gain experience in serving small business clients. A goal during this learning period is to have them assist in each of the firm's departments in order to give them a broad background of firm services. New personnel should be reviewed within the first 90 days of employment and again at the end of six months. After six months, they can be assigned to one of the departments.

I suggest you consider starting new employees after Labor Day rather than in July, after graduation, as is normally done. Since the summer is usually a slow period, it may be difficult to keep entry level people busy during that time. However, if they begin in the fall, they are working into tax season right after training. You may suggest to your entry-level people that they take a vacation after graduation since it may be their last opportunity for an extended vacation for a number of years to come.

Employee Benefit Programs

You probably won't win over any potential employees because of your benefit programs, but you sure are likely to lose some if you are not competitive in this area. Following is an example of one extensive benefit program. Some of the items are typical, some rather unusual, while others are a mixture of both.

INSURANCE

- Group health and hospitalization, for which the firm pays the employees' coverage and employees' pay for dependent coverage. *Unusual:* A dental plan included.
- Life insurance (probably unusual). The firm can provide life insurance coverage equal to the employee's annual compensation. This can prove to be a very low cost but rewarding benefit.
- Disability insurance (probably unusual). After one year with the firm, you can consider providing disability coverage. After a waiting period it pays up to 65 percent of salary in the event the employee is unable to work due to sickness or injury. This too can prove to be a rewarding program.

BONUS DAYS (UNUSUAL)

In addition to stipulated paid holidays, each person in the firm can be permitted two *paid* bonus days per fiscal year. Employees may wish to choose the Friday after Thanksgiving, a shopping day before Christmas, or perhaps a birthday or a vacation extension.

VACATIONS

One week the first year; two weeks per year for the next four years; three weeks thereafter.

SICK LEAVE

Sick leave (which includes family emergencies) can accrue at the rate of one half-day per month and can accumulate permanently to accomodate for such emergencies. This is similar to a reserve savings account. These days should not vest when an employee leaves the firm.

CPA EXAM

Staff professionals can be credited with regular time for the days they sit for the CPA exams. In addition, upon passing the exam, they can receive an automatic salary increase and a personal letter from the managing partner, welcoming them to the profession, telling them about the raise, and advising them that the firm will pay their dues in the AICPA, as well as in the state society and the local chapter.

TAX ASSISTANCE (UNUSUAL)

The firm can offer professional tax assistance to its administrative personnel.

It is important to offer competitive employee benefit programs and it is essential that your programs be implemented uniformly (without favoritism) throughout the firm and communicated to all personnel. This can be done through an office or personnel manual provided to all members of the firm. A loose-leaf notebook format most readily accommodates for inevitable changes in this type of manual.

Review Program

If there is one thing an individual hungers to know, it is: How am I doing? This yearning prevails at all levels and is a particular concern at the lower staff levels. Unfortunately, there is an almost universal lack of documentation in personnel files from which such a question can be authoritatively answered for the employee. A firm can address the issue of evaluating and documenting performance with four recommended types of reviews: first 90 days, quarterly, post-engagement, and spot review.

FIRST 90 DAYS

The first 90 days of employment can be considered a probationary period. Before a new employee has completed 90 days, the employee should be reviewed by the department head and often by a principal or manager in the department. The review is to be carried out on an informal basis, though a record of the review is made by the department head for the personnel file. The department head may also request others to complete an abbreviated critique of the new employee using the review procedure form in Exhibit F-1.

QUARTERLY

All employees should be reviewed quarterly, with each quarterly review focusing on different considerations. For example, the review for the second

TABLE 4-3. **Schedule for Quarterly Reviews**

Quarter	When Conducted	Conducted by	Review Evaluation	Topics Covered
1. July, Aug., Sept.	Oct.	Section or department heads	Section or department heads, with one or two top-level department members, review personnel files, make inquiries, complete forms*	Career progress
2. Oct., Nov., Dec.	Jan.	Section or department heads with a principal or manager*	Information obtained from partners, principals, managers, and staff members who have supervised the individual in the past six months†	Compensation, career progress
3. Jan., Feb., March	April	Section or department heads	Section or department heads with one or two top-level department members review personnel files, make inquiries, complete forms	Career progress
4. April, May, June	July	Section or department heads with a principal or manager*	Information obtained from partners, principals, managers, and staff members who have supervised the individual in the past six months†	Advancement, career progress

*Advancement and compensation changes should be approved by the partners (through action of the managing partner).

†The form in Exhibit F-1 can be used. A summary (or average) of all the review forms is then posted to an annual summary, by quarters, in the personnel file.

quarter can consider compensation, while the review for the fourth quarter can concentrate primarily on advancement. Table 4-3 shows a schedule for quarterly reviews that covers the major topics.

POSTENGAGEMENT

In addition to the quarterly reviews, a review should be required of all staff personnel for any engagement which exceeds 40 hours. The senior staff person will complete the personnel form for each staff person on the engagement. The form is to be reviewed with the staff person, and both should be required to sign it before it goes to the personnel file. This review is also handled by the form in Exhibit F-1.

SPOT REVIEW

Another opportunity for a review arises when an employee's performance is better than anticipated, or, conversely, when performance indicates a need for improvement. The spot review form (Exhibit F-2) can be used by anyone at any time provided that:

· It is discussed with the person evaluated
· Positive action is indicated by the department head

This completed form also becomes part of the personnel file.

RAP (Responding as Professionals) Program

A RAP program is designed to provide a personal channel of communication for every member of the professional staff. Ours evolved out of the following experience.

Monday is the day when most crises occur for the managing partner because people have had the weekend to consider such soul-searching questions as: Am I in the right profession? Am I tired of living in this city? Is my career progressing as fast as I expected? On this particular Monday morning, I arrived at my office to find a plain white envelope on the desk. Its contents were the resignation from a senior staff member who had "grown up" with the firm: She had started with us from college some five years before. She was the kind of professional a firm hates to lose. The letter of resignation contained no specifics, and when I called in the staff member to discuss the matter, I learned that she did not have another job, that we could have as much notice as necessary, and that her primary complaint was frustration with the firm. She had been placed in a particular department with no one having discussed the change with her. In fact, she had first learned of it by reading a new edition of the company roster. She had wanted to quit for two weeks and had carried her letter of resignation around all that time, *because she didn't know whom to tell.*

Fortunately, I was able to handle the situation in such a way that the staff member chose to remain with the firm. This experience prompted us to create the RAP program, through which every professional in the firm has someone to go to—a "RAP partner" who is a partner of the firm—to talk about what is on his or her mind. Our guidelines for the RAP program are:

1. The RAP partners must meet at least once a month (usually at lunch).
2. The RAP partners cannot be from the same department.

3. Technical information is not discussed; personal matters, firm policies and procedures, sports, and general good and welfare are the order of the day.
4. A brief handwritten report from the partner is made to the managing partner, which:
   a. Confirms the implementation of the program
   b. Alerts him to any areas that need attention
   c. Indicates what the partner told the staff person
5. Semiannually, either party has the option to request a RAP partner change. This is rarely done.

Then there is *super RAP!* Professional staff know that technical and personnel matters are to be discussed with department heads, and personal matters with either the department head or RAP partner. However, if there is a difficulty in discussing any matter with either of those resources, they are free to request a super RAP with the managing partner. The managing partner serves as the judge of last resort, the resident chaplain, the ombudsperson, and the in-house "shrink" to all personnel.

The RAP program can be a great influence in stabilizing staff attitudes and can provide an outlet for petty frustrations before they develop into major outbursts.

Communications

Many difficult situations arise merely from lack of knowledge of what is happening in the firm. As your firm grows into a multimillion-dollar practice, the problem of "keeping in touch" also grows. You can respond to this condition in a number of ways.

• **Internal journal.** An internal house organ can be distributed monthly or semimonthly. It publishes firm news, CPE programs, firm policies, rosters, commendations, as well as birthdays and anniversary dates with the firm. (This is in addition to a firm newsletter, which goes to clients and firm personnel.) In addition, an update can be distributed to partners, principals and managers for dissemination of management topics.
• **Departmental meetings.** Each department should conduct regular staff meetings for answering questions about and discussing technical matters, scheduling, firm policies, and announcements.
• **Annual meetings.** An annual meeting for all personnel, conducted during the last week of the year, can include a "holiday cheers" lunch. The business purpose of the meeting can be a state-of-the-firm annual report by the managing partner and heads of each department. The reports should include a review of the past year and should also let everyone in on the firm's plans for the coming year (and the five-year plan as well).
• **Evaluation of firm.** Every other year the personnel of the firm can be asked to evaluate the firm's policies and procedures on a confidential survey form,

responding to questions with plenty of room for additional comments. The signature line on the form should be marked *optional*. You may be surprised when a majority of the respondents sign it.

One of the questions on the form should be: "Do you believe that the firm will make changes based on the results of this survey?" It is important to understand, before embarking on such a survey, that the firm is prepared to respond in a positive way as a result of the replies.

"A Little Bit More"

Undoubtedly, most firms do follow some of the procedures listed. Some may even do all or most of them. Doing a little bit more is even possible.

The first "more" is *attitude*. Make the theme of your firm's philosophy one which is oriented to the human equation in public accounting. This philosophy should apply as fully to staff personnel as it does to clients. This means that staff, both professional and administrative, are not subordinates meant to serve partners. They are part of a team which works together to service *your* clients (yours and theirs together). It also means that partners do not sit in regal offices from which to command the troops. It means they work with the staff, they take them to lunch, they visit in the staff area and find out not only how a job is going but also how the new baby is doing (and whether help is needed in getting ready for the CPA exam).

Your personal attention to staff members can have effects more far-reaching than you'd ever expect. An example of this is the occurrence which took place at the time a manager left the firm just prior to completing the fiscal year-end work for our largest client. The client had a complex company and his business involved real estate development and installment reporting with significant variances between financial statement reporting and income tax reporting. The partner in charge of the engagement called in a young member of the staff, a senior who was in his third year of public accounting. The partner reviewed the files with the staffperson and asked if he was interested in accepting the challenge of completing the engagement. He enthusiastically agreed.

The senior proceeded to do a job of such excellence that the client called the partner to compliment him on the manner in which the work was completed and to add remarks about perception and attitude. As a matter of fact, the senior had even brought the job in well before the due date and under the budgeted time. We realized that to accomplish this, he and the others working with him had had to put in considerable extra time.

The partner in charge and I felt that the firm should express its appreciation to this young staff member and we decided to give him a special bonus check (which was equal to one week's salary) and enclose it in a personal letter describing our appreciation. The envelope was sent to his home. The interesting part of the story is that long after the staffperson had thanked us for the check, he was still telling people about how nice it was to have received that personal letter of commendation.

You may wish to give a firm award every month to honor outstanding service. The winners, who will come from all staff levels, can be selected by the operations committee (made up of department heads and the managing partner). They can be given a cash award, a signed certificate, and an announcement in the internal journal; you might even have a plaque designed for your reception area on which their names can be inscribed. Or you might throw in a lunch invitation from the managing partner. The firm can sponsor several athletic teams (such as baseball and basketball) and conduct golf, racketball, and tennis tournaments. An annual picnic can be held for all employees and their families. In addition, a dinner dance can serve to celebrate the end of tax season. Sports trophies can be awarded, as well as special honors such as election of staff persons of the year.

Staff personnel can participate on firm committees (such as the editorial board and a committee for practice retention and development), serve on the inspection team, and take part in planning sessions with clients and partners. At the firm's annual planning session, suggestions from staff should be encouraged and several staff representatives selected to make presentations.

In spite of all this, even with the "little bit more," there will still be turnover of personnel. People move to other communities, to industry or government, and even to other firms—and this is to be expected. However, the more accomplished you become in the development and implementation of your staff program, the longer you will retain staff members—and fewer will be lost as a result of internal causes.

Please note that we have nearly reached the end of the chapter and have not once mentioned the word "compensation." There is little to say about it except that it appears to be almost universal, it is difficult to do without, and some may well be better than none. The amount of compensation is rarely a motivator. A viable policy is to be competitive and to be currently aware of what is happening in the professional employment marketplace.

I am reminded, in fact, of a survey conducted by the U.S. Chamber of Commerce.[1] Management and employees were asked to rank employees' priorities in job satisfaction. *Management's* order of rankings were:

1. Good pay
2. Job security
3. Promotion and growth

Notice how different were the rankings by employees:

1. Full appreciation of work performed
2. Feeling "in" on things

---

[1]Quoted in "How to Motivate Your Staff," by Robert P. Levoy, *The Journal of Accountancy*, Nov. 1972, pp. 87–89.

3. Sympathetic help on personal problems
4. Good pay

Thus it should be clear that compensation is not a major motivator. It is hoped that some of the suggested policies and procedures may be adaptable in the building of your staff program for the eighties. And then start planning for the nineties.

Following are a few case studies based on the author's experiences in staff situations. You should be getting skillful at evaluating these studies by now and be able to quickly establish a plan of action as the managing partner of the firm.

Case Studies in Building Your Staff

These are exercises designed to test your abilities *and* imagination at handling the kinds of personnel situations that typically arise in a large practice. They are not far removed from actual experience. In each example, imagine yourself as the managing partner of a large firm in which it is your responsibility to resolve the situations presented.

Case 1
A FEW DOLLARS SHORT

It is payday and the office manager has just put the paychecks on your desk for signature. You have been somewhat concerned about the collection of accounts receivable lately and ask him about the bank balance. He indicates that collections are always slow at this time of the year and that the bank balance is overdrawn, "but only by a few dollars." You quickly realize that banking hours for the day have ended and remember that the friendly vice president of the bank, with whom you occasionally play golf, is away on vacation.

Discussion

To begin with, you, as managing partner in this case, should never have allowed yourself to fall into this predicament. If you had carefully projected and budgeted your cash flow, you could have averted the crisis altogether or, at least, anticipated it well ahead of time. Your constant policy should have been to encourage the partners to more aggressively collect the accounts receivable.

As an insurance measure against such crises, you could have set up an open line of credit at your bank so that you could call any one of the officers to have funds credited to the firm's account. Furthermore, you could also have regularly withheld some distribution of the partners' draws to establish a cash reserve for use in such emergency situations. Finally, as managing partner, you should have constant knowledge of the bank balance and be kept up to date by the office manager on a daily basis. Having failed all this, and having to react to a crisis, you must now try to reach the banker who is on vacation, or convince another officer there to fund you, or simply hope you have sufficient funds to advance from your personal account. Although it may be highly injurious to staff confidence in the firm—and therefore to morale—you could (finally) explain your embarassment to the employees and ask their *temporary* indulgence. I hope none of these will ever be necessary! As a manager, always have "plan B" ready should "plan A" fail.

Case **2**
HELP WANTED—RIGHT NOW

It is Friday afternoon and a senior accountant needs the assistance of a junior accountant right away for a job that will only require a few hours' time. Knowing that several people are available, the senior accountant approaches the office manager who schedules the staff. The office manager, who is known for being temperamental, claims every member of the staff is occupied and that none of the junior accountants will be available until the middle of the coming week. The senior accountant insists that there are at least two people she herself knows of who are working on lower priority assignments or have extra time. The office manager refuses to relent. The senior accountant, in a state of anger and frustration, brings the problem to you.

Discussion

As the managing partner depicted in this situation, you were remiss in not having spent more time with your office manager, communicating to him the high priority for both client service and team spirit, and stressing the absolute need for cooperation. Temperament has no place in achieving the primary responsibility of the firm.

It appears that ultimately this firm will need a different office manager, someone else who understands priorities in scheduling personnel. In this instance you will have to instruct the office manager to reassign the staff in such a way as to make a junior accountant available to the senior accountant.

Case **3**
IT'S NOT MY JOB

Two secretaries in your firm, whose working spaces are closely neighboring, were formerly good friends. They often lunched together and occasionally socialized on weekends with their families. At the last staff evaluation, one of the secretaries (Susan) was given a considerably better rating than the other (Mary), along with a sizeable raise. Since that time, their relationship

has cooled and Mary has been belligerent from time to time. On this particular day, Susan is overloaded with work and asks Mary, who obviously has
some free time, to please help. Mary adamantly refuses with the statement
that she has plenty of *her own* work to do. Susan, confounded, takes the
problem to you.

Discussion

This situation is similar to that of the second example. Once again a non-
cooperative member of the organization, Mary, has not learned the spirit of
flexibility necessary to make a firm function effectively. However, this could
be as much the fault of the firm as the individual. Indoctrination and training
programs are as important for administrative personnel as they are for
professional staff. People must understand what is expected of them before
they can be criticized for not meeting those expectations. These matters
should also be brought up during the evaluation periods.

Concerning the situation at hand, you, as managing partner, along with
Mary's supervisor, should meet together to discuss her attitude, and, if necessary, her relocation.

Case 4
RETURNS AND ALLOWANCES

Renee Legrand was in the tax section of a large national corporation and, for
a number of years, worked for a national tax preparation firm during tax
season to earn extra money. When she moved to your city she decided to try
to get a job in public accounting since, among her credentials, she did have
a CPA certificate from her home state. She was hired immediately for your
tax department and did an outstanding job in the preparation of tax returns
and in the review of tax returns prepared by others. She was well liked by
both her peers and the partners, being capable, diligent and hard working.
She received regular increases in compensation but showed no desire or
ambition to advance to a supervisory level, did not want to be responsible
for other people, and certainly had no ambition to become a partner in the
firm.

After two years with the firm she suffered a major illness and was inca-
pacitated for about two months. During that period the firm followed its prescribed sick leave and compensation rules as published in the office manual.
The firm's group insurance covered a good deal of the medical expenses.
However, Renee felt that the firm should have done more for her under the
circumstances and upon her recovery she told the firm she was not returning.

You thought that was the last you would see or hear of Renee Legrand.
Not so. About 18 months after her separation from the firm, she called the
senior tax partner. She related to him how unhappy she was at her present
job with another large local CPA firm. Her major complaint was that at her
present firm people were treated like replaceable machine parts rather than

as individuals. That is what she really missed about not being with your firm and she wanted to come back. The senior tax partner, hardly an individual of incisive perception and fast, astute decisions, replied, "Gee, I don't know, but let me talk to our managing partner and I will get back to you."

Assuming that your office manual states that the rehiring of a former employee is subject to the approval of the managing partner, how would you respond to the senior tax partner when he presents this proposal to you?

Discussion

We have had numerous experiences with "returns and allowances," that is, employees who leave the firm and then ask to return. There has been a mixed bag of results: Some have worked out remarkably well, some have worked out reasonably well, and others have failed. The only rule we have developed from our experience is that we will not actively seek out former employees in order to ask them to return. But if a former employee does contact us with a legitimate reason for wanting to return, and if that person was considered a good to excellent employee while with the firm, we will certainly consider readmittance, particularly if there is a need at that level at the time of reapplication.

Renee Legrand met all of these standards and should prove to be a good to excellent staff member once again. This case study also presents another interesting point of consideration—should an accounting firm consider a "career employee." The theory in the national firms seems to be "up or out"; that is, if an employee does not continue rising through the ranks with partner potential, that employee should be separated from the firm. I do not believe that this theory should apply to local firms.

A local CPA firm should be able to accommodate a person who does a solid, steady job at a particular function. There is no reason why that person cannot continue indefinitely with the firm, receiving adequate annual compensation increases and other fringe benefits, without the necessity of striving to become a partner. Some people do outstanding jobs at particular levels, but do not have some of the capabilities nor the ambition to become partners in the firm. This concept has worked well for us in the past, improved productivity, reduced turnover, and proved to be an effective morale builder. I must add, however, that it doesn't always work and that there is an attendant risk factor. In fact, a returned employee was once placed in a high managerial position, only to leave subsequently to become a key individual in a new firm. Nevertheless, considering the overall risk-reward evaluation, we have opted to take the risk.

Case 5
RETURNS AND ALLOWANCES, PART II

Manuel "Manny" Lopez started with your firm fresh out of college. He is very gregarious and well liked—a sparkling personality. He also happens to be a good accountant. His only problem is that he would much rather socialize than do accounting. You see in him great potential for bringing in business for the firm someday. He also likes to busy himself with organizing extracurricular activities such as picnics and sports tournaments. At his semiannual review everything usually goes along well until salary is discussed. He is never satisfied with the amount of his increase, citing the fact that others are getting more than he and that he can earn a lot more money if he jumps to another firm. It is obvious that his socializing with other staff members includes salary discussions.

After 2½ years with the firm he gives notice and leaves to join another firm.

Two years later Manny calls one of the partners of the firm and asks to visit with him. The topic of conversation is his possible return to your firm. It seems that since leaving your firm he has had positions with three other CPA firms in a period of two years, including another local firm, a small national firm, and a "big 8" firm. Each change has seen an escalation in his salary, even though he has yet to pass the CPA exam. He would like to return, he says, because he likes all the people in your firm and he likes your professional atmosphere.

The partner comes to you as the managing partner with a proposal for Manny to rejoin the firm because personnel at his particular level is desperately needed. They have agreed on a salary, which is about 10 percent higher than anybody else's at that level, with a proviso that there will be no increases for a period of one year. Keenly aware of the staff level shortage, you agree, and Manny rejoins the firm.

The scene changes. It is now a little over a year later. Manny has worked out very well, except every once in a while he has to be cautioned to devote more time to client service and less time to office gossip. He was not satisfied with his annual review or with his increase in compensation. He was held back from promotion because his next level would have required him to be a CPA and he still has not passed the examination. Two firm members who were above him in his department recently left the firm.

Several months after his review he makes an appointment to see you, the managing partner. This is what he has to tell you: "I just passed the CPA exam! Don't you think I should be promoted now? There are big vacancies in my department. I know that the firm policy is to make promotions only once a year, but I think my case is an exception. Anyway, I have been getting calls from other firms. I don't know how they know about me, but these are good firms and they all seem to know how to reach me. They are offering me *30 percent* more than I am making here. I really don't want to leave because I like the firm, but it just looks like I could do a lot better for myself somewhere else. What do you think the firm can do for me?"

Now that you have the story, managing partner, how would you handle it?

Discussion

While this is similar to the previous case study, it is presented for your consideration because of the different elements which have been introduced, elements which have led to different conclusions. Manny appears to be a restless individual who is never really satisfied with his position. Not only will all of his raises be less than he expected, but all of his promotions will inevitably come later than he expected them.

It becomes obvious that Manny's personality compels him to gain recognition beyond that of his peers and, quite likely, beyond that of his capabilities. The rehiring of Manny was probably a good decision at the time. But his past dissatisfaction with his other employers and his own slow rate of maturing indicate that he is not equipped to develop a lasting relationship with the firm. By examining Manny's personality, you might project that he will eventually become quite successful in some other field, one that involves more direct personal contact in which accounting will play a supporting but not predominant role.

Case 6
A STUDY OF OFFICE MATES

George W. Turner and Billy Lee Jackson joined your firm together as junior accountants two years ago. They shared an office and got to be close friends. However, Jackson progressed much faster than Turner and, in fact, has recently been promoted to senior while Turner still remains in a junior category. In addition, he received a much larger increase in salary, which Turner has found out about. In his position as senior, Billy Lee Jackson has been assigned to do an audit of a small local company and the office manager has scheduled George W. Turner to assist him on the engagement.

As soon as the schedule is posted on the bulletin board George charges into your office and says quite angrily, "I don't want to be carrying Billy Lee's audit bag around, and in fact I don't even want to share an office with him anymore. We started at the same time and I am just as good as he is and I don't want to be his flunky on a job!"

How would you respond?

Discussion

This case study may have a familiar ring to you since it is quite similar to that of the two secretaries who had been friends but could not seem to work together. Here George Turner's problem may not actually be *his* problem but, rather, a problem of the firm. He appears to lack adequate supervision and training, and obviously has not yet learned the firm's standards and policies for promotion within the organization. Nor has he been adequately motivated to adopt the firm's philosophies of team effort in its dedication to accomplishing service to clients. Once the firm has invested its time and effort in the training and supervision of this type of employee, the rest is up to the individual. If George is either unwilling or unable to learn from the teaching given him, then perhaps he should consider employment with another firm or maybe in a field other than accounting. Nevertheless, the employee is entitled to the benefit of exposure to what is expected of him, and how it is to be accomplished, before criticism for failure to perform is justified.

The other important point revealed in this story is a major protocol problem. No staff person should feel entitled to the liberty of barging into the managing partner's office to confront him with this type of problem. Staff people should be taught that there is a proper protocol and he must learn to respect that procedure within the organization. The proper approach would have been for George first to have discussed the matter with the head of his department. If, then, he did not feel satisfied, he could have arranged for an appointment to meet with you, the managing partner.

Case 7
THE CASE OF THE SADISTIC TYPIST

Let's talk a little about administrative staff, which unfortunately some firms still refer to as "clerical people," or some other title indicative of lesser importance than professional staff. A firm should address them as administrative staff to put them on a par with all other employees. This story is about Mary Wellington Longworth. She is the statistical typist of the firm, who in this particular case study is sometimes referred to as a sadistical typist. Mary originally started in the firm with the founding partner, some 25 years ago. She is probably the fastest and most accurate statistical typist in town, and is also just as likely to be nominated as the most miserable personality in town.

On this particular day Mary is busily typing away at a voluminous report for one of the senior partners. It is an internal report about the firm which the senior partner needs for a partners' meeting which is scheduled in three weeks. The report should take her about 2½ days to complete.

One of the managers rushes in to Mary with a financial statement, which would probably take no more than two hours to type, and asks if she could please expedite the typing of that report since the client needs it the day after tomorrow for submission to a bank loan committee. The client desperately needs the approval of the loan committee in order to complete the financing of additional inventory for his rapidly expanding business.

Mary looks at the manager with a pained expression on her face and says "Can't you see I'm busy doing something for Mr. Rogers? This report of yours will have to wait until I am finished."

The manager comes running in to you and asks you to fire Mary immediately for insubordination. What would you do?

Discussion

This case is similar to the one about the cantankerous office manager. Mary Longworth is an individual who has set herself up as being more important than the work of the firm (and therefore the firm itself). She has not learned the spirit of teamwork and the importance of fulfilling the firm's obligations to its clients. Certainly the work requested by the manager could easily have been accomplished and should have been if Mary had any understanding of what a CPA firm is all about.

Nevertheless, the firm itself needs to give attention to its own procedures. For efficient operation, all staff people should not be permitted to submit work directly to a statistical typing function. Rather, there should be a system of screening through a partner (or partners) as to approval of work before it goes into that department. There should also be someone in charge of establishing priorities in the completion of work to provide clarity in the event of conflict. The statistical typist is definitely not the one to determine orders of priority for production of firm reports. While, perhaps, Mary did not know any better than to abide by her self-centered attitude, the firm here also did not know how to structure its flow of work through the organization.

Some firms tolerate personalities such as Mary's because of shortages of good statistical typists. But keeping a person of this nature is counterproductive to a philosophy of service to clients. Try to instill in *every member* of the organization an understanding of this philosophy.

Since such standards could aggravate an already critical shortage, you might take the approach of simplifying and standardizing the production of financial statements so that any qualified typist would be capable of preparing them. Under this system, you advertise only for a qualified typist rather than a statistical typist. You train the typist to follow your standardized methods until he or she can accomplish the same result as a specialized typist. Not only does this overcome the scarcity problem, but it also makes an advantageous difference to you in the salary level the typist expects.

Case **8**
FOLLOWING THE BOUNCING CHECKS

Within the last few months you approved the hiring of an assistant bookkeeper to work with the office manager on the posting of the firm books and in handling the firm's payroll and accounts payable. Accordingly, the office manager has hired Maria Gonzalez, a very quiet, unassuming person with a fairly good bookkeeping background. You are quite surprised one day when Maria asks to see you privately.

You meet with her. She has trouble knowing where to start the discussion. Assuming it is her shyness, you encourage her. Haltingly, she begins: "I don't know how to tell you this. And I don't even know if it is my place to bring it to your attention."

"Whatever it is, it's obviously important to you, so let's discuss it," you encourage her further. "Is it about Susan?" (Susan is the office manager who hired her.)

"Yes, it is," she replies. "Something terrible has happened and she told me not to tell anybody about it . . . especially you!"

"Well, I think you'd feel better if you did," you offer in the calmest tone which you can possibly maintain.

"Well," she says, "Susan forgot to make a transfer to the payroll account and all of the employees' checks that were issued Friday are now bouncing all over the place and, on top of that, the checks which the employees have written on their bank accounts are bouncing too. I'm getting so many nasty telephone calls that I just can't handle it anymore. But Susan told me not to let any of the partners know what has happened. I was afraid if I did tell anyone, she would fire me, and I do enjoy working here."

Certainly, as managing partner, you have an effective response and plan of action for this situation.

Discussion

This is a particularly difficult case. It is full of nuances and presents exceptionally delicate management situations. First of all, the partner or person who signs the payroll checks should have inquired or made certain that a payroll transfer had been made before the checks were signed. Perhaps you were reminded of the several means for insuring adequate bank balance that were discussed in a prior case about lack of funds in the bank account.

As managing partner, there is reason for you to be concerned about Maria Gonzalez's ability to fulfill the role which is apparently expected of her. In all likelihood she is serving as the backup for the office manager; as such, she should be trained and capable of filling in that role whenever the situation warrants. Here it seems she is unable to speak up to the office manager, Susan, and is therefore taking a "back door" approach to vent her uneasiness and, perhaps subconsciously, to get Susan into trouble with her superiors. You need to suggest directly to Maria that she make more of an effort to assert her position and develop a better rapport with Susan so that they develop a sounder working relationship. Her ability to accomplish that may be instrumental in your determination as to which of the two employees is really better for the firm on a long-range basis.

Next, you need to discuss the situation at hand with Susan. You need not use Maria's confidential revelation as the basis for your discussion. Undoubtedly a "goof" as large as this is bound to come to the attention of the managing partner sooner or later, from one source or another. And certainly one of the employees is bound to complain to one of the partners about checks bouncing. Once armed with the slightest evidence, you should review this entire matter with the office manager.

Regarding the inexcusable failure to transfer funds, the firm may need a preprinted checklist of all steps necessary in the calculation, review, and disbursement of its payroll. Thereafter, no payroll should be released until all the steps, including the transfer, have been signed off. This is an excellent internal procedure.

Equally important, if not more important, you, as managing partner, must constantly reiterate to the office manager—as well as to all members of the firm—that you can deal with the known but can never be effective with the unknown. It is far better to reveal a mistake as quickly as possible than to try to cover it up. No one wants a Watergate on their hands. You must be able to deal with whatever events occur. Those that are not made known to you can only become compounded later, and you will be then forced to deal with them on a totally unprepared basis. I emphasize this point strongly throughout our organization. What the office manager in this case did is very offensive according to my particular style of management and would probably be offensive to most other managers. Repeated coverups, of course, lead to a dismissal of the person responsible for their perpetration.

Conclusion

Of all the people in the firm, it is the managing partner who undoubtedly devotes the greatest percentage of time to personal relationships and communications. Additionally, the managing partner has the greatest effect in shaping the image and progress of the firm through the people with whom he comes into contact. His words are weighty; they are the words of the firm itself. His is the final, authoritative say.

You have now evaluated your capacity in the role as a firm leader, your ability to deal on a peer level, and have in this chapter reviewed your personal substance in managing all the other members of the firm. Knowing and managing your staff is one base on which the firm will be able to deliver that million dollars—or more—of annual billing. There is no point to the partners marketing and developing all kinds of new business for the firm if the organization is not in a position to handle effectively, that is, professionally and efficiently, the engagements brought into the firm. Assuring that foundation is one of the major aspects of your job.

Building the Promotional Plan

Your existing client base is not only the heart of your practice, it is also what many writers and lecturers on practice management have referred to as "the gold in your back yard" and "the dollars in your files," for the additional needs of your clients (beyond basic accounting services) represent a vast potential for additional revenue. The purpose of this chapter, therefore, is not only to explore the external approaches through which you can market your firm's services and gain new clients, but also to help you expand your recognition of present clients as a *resource*.

Not only does your existing client base represent a rich resource for further revenue, it also offers opportunities for business which can be generated without promotional expenditures, without additional overhead, and frequently without additional hiring of personnel. By being constantly on the alert for suggestions and ideas which will help the client in business or in private fiscal matters, by discovering the client's needs and responding to them, by performing your services in a professional and timely manner, and by adding pluses whenever possible, you have assured that the client will be a perpetual advertisement for you, one who communicates enthusiasm for the quality of your performance.

In many situations, people often tend to see only what appears to be the obvious, and to see it strictly from their own points of view. Often they are too busy and too preoccupied to assimilate anything beyond mere surface impressions. Many clients do not realize the extent of work which has been undertaken for them in the process of completing a service, the total amount of time involved in performing that service, or the current value of such a service. In addition, most practitioners fail to communicate thoroughly. A firm may have an exceptionally competent estate planning department, but if the client does not even know that his accounting firm is involved in estate planning, he will not seek the firm's services (STEP 7). One of the most upsetting phone calls I had in my career came from a long-time client who wanted to advise me that I would soon be hearing from his attorney. "He's going to prepare an estate plan for me," the client said. "Don't you think that's a good idea?" "Of course, it's an excellent idea," I told him, "but didn't you know that we have a very experienced staff in this field?" "No," he answered, "I had no idea you did that kind of work." This incident brought home to me the point that no matter how excellent a specialization you have, unless you communicate it to your clients, your capability as a revenue producer is useless.

Making Your Services Known

There are a number of ways of making your clients aware of the spectrum of your services, all of which are in keeping with the standards of the profession. They include:

1. Fiscal year-end conferences. Rather than mailing fiscal year-end financial reports and tax returns to clients, you can invite them to your office to meet with the partner-in-charge, the senior staff person, and whatever firm specialist might be or become involved in their services. At this kind of meeting, you gain the client's undivided attention as he develops more understanding of your firm as a full-service organization prepared to fulfill his needs. It is beneficial to meet with the appropriate staff before the client meeting to ascertain a definite direction for the meeting and to develop an appropriate agenda. You should consider having the staff person take notes at the meeting in order to put into writing whatever proposals are adopted, the names of those who will be responsible for their implementation, and target dates for their completion. Once approved by the partner-in-charge, these minutes should be distributed to all the firm members involved at the meeting. A letter confirming proposals agreed upon in the meeting also should be sent to the client with copies to anyone, such as attorneys, who are professionally related to the engagement. The fiscal year-end conference is the ideal time not only to review the events of the prior year, but to develop a plan of action for the new year, and perhaps to consider some long-range planning ideas. It is at meetings such as this that the client can be made directly aware of the firm's services and how they may prove beneficial to him.

2. Regular interim meetings. Though most clients should have at least a prefiscal year-end conference to discuss tax planning, other clients may require monthly or quarterly meetings as well, depending on the type and complexity of their activities. Again, agendas, minutes, and follow-up letters are effective reinforcements to the client's perpetual question, "What is my accountant *really* doing for me?"

    These meetings provide an excellent opportunity for you to expand your communication with clients and learn about further aspects of their lives—community activities, personal aspirations, family—all of which are fields in which your services may be of benefit to clients. The better you know your clients, the more you can offer them. A follow-up report on such a meeting appears as Exhibit G-1.

3. Form 1040 time. At no other time in the year is the client a more captive audience to your recommendations than at Form 1040 time, which offers an obvious opportunity to bring up such subjects as estate taxes, tax shel- tered investments, Keogh or IRA plans, incorporating a business, and other tax planning ideas. As the client faces his annual tax bill, he will naturally be more receptive to your suggestions than at any other time of the year. Unfortunately for you, immediate follow-up will be nearly impossible at this season. However, if you make a point of scheduling a time to review these topics with the client during the off season, you will not only generate more business but also keep your firm operating at a fuller capacity throughout the year. You might also find it helpful to develop a form to be completed by the interviewer when preparing the 1040 and by the reviewer as to opportunities for tax planning after the busy season (Exhibit G-2).

4. Business seminars. By offering seminars in your areas of specialization, you not only demonstrate your expertise to clients who have an interest in those fields, but you also make your proficiency known to other members of the professional community. You can advertise your seminars with a notice in your firm newsletter and/or with flyers sent to clients with an attached response coupon (as is done for most state society or AICPA professional education programs). The topics may be broad or very spe- cialized, such as real estate investment, the current investment market, year end tax planning, estate planning, record keeping in medical offices, payroll taxes, or computer services.

5. Speeches and articles. You and members of your firm can heighten the community's opinion of your authority in your various specializations by writing articles for both trade journals and local publications and by speaking before groups. You can start small, speaking before local civic organizations, and progress to national industrial conventions. When you deliver a speech or have an article published, don't be shy about letting people know. Reprints of your articles can be mailed to clients in related businesses, your appearances can be noted in your newsletter, and pro- grams you have devised, if appropriate, can be used in presentations to prospective clients.

6. 1040-ES Vouchers. By retaining Vouchers 2, 3, and 4 after preparation of the 1040, you can give your firm three additional opportunities to com- municate with clients whom you might normally be in contact with only once a year. This is also a real service to clients since the IRS does not send out notices when these payments are due and clients might forget about mailing them. There is also the possibility that they might misplace the vouchers. Three weeks before the voucher is due, send it to the client

along with a cover letter containing instructions for filing and the due date, and an invitation to discuss amending the current voucher if changes are necessary. Add whatever other messages you might want to deliver to clients (Exhibit G-3).

7. Tax tips. As changes in tax laws, regulations, or information pertinent to specific clients become known to you, you can have that information copied and sent to the client. Not only does this extra effort make clients feel that you care about them and that their interests are of regular importance to the firm, but it also makes clients recognize how alert you are to developments in their fields.

8. Telephone advice. To demonstrate that your firm has acted professionally, confirm in writing advice that has been given by telephone. This removes possibilities for misunderstanding or doubt and serves as a record of additional services rendered to the client. An effective way of capturing this information could be a pad of forms which rests near the telephone (Exhibit D-13). As you are talking to the client, you can make notes which can be inserted directly into the client's file, put into memorandum form, forwarded to key staff members, and/or used as a basis for your confirming letter.

Perhaps the best rule to remember in expanding communication with your clients is that it is not how much you do for your clients that determines whether your fees are reasonable; *it is how much your clients realize you do for them that gives them satisfaction.*

Your Printed Image

Your printed image includes all printed communication to clients—correspondence, annual reports, management letters, tax form transmittals, and newsletters. It also includes printed material of general use, such as firm brochures and seminar materials as well as internal communications—from agendas to checklists, from forms to house organs, from memos to manuals. Printed materials offer a promising avenue through which the professional image of your firm can be consistently transmitted.

From the first time your firm's business card is put into a prospective client's hand, to the first engagement letter he receives, through the finished tax return or financial report, the presentation of your printed material is making an impression. How much attention have you given to what that impression will be? With every piece of material your client receives, he is subconsciously reacting to the quality of paper, reproduction, or binding with which you have produced it. And most of all, he is responding to the literal images you have chosen to represent your firm, starting with the logo.

There is no reason why you can't work toward having your firm's logo become thoroughly familiar to the professional community in your region.

First of all, start by taking the advice you so often give to your clients: *Engage a professional.* Do not rely on a printer or stationery store. Seek out graphic artists, ad agencies, or public relations firms that are compatible to your needs, and work with them to produce the kind of image that will give your firm the individual yet thoroughly professional identity you seek. When a logo is designed, have logo blocks printed in various sizes and in reverse. These can then be easily applied to all manners and styles of your printed materials. Your choice of stock (paper), typeface, and kind of printing (engraving, offset, or thermograph) will complete the highly professional image of your printed material.

THE FIRM BROCHURE

This publication can be your showpiece. Whether modest in execution or elaborately designed, the firm brochure encapsulates the scope of your practice and presents it in a comprehensive and digestible fashion. It can include the firm's history, philosophy, and organizational structure, and list and describe its services. The firm brochure is a prime opportunity for you to project your uniqueness. Make it the kind of product you will present to clients and prospective clients with pride and pleasure.

Again, it is recommended that an outside professional be retained to produce this booklet for you. You, however, should develop and supervise the material about your firm, because that is what you know best.

Be very careful about material which can "date" your brochure or make it obsolete. Caution is stressed against using the photographs and biographies of the partners in the firm brochure. It becomes embarassing if one of the pictured partners leaves the firm and you still have 2,000 brochures on hand. Similarly, a newly inducted partner is going to want to get into that brochure along with all the other partners.

There are several approaches which you might consider in the development of a firm brochure.

1. Prepare a separate printed piece about the partners. This could be a far less expensive printed piece, lending itself to change on a regular basis.
2. Your brochure could have flaps on the inside front and/or back covers for holding supplemental materials. One of the supplemental materials to be inserted would be a selection of separately printed photographs and biographies of partners and other key members of the firm. A separate sheet could be printed for each partner, with his or her name, current photograph and latest biographical information. In putting together a brochure for presentation to a potential client, for example, one would select the sheets of partners and key people involved in the engagement and insert them inside the cover of the brochure. This is probably the most expeditious manner to accommodate the inevitable changes occuring during the lifetime of a firm.

3. Consult with your printer, ad agency, or whoever works on your brochure, about the possibility of publishing an annual brochure. This would be similar to a corporation's annual report but without the financial data. It is an excellent way to showcase the firm, its latest accomplishments, and its newest people. It is worthy of a "cost justification review."

THE NEWSLETTER

The most important piece of regular communication with your clients should be your firm newsletter. It can be as simple as an 8½-by-11 sheet, typed at your office and photocopied, or as elaborate as a small booklet, typeset and printed in colors on quality stock (Figure 5-1). Some firms choose to make their newsletter informal bulletins, others prefer to make them polished publications. Regardless of the technique, however, your newsletter should always have a clean, professional appearance and be filled with information valuable to your clientele.

Besides being a resource for your client, newsletters also provide an opportunity for regular contact. They are a means to make yourself familiar to your client and to introduce ideas which may stimulate the client's interests in expanded services.

Whether you publish your newsletter monthly, semimonthly, or quarterly, the important thing is to publish it *with regularity.* Choose only material that is meaningful, edit carefully, and do not add copy just for the sake of filling space. You may wish to make your newsletter thematic, basing each issue on a particular topic, such as real estate, tax planning, estate planning, computer services, and so forth. This will enable you to cover topics in depth. Subjects of timely importance can be boxed or focused upon as announcements. You can also include in each issue a tax calendar which gives significant dates and designates the forms involved in meeting them.

The newsletter allows you to communicate to all your clients at one time, advising them of changes in tax regulations, business ideas, changes in the firm, and so on. It also conveys to the clients, as well as the staff, a concept of a professional organization working in unity to perform services for them. Through the selection of articles, it can emphasize both the traditional CPA services and special services. The intangible results in developing and expanding the favorable reputation of the firm through a newsletter can be enormous. Your clients will appreciate your producing a publication on their behalf and will also be able to share it with other business persons as a resource.

Your newsletter can be produced through an editorial board composed of several staff members and headed by one partner. The board should meet regularly to critique the prior issue, decide on articles for the new issue, make the writing assignments, and set the deadline for copy. Personal bylines and photos of the writers are one way of rewarding contributors.

THE RACHLIN & COHEN NEWSLETTER

NOVEMBER/DECEMBER 1981

Person to Person

THE HUMAN EQUATION IN PUBLIC ACCOUNTING

HOW THE NEW TAX LAW CAN HELP YOU

The Economic Recovery Tax Act of 1981 (affectionately known as ERTA) contains some of the most sweeping changes in our tax laws in the last 25 years. In this issue of our newsletter and the next one we will present the highlights of ERTA, along with recommended tax actions. ERTA helps individual taxpayers, corporations and estates.

Most of the changes become effective in 1982, and some are phased in over a number of years. Some of the items are effective now, and should be considered before the end of this year. The 1981 changes will be covered in some detail in our newsletter articles and are summarized below.

For 1981

- Because of the drop in tax rates effective January 1, 1982, you should follow the general rule of accelerating deductions into 1981, while deferring the taking of income until after January 1. (Special circumstances may, of course, override this general rule.)
- The maximum effective tax rate on long-term capital gains has been reduced from 28% to 20% effective retroactively to June 9, 1981.
- Two changes on sale of a residence, effective June 20, 1981:

1. The replacement period has been extended from eighteen months to two years.
2. The exclusion for those age 55 and over has been increased from $100,000 to $125,000.

- There is a one-time opportunity to earn up to $2,000 interest tax free (on a joint return) on a qualified savings certificate issued on or after October 1, 1981.

- New depreciation schedules under the Accelerated Cost Recovery System (ACRS) are available for property acquired in 1981. If you have already filed a company return for a fiscal year ending in 1981, review all assets acquired in 1981 for the possibility of filing an amended return to take advantage of the new liberalized rules.

- In consideration of the vast changes in estates and gifts, all wills and estate plans should be reviewed and modified as necessary.

Bache & Co.'s September newsletter reports "individual situations can create vastly different tax consequences. Specialized professionals in taxes should be consulted not only on specific decisions but to review an investor's overall tax picture. In taxes, what's good for one taxpayer can cost another dearly."

If you would like to have a booklet containing more detailed explanations of ERTA, please contact any Rachlin & Cohen representative and ask for a free copy of "Explanation of Economic Recovery Tax Act of 1981".

Leonard Cohen, CPA, Manager of our Tax Department prepared the material for our tax issues. Lenny first joined the firm in 1973.

INSIDE THIS ISSUE:

- DEPRECIATION, Investment Tax Credits, and the Accelerated Cost Recovery System
- Savings Incentives
- New Provisions for Individual Tax Payers
- New Estate and Gift Tax Provisions
- New Rules on Interest and Penalties

Figure 5-1. Newsletter

79

The ideas for articles come from many sources—weekly tax services, the weekly IRS bulletin, AICPA publications, tax magazines and business publications (such as *Business Week* or *Money*), the newspaper, other newsletters, questions raised by clients, contributions from partners and staff, and material received from financial institutions and stockbrokers.

To make your newsletter graphically interesting, use photographs or well-executed line drawings. Keep a photo of each partner and staff member in the personnel files to be drawn upon when needed and compile a photo file of more informal firm functions—company parties, staff meetings, and events. Rub-on type can be obtained at most art supply stores, and you can use this for headlines, borders, and illustrations. You can type your newsletter, use a word processor, or have it typeset. It is often a good idea to have a professional artist design a format for your publication. You can do your own subsequent "paste-ups" from which each issue can be either photocopied or printed.

You can maintain a mailing list on master sheets that are compatible with your copy equipment. When the newsletter is ready, the master list is automatically printed on mailing labels which are then peeled off and pasted on the mailer panel of the newsletter. One person should be responsible for maintaining the list; all notices of new clients and changes are channeled through this person. Every other year the list should be culled by partners' review. Your list can also include other CPA firms from all over the country who are interested in exchanging newsletters.

Depending on the type and quality of newsletter you produce, your publication can cost anywhere from a few cents to over fifty cents per copy. (This does not include the time spent by the editorial board, the writing, the paste-up and the mailing.) Nevertheless, when you consider its effectiveness as a communications and promotional tool, your newsletter is a modest enough investment for reaching clients and conveying your message to them.

Here are some hints on getting started.

- Don't start out too ambitiously. You cannot create another *Wall Street Journal* overnight. If you have copy equipment in your office, start out by producing it that way.
- Consider coming out with your newsletter on a quarterly basis at first. Many firms do not use the calendar concept and publish as they feel necessary to disseminate information to their clients.
- Use a mailing list and keep it current. Include all of your clients, even the smallest ones.
- Be sure you observe the rules of professional ethics in the contents of your newsletter and in its distribution.
- Consult with a local printer as to his ideas for achieving good graphic results at moderate costs.
- Consider retaining an advertising agency or artist to design your presentation. It is a one-time cost.

- If time is not an important factor, third class mail is economical. Check with your local post office.
- Get others in the firm to participate. Generate team spirit. They love to see their names and pictures in print.

FINANCIAL REPORTS

Annual reports and financial statements can be given a distinctive look through special attention to covers and binding. Make a special effort to incorporate on the report cover the logo and distinctive type style of the particular business for whom you are preparing the report; make the presentation an unusually attractive one. This is accomplished by obtaining from the client, with permission, a copy of the client's letterhead (or other material) from which you can cut out the company name and logo and paste it on the report cover master before copies are made. This not only personalizes the report for the client, but also makes your reports that much more distinctive when they are in the hands of a banker or other member of the financial community.

LETTERS

Every letter you send to a client or another professional carries promotional weight. Take advantage of this potential from the very beginning of your relationship with the client. Embossing your logo on the stationery can be effective. Use standardized letters which can be adapted for each circumstance in the case of welcome letters, thank yous for referrals, and reminder letters 30 days prior to a fiscal year end. Every new client can receive a special letter (Exhibit G-4) of welcome to the firm, which gives him a sample newsletter and conveys the firm's service concept. This conveys a large firm service capability, but with the local firm's personalized touch.

Another effective communication service is a fiscal year-end letter (Exhibit G-5). This letter alerts a client to the fiscal year-end closing, stipulates the due date of the returns which must be filed, and offers a checklist (Exhibit G-6) which effectively defines the responsibilities between the accountant and the client. It also shows just how much work the accountant has to do.

MANAGEMENT LETTERS

Management letters, which traditionally have been encumbered with professional verbiage, can be reorganized to be unintimidating and comprehensible to the client. Divide your management letter into four distinct sections: (1) the transmittal letter, (2) material weaknesses, (3) other constructive suggestions, and (4) the appendix—objective of internal accounting control (an imposing array of accounting jargon that has traditionally appeared at the introduction of most management letters). You can also implement several other unique features to make the management letter more readable and useful to the client: mark weaknesses that are uncorrected items from the previous year's management letter with an asterisk and point out to the client that failure to correct these indicated weaknesses has a direct impact on the operating efficiency of his company and the timeliness and cost of performing an audit; provide an "action taken" column in which the client can indicate whatever corrective measures he intends to undertake, returning an annotated copy of the letter to you. Make it a practice to follow up on these indications within 60 days if you have not received a response. A sample management letter of this style appears as Exhibit G-7.

BOOKLETS

Booklets and information pamphlets prepared by independent publishing houses which imprint your firm's name on the material are excellent promotional handouts. The yearly "Pocketax" and "Social Security Benefits" as well as "Tax Breaks for Buying or Selling a Home" and "Travel and Entertainment: Business or Pleasure?" are a few examples of the booklets available for your use. If you have a nicely designed logo, have it printed on the cover of the booklet. This is one of the uses for the logo blocks you order when your logo is designed.

THE INTERNAL IMAGE

Engendering respect and pride in your firm's capability does not stop with external promotion. In fact, it starts internally, and generating a professional image for the benefit of your staff can be as important as promoting that image to your clients. Remember, it is your staff who is in constant direct contact with your clients.

An "Internal Journal" can be a regularly published internal communication of announcements such as CPE programs, new personnel, changes in administrative procedures, and so on, and can serve to prevent "memo pollution." It can go to every member of the firm and can be divided into sections like: Tax Update, Update of the Professional Community, Items of Internal Interest, In the News, Birthdays and Anniversaries, and even a Classified section of which the staff can avail themselves. It is a good idea to have a specific format for your Internal Journal so that it does not become cluttered-looking and discouraging for the staff to read.

A separate PPM communication to partners, principals, and managers can also be used with information directed specifically to those members of management.

A General Ledger Referral System

Most firms don't seem to know where their clients come from, or how to take full advantage of their referral sources. For example, do you remember how many clients were referred to you by your local banker or the lawyer in your building? On the other side of the coin, do you remember how many clients you referred to them? The chances are you don't—and, in that case, you're no different from most accountants.

But who keeps score on referrals, you may ask. Are referrals supposed to be a quid pro quo arrangement with little regard for the particular needs of clients?

The answer is that keeping score can be an essential part of your firm's practice development program—especially in today's new, more competitive climate for obtaining new clients. Although clients' needs must always be uppermost, this need not prevent you from benefiting from your referrals. In fact, a systematic method of keeping track of referrals, and then following up on them, will help assure that your clients are being referred to the best professional help.

A "general ledger" referral system can be part of an "ethically aggressive" program of practice development. First, two points must be noted:

1. In making a referral, the firm's interests (namely, the possibility of reciprocal referral) are always subordinate to the interests of the client. The primary consideration in making the referral is whether you have properly determined the needs of the client and recommended the best professional talents for the client's particular circumstances. There is also an obligation to follow up the referral to determine whether the client did, indeed, receive the type of service expected.
2. The firm should recommend *at least two* potential sources when a client requests a referral. This gives the client a choice and involves him in the selection process. (It also increases the potential benefit to the firm since it increases the number of referrals made. Even though the source may not get the account, he usually remembers that you recommended him.) Moreover, giving the client a choice keeps the firm from becoming known as "tied in" with a particular lawyer, banker, and so on, to the exclusion of the other professionals in the community.

A referral ledger looks like any common general ledger—with the typical debit-credit ledger sheets filed in a loose-leaf binder. An individual ledger sheet is maintained for each source from which the firm has been favored (or hopes to be favored) by referrals, for example, for each law firm, bank, insurance broker, it has contact with. Exhibit G-8 illustrates the ledger sheet for a local law firm. Note that the heading includes not only the firm's address and telephone number but also the names of the partners and their particular areas of practice or expertise.

On the debit side of the ledger sheet are recorded the names of clients referred to the law firm. The debit entry, which puts you in a "receivable" position with the law firm, includes the date, the client's name, the referring member of the firm, the law partner who will handle the engagement, and a few words describing the nature of the service.

On the credit side are recorded the names of clients or engagements referred to you by the law firm, which puts you in a "payable" position to that firm. Information similar to the debit side is recorded on the credit side (dates, names, partner, nature, etc.).

The responsibility for maintaining the referral ledger should be vested in one partner, one who is both enthusiastic and productive in the area of practice development. This partner serves as the clearinghouse for handling all referrals, both in and out.

Where do all the "receivables" and "payables" posted in the general ledger come from? Instead of posting from journals, entries come from:

1. Referral memoranda. Referral forms (Exhibit G-8), are made available to all members of the firm and are used to enter referral information (either to or from the firm). These forms are then forwarded to the referral ledger custodian for posting.
2. Partners' meetings. At the firm's regular meetings, each person in attendance has an opportunity to discuss new business (and source thereof) and any referrals made. Minutes are kept and distributed. These minutes provide additional entries for the referral ledger.
3. New client checklists. A four-part form is prepared for each new client (Exhibit J-1). This form indicates how the client was obtained. When it was through a referral, this information is entered in the referral ledger.
4. Correspondence and memoranda. The managing partner receives a copy of all correspondence and internal memoranda. Where such documentation indicates a referral (either to or from the firm), it is forwarded to the referral ledger custodian.

For the referral ledger system to work properly, every member of the firm must know its objectives and what information is required. Here are procedures which should be followed:

1. When a client requests a referral, identify his specific needs.
2. Contact the partner in charge of the referral ledger for two or more recommendations which can satisfy these needs.
3. Respond to the client with the referrals, making sure to provide objective background information and accurate details such as names, phone numbers, and the like. Provide a specific person to contact, not just the name of a law firm or a bank. Offer to sit in on the first or any other meetings that may be necessary to provide a full and coordinated service to the client.
4. Make sure to contact the referred party to let him know that he may be receiving a call from the client and to inform him of the general nature of the subject matter.
5. Use a diary or tickler system to follow up at a future date with both the client and the referred party to see how the recommendation worked out. Again, offer to assist in smoothing out any problems, to provide the firm's expertise, or to help implement the project. It is important to indicate your attentiveness on a personal and professional level.

6. Report results to the custodian of the referral ledger, who will enter the appropriate information on the ledger sheet.

The referral ledger can be an invaluable tool for determining to whom to direct referrals. Several cases immediately come to mind, which are probably typical of situations arising in most practices. For example, a client needs a business loan and it is determined that accounts receivable financing would be the best method. The practice partner would contact the custodian of the referral ledger to determine:

• Which sources would be the best for the client? (This always comes first!)
• What is the ledger balance with that source? Is it in a debit (receivable) or credit (payable) situation?

Or, suppose a client needs an attorney to prepare a will. Whom should the firm recommend? Again, the information comes from the referral ledger. It tells (1) which attorneys are proficient at that kind of work, (2) which ones may relate well with this particular client, and (3) which ones have referred business to the firm (or which ones you want to develop such a relationship with).

It is worth repeating that reciprocity of referrals is the secondary consideration. The primary consideration in all referrals is the competence and integrity of the firm or person recommended. The firm's reputation could be damaged if a client is referred to a professional who does not perform up to expectations, and no cross-referral is worth jeopardizing a client relationship. Nor are there any cross-referrals which would be worth tarnishing the firm's reputation in the community.

If several law firms meet the competence and integrity standards to pretty much the same degree, refer the client to the law firms with the "credit" balance. Law firms are keenly aware of clients they have referred to you and it is important that you maintain comparable statistics.

How can a system for monitoring referrals be used to bring in new clients? Here are two actual examples of how our referral ledger worked for us:

THE BUSINESS LUNCH

A banker recently invited several of our partners to have lunch in the bank's executive dining room. The meeting was attended by a few bank vice presidents who had not met with us before. By the time we got to dessert, we were on a first-name basis and the conversation was sufficiently friendly for me to say, "By the way, did you know we recommended 18 customers to your bank last year?" When one of the vice presidents looked surprised, I pulled out a copy of the ledger sheet on the bank and explained how it worked. The credit side had only three entries on it. They got the message.

GETTING ON THE "LIST"

Early in my practice career, I was invited by a prospective client to visit a factory he had just opened in our area. After the customary amenities and after I gave him a brief description of our firm, he took a business card out of his pocket, studied the back of it, and said, "That's funny, you're not on the list." Result: We didn't get the account. The "list," it turned out, was a list of local accounting firms which a bank officer had written on the back of his business card. As a result of that experience, we opened ledger pages for every bank in the area. By systematically following up on these banks, which we could do easily through our referral monitoring program, we succeeded in getting on a large number of bankers' "lists," which ultimately paid off for us in referrals.

A centralized and controlled method of tracking referrals should be part of your firm's practice development program, especially in today's competitive climate. It will enable you to provide an additional service to your clients by recommending them to sources that you have screened where they are most likely to receive the assistance they need. It also provides a benefit to you in that you professionally control referral information. Using a general ledger technique can make the system work for you. If you adopt such a system, I trust you will have many rewarding entries to post.

Advertising

Since the 1977 Supreme Court decision (and the profession's subsequent concurrence) to allow CPAs to publicly advertise, many professionals have slowly but steadily begun to promote themselves through the media. But coming from a background in which business was sought indirectly—through referrals, public speaking engagements, organization memberships—the transition has been a cautious one. In keeping with the low-key profile with which they have so long been associated, many firms originally chose to design their ads with an emphasis on informing rather than persuading. Nevertheless, accounting firms are in a highly competitive situation for the same and new business, and the need to project individual identities is causing firms to reach beyond traditional reticence toward promotions of more aggressive distinction. (*Note:* Ironically, our colleagues at the beginning of this century had comparatively few legal or traditional inhibition about advertising their services. The ads in Exhibit G-9 date from February 10, 1921, when they appeared in *the New York Times*).

One fact, above all, is stimulating a change in attitude: The returns on well-conceived, well-placed ads can generate far more than the expenditure of producing and running them.

Should you advertise? The decision to advertise is indeed a weighty one. It may not be the best decision for every firm. Lawyers have been permitted to advertise for several years now and most of the advertising seems to be from the newer and smaller firms.

This is a difficult area for those practitioners who have spent their careers under the aura of professionalism. It would seem that any program of advertising should be balanced with two other considerations:

1. What is the firm's overall long-range plan, and how can advertising help to fulfill those goals?
2. What is the firm's marketing strategy? Both advertising and public relations should fall within those guidelines.

Fortunately, we are seeing more and more information on this topic (including professional services); it is hoped that this will help in the decision-making process.

Depending on your budget and the type of market you are trying to reach, you could consider advertising in anything from concert programs to the yellow pages to newspapers to magazines to television or radio. The idea is to give your firm the kind of exposure you need and to gain the professional community's recognition. The particular market you wish to target will be the significant factor in determining which media sources you choose. City magazines, for example, reach the top 19 percent in income, corporate decision makers and people who require financial planning. For the local CPA who wants to capitalize on this market, there is the choice of these magazines' classified sections or half- and full-page ads in the front of the magazine. One Texas practitioner had excellent responses to his newspaper advertisement for tax work. He targeted people who had just moved to the state as his market and advertised repeatedly in the same place to generate results. Some practitioners encourage follow-up on their ads by using coupons and mentioning firm brochures.

You will need to delegate the responsibility of researching matters related to advertising and marketing to one partner. To avoid the pitfalls of committee decision making, this partner should assume full creative control. He should investigate and engage a professional agency and work with them to develop an image for your ads that is most appropriate in communicating the kinds of services you provide. In essence, your ads will be putting your firm's identity down in black and white, and if they are not carried out with the utmost sensitivity to your professionalism, your reputation can suffer.

By all means, your advertising efforts must conform to the standards and guidelines established by the ethics committee of the profession. The quiz in Exhibit G-10 may sharpen your awareness as to what is and what is not allowed in today's environment.

Even before CPAs themselves had permission to advertise, many state societies campaigned to boost the image of the CPA and to make the public aware of specific services. Part of the intention of the state societies has been to develop a public awareness of the local practitioners similar to that of the national firms. State groups sometimes make their ads available to local firms who then run the ads with their own logos in hometown publications.

It is recommended that the partner in charge of advertising also develop a *written* program for practice retention and development. Retention is an important word here because you don't want to jeopardize clients you already have (gained through years of hard effort) in your zeal to pursue the new ones. A suggested format for such a plan appears as Exhibit G-11.

It is probably true that underneath the professional reserve of most CPAs is a businessman as eager as any to take on the competition. The field for promotion in public accounting is broader than ever. By beginning with the resource of your present clientele, you take the most important step in attending to the business of your profession. And by projecting your image in the community—with speaking engagements, published articles, and advertising—your promotional efforts will bring measurable profits.

6

Building a Profitable Tax Department

A separate tax department for a local CPA firm not only can provide beneficial services for its clients, services that are easily recognized and tangible, but also can prove instrumental to the growth and profitability of the firm. A tax department particularly lends itself to the promotional techniques discussed in the previous chapter in regard to retaining good clients, stimulating additional services, developing work for the nonbusy season, and encouraging referrals of new clients.

Determine a Philosphy for your Tax Department

A wide range of professionals is available to taxpayers for preparation of their tax returns, including in-house bookkeepers, nationally advertised services, and accounting firms. What will you offer to make your firm an outstanding choice for the taxpayer?

A tax practice philosophy might be expressed as follows:

> We care not only about the accuracy of the return (for which we undertake many review procedures) and the appearance of the return (which we have computer-printed), but, most important, we care about achieving the lowest possible tax. This is accomplished through a two-step process. First a list of alternatives is selected by computer; second, it is reviewed by our tax professionals. And our concern goes even further—we care about the family's entire financial planning! Like the old-fashioned family doctor, we care about fiscal health. This means estate planning, investments, IRA accounts, family trusts, and all the other recommendations we can develop for each client's unique financial and family circumstances.
>
> Our work does not end when a return is completed—that's where it begins. Many companies prepare returns. We serve a client. And we do it on a year-round basis by communicating, planning, and showing that we care.

We think about this philosophy every time we pick up a pencil to prepare a tax form.

We hope you will think about it, too.

Structuring the Tax Department

In order to organize a tax department effectively, you must decide which functions you want your department to perform and which it will be responsible for. For example, a department need not prepare returns for business entities (corporations, partnerships, or proprietorships) nor need it prepare individual tax returns. But it can:

1. Review all tax returns and control due date compliance
2. Prepare designated tax returns:
    • For estates and fiduciaries (Forms 706, 1041, and related forms)
    • The most sophisticated and complex individual tax returns
3. Tax research for all firm members
4. Handle tax examinations
5. Review tax provisions and tax accruals
6. Conduct the tax person in charge (TIC) program—which will be explained later in this chapter
7. Supervise the firm's 1040 services
8. Provide tax education for the firm—through CPE programs and internal bulletins
9. Maintain the tax library for the firm
10. Market the firm's tax capabilities—through outside seminars, articles, and community activities

A fully developed tax department can include tax partners, a secretary to the partners, a manager, supervisors, researchers, staff persons, preparers (in tax season), an administrator, and a clerk.

Background of Client Service

A firm's success can be enhanced by the concept of the person in charge (PIC), that is, the person in charge of the firm's relationship with a client. This concept emphasizes communication, concern, and confidentiality to provide effective service and to amplify practice retention and development. A PIC is responsible for the effective and efficient service rendered to each client. This includes the widest possible range of service—from preparing a 1040A for the business owner's college-age child to the preparation of a 10K for the SEC. The PIC does not necessarily do the work, but is responsible for its completion. The timely delivery of those documents, prepared properly, is important in the measure of the firm's performance.

Equally important to the PIC concept are the consultation services which provide for planning with the client *before* tax deadlines arrive, planning jointly for an annual audit, and business planning and tax planning on a year-round basis. Since most any CPA firm can prepare a tax return or do an audit, the quality of your service can be distinguished by the uniqueness and usefulness of your consultation services. It is not the computerization of tax returns nor the neatness of the typing on your reports (though they certainly make an impression) that "sells" your services. It is what you *do* with that information that makes the difference. Using the prior year's information in a planning session to save $10,000 of the current year's taxes will be remembered long after the literary excellence and professional brilliance of footnote G to the financials is forgotten.

The best way for both the client and the firm to capitalize on these consulting and planning services is to follow these guidelines:

· Conduct planning sessions before an extended engagement.
· Conduct a postaudit review session.
· Conduct planning sessions with the client *prior* to the fiscal year end.
· Conduct other planning sessions with the client during the year.
· Involve a tax person as TIC in these sessions.

The Tax Person in Charge

Involving the TIC is important because:

1. Tax savings are a highly visible and tangible measure of unique service to a client.
2. Taxes are a highly specialized area of knowledge, requiring time, study, and continued education for the specialist to remain proficient. This responsibility is assigned to the tax department.
3. One-on-one planning sessions with clients have proven to be the type of service most appreciated by clients and most easily billed and collected.
4. PICs are more successful when they avail themselves of tax department expertise.
5. A continuing relationship between a tax person and a client provides consistent and thorough knowledge of the client and the client's business. This enables the TIC to do the most effective tax planning in the most expeditious manner.
6. Using a TIC as part of the professional team enables the firm to provide the most beneficial services to the clients while reinforcing its reputation for being responsive to the client's needs.

Here's how a TIC program works:

1. The following should be eligible to serve as TICs: tax partners, principals, managers, and supervisors.

2. It is the responsibility of the PIC to select, assign, and work closely with the TIC.
3. A TIC should be assigned:
   a. To regular business clients with gross annual billings of $5,000 or more.
   b. For all audit engagements.
   c. To special engagements where there is a need, there appears to be a need, or there is an opportunity for tax planning. This includes legal support engagements involving tax matters and/or tax consequences.
   d. To any clients of the firm who have a current or pending tax problem, or any client who may benefit from tax planning.
4. The designated TIC information becomes part of the client data base.
5. The TIC should attend the following meetings:
   a. Audit planning (in part).
   b. Postaudit review (in part).
   c. Year end planning session with client.
   d. Other planning sessions with client.
6. Other functions of the TIC:
   a. Review tax provision workpapers, as required.
   b. Review the client's tax returns.
   c. Supervise the conduct of client's tax examinations.

It is imperative that the TIC and PIC work closely together in servicing the client. This necessitates copying and sharing memos, letters, records of conversation, and so on. It is also important that the TIC receive copies of financial and management reports.

1040 Marketing Program

PRE-TAX SEASON MATERIALS

Distribute to all Form 1040 clients, prior to tax season, a workbook for accumulating tax information, which includes computer-printed data and numbers from the prior year's tax return. This serves as both a checklist for inclusion of all information, and as an excellent comparative analysis: Was a quarterly dividend missed on a particular stock, or was the stock sold during the year? It also puts the material in an excellent form for preparing the return.

You might consider including with the workbook a flyer containing the following information:

• Tax practice philosophy (previously stated)
• Effective use of tax planning workbook
• How to compile your tax information
• Estimated tax declarations
• Use of computers in preparing your return

- Information for state tax returns
- Fees for tax preparation
- Tax examinations
- Deadlines for information

The flyer can contain a preaddressed postage paid card to your firm; the card is perforated for easy removal and mailing. It can list a number of tax planning and financial planning services available from your firm, to be checked by the respondent. There is also room to enter name, address, phone number, and time to contact (Exhibit H-1).

QUALITY CONTROL VERIFICATION?

Another post card marketing opportunity occurs after the return is mailed. A week after a client's return is mailed, the tax department can mail a two-part perforated card to the client. The card can state that, as part of the firm's quality controls, you are concerned that the tax return recently mailed was received and received in good order. The detachable portion is a card preaddressed to the firm, requiring no postage, which allows the client to respond to that request as well as to an invitation to discuss with them areas of tax planning which may be useful to them. The suggestion is made that such a meeting occur after the "hustle and bustle" of tax season. This portion of the card is reproduced as Exhibit H-2.

VOUCHER MAILINGS

As mentioned in a previous chapter, voucher mailings are an opportunity to communicate to all of your 1040 clients three times during the year. The IRS does not send notices to the taxpayers to alert them to filing dates for 1040-ES Vouchers 2, 3, and 4, and there is always the danger that the client will forget to pay the voucher on time or will lose it. You can, therefore, withhold vouchers and send each one to the client several weeks prior to the filing date, accompanied by a letter from the firm (Exhibit G-3).

Packaging Your Tax Product

Again, as the previous chapter emphasized, the importance of product packaging in our heavily commercialized world is obvious. To relate this to tax practice, visualize a client receiving a bulky envelope during tax season from your office. As he opens it, the contents spill all over the floor. He gathers up the mess of papers and tries to sort out where to sign, how much to pay, and when and where to mail. Frustration grows and he finally exclaims, " . . . and this is what I paid that accountant so much money for?" The point, of course, is that you can destroy the significance and effect of a well-prepared technical product with shabby packaging. The following is a list of tips for your firm to consider in putting together material which goes to the client:

1. Use a large, sturdy envelope for mailing to the client, prominently marked *personal and confidential.*
2. Attach to the top of the copies to be retained by the client a clear, but comprehensive, set of instructions. The client is cautioned to use separate checks for Forms 1040 and 1040-ES and to record his social security number and form number on the check. There are appropriate boxes for recording dates and check numbers of payments. And at the bottom of the form is usually a "commercial," such as: Is your will up to date? Has it taken into account changes in the family, in financial circumstances, and in residency?
3. Clipped to the tax return which is to be signed and mailed is an envelope preaddressed to the proper taxing authority. This helps the client in two ways—the envelope is designed to accommodate the form with a single fold, and the client doesn't have to search for the correct mailing address. (When I first started in practice I even affixed the proper postage to these envelopes as another plus service. But we all know what has happened to postage rates.)
4. Items 2 and 3 can be placed in a folder before the entire package is placed in the mailing envelope. The folder should be attractively designed and coordinated in color and appearance with the envelopes and instruction forms. If there is a pocket on each side of the folder, one can be used for the tax forms and the other for the client's worksheets or other material which relates to the return.

BUSINESS RETURNS

The same packaging philosophy should apply to business returns (corporations and partnerships) as to individual returns. Again, the instruction forms should be designed to be clear and explicit, and preaddressed envelopes should be enclosed.

There should, however, be a few differences in the procedure for business returns.

· **Review checklist.** The business returns should go through a review checklist. If the review indicates a need for tax planning, the PIC or TIC should contact the client, sometimes using a letter similar to the following:

Dear Client:

Upon completion of your current fiscal year-end tax return, it came to our attention that the following tax planning suggestions might be worth your consideration:

[The items would then be listed from those checked on the planning checklist.]

We would be pleased to review with you these matters and the potential tax deferrals or savings they represent. A call to _____ at _____ (or to any partner or member of our tax department) would provide for discussion of these potential tax planning areas.

Very truly yours,

Signature

· **Tax planning card.** Enclosed in the envelope with the business return can be a card preaddressed to the firm containing a checklist of financial and tax planning concepts which the client may wish to review with you (Exhibit H-3). This card is also enclosed with the mailing of financial reports.
· **Special handling of K-1.** In the case of partnerships and Subchapter-S corporations, there should be a separate instruction sheet addressed to each partner or stockholder. The K-1 and the instructions should be put in individual envelopes (your firm's), and addressed to the individual taxpayer. These envelopes can then be enclosed in your tax folder. The corporation or partnership can then hand them out, or mail them (again, in your envelope) merely by affixing postage. (*Procedure note:* If the partner or stockholder is a client of the firm, a copy of the K-1 should be forwarded to the client's 1040 file for the appropriate reporting year.)

Tax Department Controls

With such a volume of work flowing through a department, it is essential to establish controls in order to monitor the status and assure compliance with due dates. The tax department should maintain four control logs for each PIC of the firm:

1. Tax return log (other than 1040)
2. Tax examination update sheet
3. Research summary sheet
4. Tax extension control

Each item entered into a log should be assigned a tax department control number. A log essentially is a historical listing of each item entering the department, indicating name and number of the client, due date, and to whom assigned, and listing the steps through review and to the client. Semimonthly each PIC should get a copy of the four control logs which covers his area of client responsibility (Exhibit H-4).

CONTROL OF 1040S: TAXTRAK

TAXTRAK refers to the computerized log our firm uses for the control of 1040 returns. This computer printout indicates the current status of every 1040 return. Each PIC and staff person is regularly furnished with a copy of the printout (semimonthly, except March 1 to April 1 when it becomes weekly) listing their respective client responsibilities. The tax department gets a printout of all returns.

DUE DATES

One other responsibility of the tax department is to monitor the due dates of business returns. Sixty days prior to a client's fiscal year end, our computer department prints a fiscal year list for the tax department (along with forms we use for continuation of clients under our quality control system). From these lists the administrator of the department monitors the due dates, and assigns staff personnel to follow up on extension requests, as necessary.

Research Projects

One of the functions of a tax department is tax research for the entire firm. You may have noticed from our log report (in Exhibit H-4) that partners should be alert enough to tax planning opportunities that one research project a month should be the average. Some PICs are particularly effective in producing well above the average.

Work on a research project should be generated by the PIC when he prepares a Tax Research Request form (Exhibit H-5) and submits it to the department. The form indicates a due date and a time budget. If they cannot be met, the PIC is to be alerted. A tax partner reviews the request and then assigns it to a member of the department. The tax person assigned to the project may find it helpful to discuss the subject with the originating PIC.

A report is prepared in the following form:

Statement of facts
Question(s) posed
Answer to question(s)
Discussion (with citations)
Summary

The report is reviewed by a tax partner and then submitted to the PIC. The method in which the research project is presented to the client is then at the discretion of the PIC.

FIRM PARTICIPATION

The success of a tax department depends not only on the efforts of the personnel in that department but on the participation by the entire firm, based on the firm's awareness of how important the tax department services are to your clients.

One method of achieving this participation is the use of in-house seminars.

The tax department can present a pre-tax season seminar on preparation and review of 1040s, as well as covering any changes during the year in the tax law, regulations, or procedures which staff personnel should know about.

During the year, as part of the CPE program, the tax department can present seminars on tax topics such as: estate planning, corporate liquidation and reorganizations, pension and profit sharing plans, and year end tax planning. (Tax partners should also be active in presenting programs outside of the firm.)

Firm participation can also be encouraged by the publication of tax department bulletins in your internal journal; articles on tax subjects written by members of the tax department and a calendar of tax due dates in your regular client newsletter; mention of the tax department services by the managing partner in his welcome letter to new clients; and a detailing of tax department services in your firm brochure.

A CASE STUDY FOR PICS AND TICS

Your secretary has just received an irate call from a very old, very good client. When the call is forwarded to you, the client complains that: (1) your fees have become so high that he will no longer pay them; (2) you haven't visited his office in over a year; (3) one of your accountants insulted his faithful bookkeeper; (4) his tax return was delivered on the last day of the last extension, and he didn't have time to arrange for payment of the substantial tax, the amount of which came to him as a complete surprise; and (5) he feels that you've become "too big to bother with me now."

How would you respond to this series of irate comments?

Discussion

Number 1: Don't panic. Number 2: Recognize that you cannot refute these angry charges on the telephone. Therefore, allow the client to calm down and give yourself the opportunity to gather the necessary information to respond.

Incidentally, you were wise to have advised your secretary to put through calls of this nature, since an upset client should never be told you are too busy to talk. You may even wish to educate other members of your staff who handle phone calls about dealing with this sort of situation.

You first need to have a meeting of the staff people who worked on this engagement and find out from them the validity of the charges. The problem might be the old bookkeeper who never has the records ready on time, or the client's record keeping, which should be automated. Perhaps the client himself has changed the inventory figures several times while his tax return was being prepared. There is usually another side to the story, and additional facts which you must be aware of before you can meet with the client.

Make sure that when you see him, it is at *his* office. This shows that you thought enough of him to travel to his place of business. Encourage him to show you whatever is new there, and allow him to take pride in his company's growth. Remind him of the "good old days" and the many years you worked together hand in hand, exclaiming about how fortunate it is that you've both been able to grow in your businesses. Point out that just as he no longer personally operates one of the machines, you no longer personally do all the accounting work. Nevertheless, assure him that you are aware and interested in everything that is going on, and that you are always available for consultation on important matters. It is extremely important in these discussions to avoid sitting across the table from your client (this gives the physical inference of "taking sides"). Try to sit next to him, emphasizing that you are both on the same side. Putting your arm around him or touching him (only if you are comfortable with these gestures) is effective body language which emphasizes a close relationship.

Finally, point out to your client that his office needs modernization, just like his plant, which has been modernized. And it just so happens that you have with you a new engagement letter for him to sign for a systems study and computer feasability report. This is the *positive* approach.

Building an Estate Planning Specialty

Developing an estate planning specialty for your practice can fulfill a number of important needs for both your firm and your clients, the most fundamental of which are: (1) your need to expand your practice and be consistently rewarded professionally and financially, and (2) your client's need to conserve his estate. Because the standard services you provide enable you to see your clients regularly, you can develop familiarity with their personal and business economic conditions. And because of the independence and integrity intrinsic in the profession, you are in a position to be totally objective in evaluating the client's estate, thus assuring your client that your recommendations are never self-serving.

How Do You Introduce Estate Planning Services to the Client?

Estate planning is not a one-shot package. It is a program which requires continual updating to monitor changes in the client's needs and circumstances as well as changes in applicable laws and regulations. The program you offer should arise normally from your service to the client, whether that service is accounting, auditing, taxation, or management consulting. Asking certain questions will help the client recognize a need for your estate planning services, for example: Would a pension or profit sharing plan help your company? Could you use a Keogh or IRA plan? Do you have a current will? Other pertinent questions to pose to a client might be:

- Do you have any idea how much of your estate would go to estate taxes and administration costs if you died tomorrow?
- If that property were in a short-term trust, do you know how much tax you would save?
- Do you really have enough life insurance? Who owns it?

· How would your family get along financially if you were to die unexpectedly tomorrow?
· What funds would your widow (or widower) have available for debts, funeral costs, and other expenses?
· What income would be available to support the children during infancy and their adolescent years?
· How would your spouse manage after the children have grown and left the family home?

Most business persons are so busy accumulating property that they seldom take the time to take the proper steps to conserve it. You must impress upon your clients that without an estate plan, they may well be allowing unsuspected heirs to take parts of the estates they had assumed would go to their families. Those unsuspected heirs could be:

· The United States Department of the Treasury
· Tax collector of home state
· Tax collectors of other states
· Avoidable probate costs
· Avoidable and unnecessary administrative costs
· People who benefit from forced sales of estate assets
· Creditors who discount collection on estate receivables and business receivables to make cash available

Thus, your clients need you to make them aware of this problem and to recommend a plan of action which will protect them from it. These various factors, though they do not occur until death, need to be considered in the same light as income taxes and dealt with in a similar timely manner. This is especially true since your expert assistance can often result in even greater savings here than in the income tax field.

As every client is unique, so is each client's estate plan. A good estate plan takes various personal factors into account and involves calculated risks. Those factors include:

1. The ages of the people concerned
2. The size of the family
3. The nature of the main sources of income—whether salary, business, investments or a combination
4. The presence of any moral or legal obligations of a financial nature
5. The attitude of the family head on the manner and extent of providing for the members of the family after the death of the family head.

The following case studies should make apparent to you how estate planning opportunities could be staring you in the face when you have a close relationship to your client, especially if you have been preparing the client's income tax returns for a number of years. In the case of Nat Nelson, for example, you are in a unique position to calculate the dollar amount of his taxable estate and determine whether he has an estate tax problem. Once it is determined that Nat indeed has such a problem, the benefits of various plans and recommendations should be considered. Thus you provide an important tax-saving service for the client which will result in a professional fee for your firm.

Case 1
NAT NELSON

Nat is 58 years old. His wife died three years ago. Their three children are all married now. Last year he married a younger woman, a widow, who has two children, ages 16 and 12, both of whom Nat adopted.

You recall that about five years ago an attorney called you to get some information about Nat's assets for a will he was rushing to prepare before Nat and his first wife left on an extended vacation trip.

In preparing the individual tax return for Nat, an annual service you have performed for the past 15 years, you find the information shown in Table 7-1.

You are well aware that the municipal bond interest is not taxable and that Nat had an excellent year and is probably an outstanding candidate for income averaging this year.

OTHER ASSUMPTIONS:

Value of interest in Subchapter-S corporation $500,000
All other assets are worth the capitalized amount. (An asset with a 10 percent return is worth 10 times the earnings; a 5 percent return is worth 20 times, etc.)
Wife receives one-third of estate in accordance with state law.
Life insurance (owned by Nat with wife as beneficiary) $100,000
Residence (held jointly with right of survivorship) net value above mortgage. $120,000
Administration expenses $65,000
Nat contributed 100 percent to the acquisition of all assets, and Mrs. Nelson never earned any income of her own and never had assets of her own.

TABLE 7-1 **Information for Nat's Individual Tax Return.**

Sources of Income (All in Nat's Name)	Amount	Assumed Rate of Return, Percent
Dividends	$15,000	10
Certificate of deposit	15,500	15½
Savings accounts	6,600	5½
Interest on mortgages	12,000	12
Municipal bonds	8,000	8
Rents	8,000	10½
Subchapter-S corporation	20,000	—
Salary (same corporation)	30,000	—

Questions:

1. What is Nat Nelson's estimated estate tax (assuming death in 1982)?
2. Does he need estate planning?
3. How would you bring up the subject?
4. What suggestions would you make?

Answers to the Case of Nat Nelson

1. Stock ($15,000 ÷ 10%)	$ 150,000
Certificates of deposit ($15,000 ÷ 15%)	100,000
Savings accounts ($6,600 ÷ 5½%)	120,000
Mortgages ($12,000 ÷ 12%)	100,000
Municipal bonds ($8,000 ÷ 8%)	100,000
Rental property ($8,000 ÷ 10%)	80,000
Subchapter-S corporation	500,000
Life insurance	100,000
Residence	120,000
Total Assets	$1,370,000

Under the 1981 Economic Tax Recovery Act the calculation is

Gross estate	$1,370,000
Less: Administration expenses	65,000
Adjusted gross estate	$1,305,000
Less: Marital deduction (⅓ of $1,195,000)	434,000
Taxable estate	$ 870,000
Tax before unified credit ($248,300 + 39%)	$ 295,100
Less: Unified credit (assume maximum)	62,800
Estate tax payable	$ 232,300

With an estimated estate tax of nearly $232,300 and estimated administration expenses of $65,000, approximately $297,000 is payable almost immediately out of Nat's estate.

2. Does he need estate planning?   *Yes!*
3. The "how" of bringing up the subject of estate planning may be somewhat foreign to CPAs who wait for a client to come asking for service. If you are asked about either estate or gift tax by the client, the door is open for a discussion of estate planning. However, many people who could benefit from a good estate plan will not bring the subject up of their own accord. It will be up to you to broach the matter by asking questions that will encourage interest in your estate planning services. Some questions you can ask are:

> • Have you reviewed your will lately? (Surprisingly, the reply may be, "What will?"

• How much estate tax do you expect to pay?

• How much will your family receive after your death?

These blunt questions will force the client to consider estate planning or at least to state that he isn't interested in estate planning.

4. Problems and suggestions include:

a. The estate is lacking liquidity for taxes, expenses, and support of widow and children.

b. Nat had a will, but that was when he was married to his first wife. Undoubtedly she is the beneficiary under that will. An *immediate priority* is to recommend that a new will be prepared.

c. A program of gifts should be considered to give some of the assets to Nat's heirs. This could include stock of the Subchapter-S corporation.

d. Trusts for the benefit of the young wife and young children should be considered.

e. Other considerations for the Sub-S corporation:

(1) Possibly revoke the election

(2) Pension or profit-sharing plan

(3) Key-person insurance

f. Consider a private annuity or installment sale on rental property.

Case 2
FRED LOMBARDI

Fred Lombardi has been your client for a number of years and you have a very close relationship. When you first met him ten years ago, he operated his plastics extrusion business from an old garage as an individual proprietor. You helped him through the growing pains of moving into a new factory building and of incorporating his business as Lombardi's Plastics, Inc. You recall that at that time the corporation issued 50 shares of no par value stock to Mr. and Mrs. Fred Lombardi in exchange for the net assets of the proprietorship, having a book value of $24,500.

The business has prospered beyond Fred's wildest dreams in the past five years (Table 7-2).

You have been with Fred in the good times and the bad. Two years ago, his wife died when their three children were 10, 14, and 18. Since she had no separate assets to speak of, there was no probate and no estate tax return

TABLE 7-2 **Lombardi Plastics, Inc., Five-Year Record**

Year	Sales	Net Income After Tax	Retained Earnings	Fred's Salary
1978	$ 350,000	$20,000	$ 65,000	$20,000
1979	500,000	40,000	105,000	20,000
1980	700,000	65,000	170,000	25,000
1981	900,000	80,000	250,000	30,000
1982	1,300,000	90,000	340,000	40,000

was filed. Mrs. Lombardi was not gainfully employed during the marriage and had no separate income.

In reviewing the 1981 results with Fred, he finds it difficult to believe the profits were $90,000 after taxes since his cash position is very poor and he is beginning to feel some pressure from creditors. You explain that his inventory increased substantially to meet the volume of business, that he bought a great deal of new equipment, and that he is paying off both the mortgage on the factory building and the bank loan he obtained for the major addition to the factory two years ago.

Suddenly, Fred says, "Hey, what happens to my kids if something should happen to me? Do they get the business . . . and then have to worry about all my bills?" You remind him that he has a will, prepared when the business was incorporated. It leaves everything to his wife, and on her demise, equally to the children. The wife had no will.

Now the thought runs through *your* mind . . . *what would happen?* Wouldn't the business be valued very highly for estate tax purposes? He has no other assets except the business, his home (an equity of about $25,000), and some personal life insurance ($30,000) naming the children as beneficiaries. With his wife gone, there wouldn't even be a marital deduction. You therefore respond, "Fred, you might have some estate problems here. Let me review this entire matter and I'll get back to you in about two weeks."

The case of Fred Lombardi illustrates another situation common among closely held businesses. Sometimes a business may grow rapidly, increasing earnings without a corresponding increase in working capital, which translates into a lack of liquidity for estate tax purposes. This case also illustrates the point that the accountant frequently knows—and if he does not know, he should—his client's financial background and family relationship as well as anyone.

At the meeting in two weeks, how would you categorize Fred Lombardi's tax and estate problems? What general areas would you begin to recommend for his considerations?

Answers to the Case of Fred Lombardi

In this kind of situation there is no single solution and no easy answer. Nevertheless, the case of Fred Lombardi should motivate you to discuss estate planning with your client and to consider the complexities that might arise in some estate planning situations.

1. Obviously a new will is needed to reflect the client's changed circumstances. It would include provisions for custody of the children. Second, gifts and trusts on behalf of the minor children should be considered.
2. A major problem evolves around the profitable and valuable closely held corporation. Some thought in that regard would include:
   a. Pension and profit-sharing plans

   b. Key-person insurance
   c. Arrangement with key employees to assume management of the company in the event of his death, such as:
     (1) Stock options
     (2) Installment sales of some shares
     (3) Use of an employees stock option plan (ESOP)
   d. Selling an interest in the company
   e. Acquisition by a larger entity

Since his estate appears to lack liquidity, he and his potential executor or administrator should be made aware of the relief provisions for "reasonable cause" which can allow up to 10 years for payment of estate taxes, and also the new relief provisions for closely held businesses which allow up to 15 years for payment of estate taxes. (Sections 6166 and 6166A of the Internal Revenue Code allow these more lenient terms for paying estate taxes if the estate consists largely of a closely held business.)

Gathering Information on the Financial State of Affairs

Your initial interview should be with the client (Exhibit I-1); then, with your client's permission, you can speak with his attorney, insurance representative, banker, investment counselor, stock broker, and other accountants (Exhibit I-2). When you do, you should keep in mind these two important points: always think of these individuals as your client's estate planning team and be aware that these sources of information can become important contacts for your practice development. Subtly, but unmistakably, let all the members of the estate planning team know that you are actively pursuing estate planning engagements.

Many practitioners use a printed questionnaire to gather information for estate plans. The questionnaire serves first as a means to inventory assets and get one's house in order. Second, it serves to help identify the firm's capability in estate planning. Exhibit I-1 is an example of such a questionnaire which you can use in your own client interviews.

THE WORKSHEET

The worksheet (Exhibit I-3) is an important tool in gathering information for projected cash sources and cash needs of the client's heirs. The information in the worksheet will be used to plan against any disaster that should befall your client, to be sure that the spouse and children will get by in the daily business of living and paying the bills. This projection is needed in planning the estate from a cash planning point of view. Standard worksheets make the job easier, and they are useful for discussion purposes. They, too, graphically demonstrate your concern and your professionalism, and so are beneficial to your practice development.

THE WILL QUIZ

A will quiz (Exhibit I-4) is a series of yes-or-no questions concerning your client's or potential client's will. Each "yes" answer is a danger signal, one that indicates a problem with the individual's estate, and therefore a need for a good estate plan. You can distribute the quiz as a special mailing or simply make it part of one of your regular newsletters.

Presenting the Plan

After all of the information on the client's estate has been gathered, the next step in the estate planning process is to calculate the estate taxes and the administration costs, based on the assets as they are presently held. First, assume the husband predeceases the wife. Then repeat the calculations assuming the reverse. Next, consider some of the alternatives in planning, such as trusts, gifts, title corrections, annuities, installment sales, insurance contracts, insurance trusts, a marital deduction qualification, legal domicile, and business agreements. Also, review the recommendations of the estate planning team. Then, when you have put together what you think is a good plan, you should present it to the client.

This meeting should be an uninterrupted one, each item being carefully explained. Your service, however, does not end with the presentation. The plan must be completed and implemented, and it must be reviewed regularly with your client.

Although this may sound like an obvious comment, it is necessary that the estate plan always be written. Too much is involved with developing an estate plan to not put it in writing. And when the writing is finished, the estate plan should be read by all members of the estate planning team, as well as by the client. At some future time, the estate plan will have to be reviewed for changes in circumstances and for changes in laws. To do this intelligently, each member will need the exact details from which to work. An oral estate plan is just not feasible from any point of view.

The estate plan is usually written by the CPA or the attorney. Which one writes it depends on the competence of each in that area or on the client's discretion. It is here that the CPA who is competent in estate planning can take charge and be the prime mover in the assignment.

No two clients are alike. No two estates are alike. Therefore no two estate plans should be alike. There is no such thing as a standard estate plan. Each should be tailor-made for that particular client, taking into account the client's specific assets, circumstances, and goals. Anything less would be unprofessional and not in the client's best interest.

The estate plan is presented to the client at a meeting attended by yourself, the attorney, the trust officer, the life insurance agent, and any other members of the estate planning team. Either you or the attorney, depending on who wrote the plan, presents the plan to the client and the others. During the presentation, the client and others voice their reactions and questions. Thus, all parties are able to exchange their ideas. The final product will be an estate plan acceptable to all. At the end of the meeting, the client should direct all members of the team to carry out the provisions of the plan upon which agreement has been reached. Sometimes certain provisions of the plan will not be agreed upon at the the initial meeting and you or the attorney will have to review and revise your recommendations to be presented at a future meeting.

It is almost always advisable for the spouse to be present at the meeting so that he or she can learn about the family financial affairs and can contribute to the implementation of both the plan and the necessary postmortem responsibilities. However, as a word of caution, first clear with your client the proposed invitation to the spouse. Some clients are very sensitive about sharing this information.

Should You Serve as an Executor or Administrator?

Some practitioners encourage being named as executors and administrators because they feel that it:

1. Lends to a long and close relationship with the client and his family.
2. Provides the objectivity and independence of an audit-oriented person.

Other practitioners believe the CPA should not serve a client in that capacity because of these considerations:

1. His ability to serve as executor.
2. The CPA's fee as executor vis à vis his fee as accountant for the estate. (Is he entitled to two fees?)
3. The CPA's independence as accountant for the estate and executor. (See ET 101.01 and ET 191.022 of the AICPA which state that the CPA's independence is impaired.)
4. His liability as executor.

Opportunities for Estate Planning

The Economic Recovery Tax Act of 1981 brought about wholesale changes in the taxation of estates and gifts. Its passage opened the door for new estate plans for almost all clients who have existing plans. It has also brought estate planning into the spotlight for many individuals who do not have estate plans.

Fewer estates are subject to tax under the current federal law. However, the ones that are must be reviewed, and, if necessary, must have new or revised plans drawn up. You should notify your clients of changes in the law and suggest a review of their estates to determine if revisions are advisable.

Billing for Estate Planning Services

Because of the many skills required in the estate planning process and the high levels of technical knowledge required, many practitioners believe that billing rates for this type of work should be at a premium above standard. Some say perhaps as much as 150 to 200 percent above. Traditional criteria for setting fees include:

1. Value to the client of the service rendered
2. Technical importance of the work and amount of responsibility assumed by the CPA
3. Difficulty of the engagement
4. Ability of the client to pay
5. Acceptability of the fee to the client
6. Urgency with which the work must be done
7. Community standards or fees for similar work

Other considerations that influence the setting of your fees for estate planning are:

1. Is the engagement for a long-time client or is it a "one-shot" engagement?
2. Should a minimum fee standard be established for estate tax returns?
3. If there is a fixed fee, there should be a preliminary time devoted to a cursory projection of what the estate plan might achieve.
4. It is important to show the relationship of the fee to the size of the estate taxes or potential tax savings.
5. Have a sound understanding with the client before the plan begins.
6. What will be the contribution of the attorney and his relationship to the firm?

The following case study will give you an opportunity to determine how much you would bill for an estate planning client.

Case 3
BILLING FOR ESTATE PLANNING

Stan Petrovich has been your client for several years. He has recommended a number of clients to you. Last year the firm realized $12,000 in fees from

EXHIBIT 7-1 **Billing for Estate Planning**

Hours Spent In	Schedule				
	Tax Partner	Practice Partner	Tax Staff	Audit Staff	Administrative
1. Initial interview with client		1			
2. Review of completed questionnaire		2			
3. Calculation of estate taxes, as is			4		
4. Check of math				2	
5. Estate plan conference	2	2			
6. Calculation of revised estate taxes			3	1	
7. Preparation of report		3			
8. Review of report	2				
9. Review of recommendations with attorney, banker, insurance representative		3			
10. Typing and processing					6
11. Conference with client and spouse		2			
Total hours	4	13	7	3	6
Standard rates	—	—	—	—	—
Calculations:					
	Proposed fee......$				

him, his family, and his business interests at rates very close to standard. It appears that the estate plan which you have just prepared for him may save about $100,000 in taxes and administrative expenses, and perhaps lead to saving a few thousand dollars a year in current income taxes. Using the schedule shown in Exhibit 7-1, how much would you bill Mr. Petrovich?

Answer to the Case of Stan Petrovich

You should have multiplied your actual hours times your standard rates, plus a markup percentage based on the criteria previously mentioned. The fee should range anywhere from 100 to 200 percent of standard. You also could consider a *minimum fee* for this type of service.

Opportunities after Initial Planning

In addition to the original estate plan and its implementation, there are other services you can offer your client such as:

1. Assisting the client when he is an administrator, executor, or personal representative
2. Working with the client and his attorney when he is an heir in a contested estate
3. Eleventh hour planning (deathbed planning)
4. Postmortem tax planning

Postmortem tax planning by the executor or administrator can prove very beneficial to all the parties who have an interest in the estate. It may involve prudent decisions on certain tax elections available under the Internal Revenue Code as well as choosing among alternatives for maximizing the estate's net remaining assets to be used for paying debts, expenses, and taxes, and for distribution to heirs.

An estate is a separate tax-paying entity that must file, in addition to the decedent's final individual income tax return Form 1040, two other returns. The estate must file: Federal Estate Tax Return Form 706, a one-time filing that lists in detail the assets and liabilities of the estate and computes the estate tax, which is a tax on the net taxable assets of the decedent at the date of death or at the alternate valuation date (because it deals with assets, Form 706 is entirely different from Form 1040), and fiduciary income tax return Form 1041, which must be filed every year until the estate is closed. This form reports the taxable income and deductible expenses of the estate. Any income received or expenses paid before the decedent's death are reported on the decedent's final income tax return, Form 1040. The timing of filing of these returns can result in substantial savings on tax dollars. The executor of the estate can choose a year-end date as the last day of any month of the first twelve months immediately following the decedent's death. One important factor to consider in this selection is the beneficiary's taxable year. Any distribution from the estate is deemed to be made on the estate's taxable year end, regardless of when the distribution was actually made. Thus, if a beneficiary is on a calendar year, and the estate selects a January 31 fiscal year, the payment of taxes by the beneficiary on distributions received during the estate's fiscal year could be deferred for as long as 26½ months after receipt of the distribution. In this way, the beneficiary has unrestricted use of the cash or property distributed for this period of time.

A different kind of election is available in preparing the Federal Estate Tax Return Form 706. Here the executor can alternately elect to value all of the estate assets at date of death or six months later. This is known as the alternate valuation date. Many factors must be considered in deciding whether or not to use the alternate valuation date. For example, if an asset's value decreases after the date of death, the lower estate taxes must be weighed against the possibility of the larger capital gain upon subsequent sale since election of the lower value carries with it a lower tax basis.

There is a special type of income referred to as "Income in respect of a decedent." Some examples are undistributed partnership income, dividends declared but unpaid at the date of death, and accrued bond interest. Income in respect of a decedent is both an estate asset and income to the estate. It is therefore potentially subject to double taxation, estate and income tax. To prevent this, the law provides that the recipient of the income may deduct from his income the estate taxes paid by the estate attributable to the income. The executor must decide when to distribute to the beneficiary the asset which produces the income in respect of the decedent. A guide to making this decision is to compare the estate's tax bracket with that of the beneficiary.

When and where to take deductions for maximum tax benefit and how to generate funds to pay expenses and taxes of the estate which has insufficient cash for living expenses for the spouse and children are also important aspects of estate planning which the administrator, executor, or tax advisor needs to consider. From this discussion, it should be evident that it is almost never too late for estate planning and, by the same token, it is never too early. Likewise, there is never a limit to what you can learn about tax planning for your firm's present and potential clients. You can be a part of the planning required at all stages.

What Do You Need for an Estate Planning Practice?

Fundamental to any estate practice is a thorough knowledge of the preparation, calculation, and filing of the necessary tax returns: Form 706, Federal Estate Tax; Form 1041, Fiduciary Income Tax Return; Form 709, Quarterly Gift Tax Return, and the additional forms required by each state.

In order to become well versed in the technical information which makes for a strong background in estate planning, you may need to attend technical programs and courses relating to estates and trusts; maintain and use a library of technical information; read current estate planning publications; join an estate planning council; develop consulting relationships with other professionals; and engage in a practice development plan with estate planning objectives. The AICPA offers a number of interesting and informative estate planning courses, including Basic Concepts in Estate Planning, Estate and Gift Taxation, Estate Planning Workshop, and Income Taxation of Estates and Trusts. All of these programs, as well as the many others that are available, can be of great value to you.

There are also many terms you will need to understand and use intelligently in your estate practice when dealing with your clients and their lawyers, bankers, life insurance people and other professionals.

Case 4
PLANNING FOR A PROFESSIONAL

"I just can't believe that I owe $32,000 more in income taxes!" That's the response you receive from your new client, Dr. Karim Singh, a well-known local surgeon, when you deliver his 1981 tax return.

You patiently explain that his practice (a partnership) is extremely lucrative, and that his outside investments (the clinic building, stocks and bonds) are also very profitable.

To this Dr. Singh replies, "I didn't hire you to tell me what I owe, I want you to tell me how to save on taxes and how to keep more of my income."

You reflect on the doctor's personal statistics. He is 55 years old, his third wife is 48. His children, all from his first marriage, are Bob, age 30, a high school teacher who is married and has two small children, and twin daughters, Jan and Jane, who are sophomores at a private college.

He has given you the perfect opening, you think. "Doctor," you respond, "you're absolutely right. In fact, I was going to recommend that for you myself."

"Recommend what?" he asks.

"Why, an estate plan, of course. I can do an outstanding job for you."

"I don't need any fancy *estate plan*," he says quite angrily. "I've been reading some books and I know all about how to avoid probate and all that kind of stuff." This reaction makes you pause and wonder how to respond.

In your prior meetings with the Doctor, you had developed the following facts:

- Dr. Singh is the senior partner of a three-man medical partnership. His interest is 60 percent and the two younger doctors hold 20 percent each. For the past three years he has averaged $150,000 from the practice.
- The net worth of the partnership, on the cash basis, is about $60,000, representing primarily the equity in medical equipment and office furnishings.
- Dr. Singh owns the clinic building in which the partnership practices. The net annual taxable income from all the tenants is $45,000. There is no longer a mortgage on the property. It originally cost him $200,000; the present book value is $100,000 and the market value is $345,000.
- He owns stocks and bonds at a tax basis of $125,000, having a market value of $200,000. His taxable income from these sources is $12,000 per year.
- He receives $18,000 per year interest from municipal bonds (basis— $180,000).
- He has two $50,000 life insurance policies, each with a $12,000 cash surrender value. The policies name his present wife and the three children as beneficiaries in equal shares.
- They live in a rented apartment. His present wife has no independent income or assets. His first wife is living but receives no alimony. He pays her $600 per month child support for the twins for four more years and is obligated to pay their college costs. The second wife died. He inherited the securities and municipal bonds from her.

Questions

1. How would you respond to Dr. Singh?　　　**Yes**　　**No**　　　　**Why**
   a. You better go see your lawyer about this.　＿＿　＿＿　＿＿＿＿＿
   b. An estate plan is an *investment*, not a
      cost.　　　　　　　　　　　　　　　　＿＿　＿＿　＿＿＿＿＿

c. An estate plan could save you thousands of dollars in potential estate taxes. _____ _____ _____

d. I know an insurance company which will do a computerized plan for you, at no charge. _____ _____ _____

e. In reviewing your assets and income there is an excellent chance that income tax savings opportunities will also develop. _____ _____ _____

f. I guarantee you, the estate tax savings will be at least double my fee. _____ _____ _____

g. Working together with your attorney, banker, and insurance counselor I am sure we can develop some excellent recommendations not only for tax savings, but toward family financial security. _____ _____ _____

h. It might be a good idea to calculate your potential estate tax exposure. I have all the necessary information to do that. Can I get together with you in two weeks and review the results? _____ _____ _____

2. Would the following suggestions be appropriate for Dr. Singh?

a. Incorporate the medical practice.
  (1) Include the receivables. _____ _____ _____
  (2) Set up pension and/or profit-sharing plans. _____ _____ _____
  (3) Take advantage of other employee benefits. _____ _____ _____
  (4) Elect an effective fiscal year. _____ _____ _____

b. Regarding the rental property:
  (1) Mortgage the property, tax-free. _____ _____ _____
  (2) Consider selling the property to family members on an annuity contract basis or on an installment sale.

c. Gift securities to his children, using the annual exclusions, and perhaps some of the unified credit. _____ _____ _____

d. If it would not create a personal holding company, put the rental property and some of the securities into a corporation. Dividends would have an 85 percent exclusion, and the corporation's tax rate would be far lower than his. _____ _____ _____

e. His wife and children, either directly or

indirectly, should become the owners of
the life insurance policies.   ___ ___ _____

f. Trusts for the children should be considered so that some of the assets will not
become diluted by passage through both
his estate and his wife's estate.   ___ ___ _____

Answers to the Case of Dr. Karim Singh

1. Clearly, your first task is to overcome Dr. Singh's resistance to discussing potential estate problems. To do this, it might be worthwhile to voluntarily project his estate taxes and potential administration and probate costs. He might also be interested to learn that in developing an estate plan, income tax savings on an annual basis could also result. Another advantage you could mention would be the opportunity to get his affairs in order.

2. a. Yes, it would be a good idea to incorporate the medical practice. This might include the receivables. Dr. Singh could also set up pension and profit sharing plans as well as take advantage of other corporate fringe benefits.

   b. Dr. Singh was probably paying 70 percent tax (now 50 percent) on the rental income. He could mortgage the property up to $100,000 and keep the cash tax free. An annuity sale or sale of the property to family members would then also be worth considering.

   c. Dr. Singh is also paying maximum tax rates on his income from securities. A portion of this income may be gifted to his children, using the unified credit and the annual exclusion.

   d. Yes, indeed.

   e. Again, yes.

   f. Another idea which could be extremely beneficial to Dr. Singh's financial estate.

Summary

You can fill many important needs by developing a good estate planning practice. Helping a person to plan his or her estate is one of the most important services you, as a CPA, can perform. Develop proficiency, promote your capacity to fulfill this service, and you will be implementing a large part of your goal towards building a big practice in public accounting.

Building Opportunities in Litigation

"Sue the bastards." How often have you seen that supposedly humorous sign in law offices? Did you ever consider that those words could be intended for you? Unfortunately, we seem to live in a litigious society and CPAs are no less targets for law suits than doctors, hospitals, and other professionals. Those who carry liability insurance and have assets are known as the "deep pockets," or those to get when others have fled or have nothing left to attach. One of the unfortunate aspects of our system of jurisprudence is that it takes relatively few dollars to bring a law suit, but usually many thousands to defend it (only to prove that charges against you were unfounded in the first place). Thus, as public accounting practitioners it is especially important to take precautionary measures to avoid litigation.

These measures include knowledge of your clients (and periodic evaluation of them), professional performance, engagement letters, use of an attorney, and adequate professional liability insurance.

Knowledge of Your Clients—and Periodic Evaluation of Them

You should certainly not represent clients who are dishonest or do not live up to your standards of moral integrity. Unfortunately, while most CPAs would agree with this statement, very little is done about monitoring a firm's policy to concur with that statement.

Auditing standards now contain provisions for a firm's system of quality control to provide reasonable assurance that it is conforming with generally accepted auditing standards. One of the elements of quality control requires policies and procedures for acceptance and continuance of clients. The Exhibits in Appendix J provide a means for a firm to enforce and monitor a program which should be critical in the firm's efforts to avoid clients who might prove to be sources of future litigation.

Law suits against accountants often follow some significant disaster to the client. When desperate for a leg to stand on, many failing businesses, their creditors or their investors, may see putting the blame on the accountant as an easy way out. Although you certainly should not limit your practice to highly lucrative businesses, you should be selective in evaluating the condition of those businesses when you are engaged. And for the same reasons, disengage yourself when a client appears to be getting into *serious* trouble. This is the value of the regular evaluation of clients, which is outlined in Appendix J.

A case in point, in which our firm was involved, occurred as follows. One of our clients was going into a new venture, one totally unrelated to his existing business, and he was seeking additional capital for the venture. Since the client had not yet set up offices for the new venture, he asked if he could meet some potential investors in our office. We consented, though we had neglected to get an engagement letter about this new involvement.

The client met with one of our partners and three potential investors in our office. The investors subsequently decided to participate in the client's venture and bought shares of stock in the company. They eventually decided that they did not get what they had expected from their investment and brought suit against our client for recovery of the money plus damages. They also named our firm as codefendants in their suit claiming that they had made the investment based on our endorsement and recommendation of the venture. They cited the meeting in our office as the primary basis for this assertion. Ultimately, the insurance company and our counsel arranged to settle out of court and our client went on to win in a court trial.

In this case, we were drawn into litigation secondarily *through* a client. But often enough, the accountant can be a primary target for a desperate business person. When a client gets into trouble, he is likely to cry at you: "We're all in this together," threatening libel suits or breach of contract suits or suits for some unspecified harm that will befall him should you desert his case. In such moments of pressure, remember that your obligation as an accounting professional is not to pull a client out of a self-manufactured bind, but to exercise honest and independent judgment. Never consider the loss of a client more serious than the potential losses that could result from a lawsuit.

The extra precautions you take in evaluating clients are important to assure yourself that your clients' principals are honest. Several lawsuits which have received national attention illustrate this point. In the *Continental Vending* case, *United States v. Simon*, 425 F.2d 796 (2d Cir. 1969), for example, the principal stockholder and chief executive officer of the company diverted funds from Continental Vending to an affiliated company. That diversion of funds was the basis of the various lawsuits. In the criminal case, he testified against the accountant defendants while pleading guilty to the conspiracy charges.

In another case, that of *1136 Tenants Corporation v. Max Rothenberg &*

Co., 319 N.Y.S. 2d 1007 (App. Div. 1971), a cooperative apartment corporation brought suit against accountants who did write-up work and prepared unaudited financial statements and tax return information. The crux of the issue in the case was whether or not the accountants had been engaged to perform an audit, since the audit was based upon a failure by the accountants to discover defalcations by the president of the corporation's managing agent. The trial court found for the plaintiffs and the decision was affirmed by an intermediate appellate court and the New York Court of Appeals. Had the accountants been thorough in investigating the president of the managing agent of the cooperative corporation, they might have refused the account and avoided the costly damages directly due from his defalcations.

If you have reason to believe that the principals or key agents of your clients may be dishonest, you need not necessarily quit, but you must exercise extreme care in the preparation of any and all material for such a client.

Professional Performance

Practitioners may still be carrying the legend "unaudited" on statements, or no disclaimer on statements, oblivious to the requirements as to compilation and review services. This leaves them open to the complex and possibly injurious interpretations that can arise out of court cases. In the 1136 Tenants Corporation case again, the only identification was a legend carried on each page of the financial statements saying "subject to comments in accompanying letter," and the letter did not contain a disclaimer as such, but only, "no independent verifications were undertaken thereon." This phrase generated further dispute when an expert witness testified that in auditing, "independent verification" refers to those audit steps that involve confirmation "outside the client," and thus arose the negative implication that other kinds of verification were undertaken. The effect of the language in this case reflected that the audit steps necessary to detect the defalcation were steps involving work only on the client's records and did not require confirmation with outside parties.

The case of *Ryan v. Kanne,* 170 N.W. 2d 395 (Iowa 1969), illustrates this point well. Although the accountants in this case had adequately marked the financial statements as unaudited (the standard at that time) and carried a disclaimer, they stated in an accompanying letter that they confirmed a payables-trade. They furthermore made oral representations that the payables-trade was correct stated at $5,000. In fact, however, they had not adequately confirmed the payables, and they were understated by $49,000. As a result, the accountants had to pay a large portion of the understatement, not because the court did not recognize that they were unaudited statements, but because they had made an affirmative representation that they had confirmed the payables-trade. (The accountants were given, however, a $5,000 allowance for the margin of error acknowledged in their oral representation.)

You must be careful that the terms with which you describe your services are technically accurate. An example of the consequences of the loose application of a single technical word is evident in the 1136 Tenants Corporation case. One of the schedules attached to the unaudited financial statements listed the amount of the accountants' fees that were accrued and unpaid by identifying those fees by the word "audit." For many accountants this term has been used as a convenient way of describing accounting services, whether or not they literally involve an audit. In this case the loose application of the term proved highly detrimental to the accountants' case.

During the stock market heydays of the 1960s, our firm became involved as defendants in our first two legal actions, both resulting from similar cases. At the time, many small public companies were trying to pump up the market price of their shares through the favorable publicity of acquiring other companies. Some acquisitions were made more for the sake of announcing an acquisition than for the potential economic benefits to the acquiring company.

Two of our clients, both privately held companies, were acquired by such small public companies. Neither of the acquiring companies sent representatives to review the books and records of the operations to be acquired, nor did the acquirers see fit to review our workpapers or discuss any financial matter with us. This might have been acceptable if the acquired companies had furnished *audited* financial statements. They did not. The financial information submitted was either internally prepared, unaudited reports from us, or computer-prepared monthly general ledgers with financial statements (which today would be classified as compiled). Not only was this information compiled, but compiled with no footnotes and not in accordance with generally accepted accounting principles (GAAP). This is the type of data on which the companies were acquired.

In both cases, the parent companies soon became disenchanted with their purchases. Management of the acquirers would certainly not admit that they had made a mistake in the acquisitions, so they therefore sought to establish blame. Accordingly, our two clients were sued for misrepresentation, fraud, conspiracy and so on, and we were joined in the suits as additional defendants. Because we had malpractice insurance, our insurance carriers furnished counsel for us. Nonetheless, we retained counsel of our own to monitor the case in the event that, at some point, there might be a conflict between our interests and those of the insurance company. They never occurred.

Both cases lasted several years and significant time was expended with attorneys, interrogatories, depositions, motions filing, and infinite copy making. (Litigation is the greatest marketing technique ever developed for the copy machine industry.) Both cases ended in settlements which pleased no one.

Engagement Letters

In STEP 2 the importance of engagement letters was discussed. It is worth repeating in a chapter on litigation because, should litigation be threatened or occur, the first thing your attorney will ask you is whether you have an engagement letter.

A key issue in the 1136 Tenants Corporation case was the scope of the engagement: whether it was an engagement for an audit or only to prepare unaudited financial statements. But there was no engagement letter with which the accountants could defend themselves, no explicit evidence defining the limits of the engagement. Protect yourself; let there be no miscommunication between your firm and the client as to the nature of the services you are providing. Put your engagements in writing!

Use of Attorneys

Accountants do not want clients to prepare their own tax returns. We believe they should use a professional to render that professional service. Unfortunately, accountants are not normally such advocates of using other professionals when it comes to their own situations. As I pointed out in STEP 5, this is not in the accountant's best interest.

When most doctors, dentists, or other professionals find themselves in trouble, turning to an attorney is a natural gesture. Yet too often, accountants withhold from obtaining legal advice because they feel most attorneys do not have the familiarity with accounting practice or the expertise to be of useful counsel. Also they may think they know enough to handle the situation without incurring the costs of legal services. But there are many areas where you will need legal counsel to guide you in making decisions about problem issues, if only to prevent you from putting yourself into jeopardy. Such questions as to when and how to withdraw from an engagement, suing for fees, and drawing up partnership agreements are just a few of the areas that should be discussed with an attorney. Hopefully you will establish an ongoing relationship with an attorney who will become familiar with your firm. Take your own advice about the importance of professional service. When a legal question arises, turn to a lawyer.

Suing for Uncollected Fees

Concerning uncollected fees, the question is: Should you sue at all? It has been our experience that this kind of action can open the door to more expensive and complicated ramifications than the uncollected bill may be worth. A case in point is that of a previous client of our firm who was in the home-building business and fell into serious financial difficulty. We settled our account with him for a promissory note of $10,000, payable out of proceeds from the sale of his inventory of houses with a stipulated due date. But we were not paid out of the sale of the houses nor were we paid at the due date. Accordingly, we sued to collect on the note.

To our surprise, the client responded to our suit with an answer *and* a counterclaim stating that not only did he not owe us the $10,000, but we owed him $600,000! His contention was that since we had failed to complete the accounting work (from which we had resigned because the fees were not paid), he did not have accurate cost information and was thus forced to sell his houses at an unsatisfactory price. Eventually both suits were settled out of court to preclude protracted and costly litigation, and we never did collect our $10,000.

Rather than deal with the dilemma of suing for fees, you are well advised to determine a payment schedule with the client and bill accordingly. One of the advantages of obtaining periodic payment is that you avoid the client's accumulating a sizeable and perhaps uncollectible bill for which you might consider taking legal action. Suing to recover fees is a hazardous course for accountants, as the *Ryan v. Kanne*, 170 N.W. 2nd 395 (Iowa 1969) case illustrates. Though the accountants recovered their $3,434.67 fee, they also had to pay a counterclaim for $23,000. Insist on punctual payment of your fees and drop a client before accumulated, unpaid fees grow too high.

Adequate Professional Liability Insurance

You need this professional protection. Consider it part of the cost of operating your practice. It may some day spare you the cost of paying off a judgment (as in the 1136 Tenants Corporation case) of hundreds of thousands of dollars.

Rollins Burdick Hunter Co. (605 Third Avenue, New York) serves as the broker and administrator of the AICPA Professional Liability Insurance Program. A number of state societies also have programs which make this type of coverage available. Just make sure you have an adequate amount for your type of practice, and report all litigation or threatened litigation to your insurance carrier.

Opportunities in Litigation—Legal Support Services

There are some aspects of our litigious society which can be turned toward a positive opportunity for your firm. This might be termed turning *lemons* into *lemonade*. Consider establishing a legal support specialty within your firm as a potential service to attorneys in your community. This service can provide special assistance to attorneys in those proceedings in which your type of technical skills (not normally available within the law firm) are needed. Your professional skills include industry expertise, tax awareness, familiarity with all aspects of books, records, and financial statements and, very importantly, independent objectivity. Such training and experience, together with the ability to analyze voluminous data and communicate all obtained information to counsel and others, can be the basis of your legal support services. Support services could include compilation and organization of records, preparation of accounting-oriented questions during discovery and presentation of expert testimony during trials.

Some examples of cases where you could be of service are: frauds and embezzlements, 10b(5) cases, bankruptcy proceedings, class actions, special investigations, domestic relations, usury, money damages, lost profits, stockholders derivative actions, estate controversies, and insurance claims. Legal support services which you can provide to your fellow professionals in their practice of law can assist them in making proceedings more efficient and effective, ultimately benefiting both them and their clients.

Besides the potential revenues that can be achieved from these services on a year-round basis (not tax season-oriented), you are posturing yourself to take advantage of an outstanding practice development opportunity. It is universally accepted that attorneys can be one of your best sources of new business. In performing legal support services you are in close and frequent contact with the attorneys on whose case you are working, plus you gain favorable exposure to the other attorneys who represent the other sides. Performing effectively in legal support services can project a very favorable image for you in the legal community—a place where you would want such recognition.

Building through Acquisitions and Mergers

As the accounting profession changes in relation to both the constant flux of the external world and the proliferation of rules and standards (such as the pronouncements of the Financial Accounting Standards Board (FASB), the Securities and Exchange Commission (SEC), the IRS, and the AICPA), it becomes harder and harder for the single practitioner or small firm to keep up to date and to compete effectively.

Our firm's history includes seven mergers and one purchase, ranging from a combination with a sole practitioner with no staff to one with a firm of approximately 35 people. From the vantage point of 20/20 hindsight, most of them were *not* financial successes. Fortunately, the few successful ones more than made up for those which were not. The unsuccessful ones, nevertheless, each made its own unique contribution to the development of the firm, adding new knowledge in areas of practice management, interpersonal relationships, practice development and client service, as well as in the billing and collecting processes.

Through these experiences and those learned from other practitioners, a number of significant "rules" have been promulgated.

Rule 1. Merge for a Purpose

Do not even consider a merger until your firm has completed its long-range plan (STEP 10). Although nothing could help a plan move forward as well as a good merger, there is also nothing which could be more disruptive to your firm's progress than an unplanned merger which does not fulfill a particular need for your firm. Contemplate mergers only after you have established your guidelines through deliberate planning.

Mergers should not be made merely for the sake of merging. You should have in mind specific benefits or needs. This applies to both parties to the merger. For example, we once merged with two young practitioners who had been in practice together for less than a year, had no staff, and had little billing to add to the firm. However, at that point in time our firm had begun to grow at a rapid rate and the partners were bringing in new business faster than could be comfortably handled. We had evaluated the two practitioners as potentially excellent engagement partners. They viewed us as being able to provide them with the support of a fully developed organization. History proved out that both firms benefited from the merger.

Unfortunately, too many mergers take place because of a one-sided need. This was the primary reason for the unsuccessful mergers in which we were involved. A firm which indicates a great desire to merge into your firm and a willingness to comply with most of your demands may very well be in difficulty and looking to you to bale them out. One such merger, for example, took place with a two-partner firm, the older partner of which, we eventually discovered, had no confidence in the younger partner's ability to carry on the practice and pay out his retirement. The senior had used a merger with our firm as a vehicle to obtain a liberal retirement pay-out for himself. In fact, on his last day of active practice, his parting words were "I'm sorry to have stuck you with my partner."

When merging firms are compatible—attaining a fulfillment of mutual needs in a complementary mode—the results can be geometric rather than arithmetical, i.e., one plus one can equal more than two. Our largest merger involved a local firm which did an outstanding job in practice development, particularly in several areas of specialization. That firm's need was effective management. Its growth had been so rapid that the partnership had not taken the time to develop a plan, an organization structure, supervision, and all the other important attributes of practice management. These management capabilities lacking in the other firm were abundant in ours. We were staffed with trained personnel and had the established policies and procedures to accommodate a major expansion. The complementary skills of the two firms worked effectively and within the two years after the merger, the growth in volume was approximately 50 percent, with commensurate increased earnings for the benefit of all the partners.

Rule 2. The Name Game

One of the first decisions to be made in merger considerations is the name of the new firm. This is probably the most sensitive area of the negotiations. Each partner whose name appears in the firm name considers that name to be most important because it identifies that partner with his particular clientele. (And each partner has an ego.)

One of the ways of looking at this condition is again to go back to your particular plan. If the plan incorporates an extensive period of growth, the resolution of the name problem comes sharply into focus. For, in order to grow, one must establish an image of a firm and then institutionalize it by repetitive use, extensive community exposure, and the like. To do that requires a name of a firm which is both brief (no more than two or three names) and importantly, one which is not constantly changing. This concept of brevity and continuity is certainly evident among the national firms which have dozens or hundreds of offices organized under one name (or two or three names at the most).

At the time of our first merger, our firm had two partners and we merged with another two-partner firm, ending up with all four names as the name of the firm. It was a real mouthful, and a lot of writing for the clients on their checks. We later decided to merge with a sole practitioner and the subject of the firm name came up during the course of negotiation. It would seem that the new partner would want his name included in the name of the firm, making it the fifth, but he surprised us with the logic of his approach. He indicated the immature direction we would be taking if we changed the name every time a new partner was added or subtracted from the firm. He suggested that since at the time one partner had developed more of the practice than any of the others, we change to the single name of Rachlin & Company. The key to making that decision was the partner whose name was appearing as second of the four in the firm name. His unselfish decision to agree with the recommendation enabled us to move forward in institutionalizing and promoting the firm's name. It stayed constant, regardless of mergers or withdrawals or retirement, or any other changes within the structure, always moving forward under a single identifying banner. Once the number 2 partner had agreed to the change, all those who came after him were precluded from making a demand for inclusion of a name within the name of the firm.

Rule 3. Do Your Homework

Some people may buy an automobile because they like the color. Others, before they buy, will do research, test drive the car, and have it inspected by their favorite mechanic. Because mergers or acquisitions can be so important to the future image and liability exposure of your firm, as well as being critical in the future profits and losses of the firm, a thorough study of the other firm is imperative. This should be handled much like a peer review, with one important extension. First, in doing the peer review you would cover all nine of the policies and procedures that would be expected under a system of quality control. Then you would make a test check review of working papers and financial statements of representative types of clients as well as making sure to cover clients that are handled by each of the partners in the firm. You must have access to the files in order to evaluate the quality of service. The peer review is an excellent technique. In fact, in our merger investigations the personnel of the firm being considered for merger are advised that we will be conducting a peer review (rather than an investigation for a possible merger) and that full cooperation should be extended. This helps to prevent internal panic when personnel might learn that a merger or acquisition is in the offing.

The extension of the peer review program for a merger analysis includes the business aspects of the other firm. Billing rates, client profitability, and profit and loss are specifically excluded from a peer review. But in a merger or acquisition review, they must be included and done so with the same planning, thoroughness and objectivity as if you were doing an audit of a client. You must get into the nuts and bolts of the practice's operation—its billing rates, salary structure, chargeable hours, realization rates, collection procedures, ratio of receivables to billing, and other analyses. The best approach would be to assume that you are being retained by an independent client (your firm) and that client is paying you a handsome fee to determine whether or not they should buy this particular business. Remember, a great deal of money plus your professional reputation is at stake in making this evaluation.

One of the elements of doing your homework is to find out as much about the other firm as possible. Each of your partners should be directed to poll their acquaintances, particularly in the financial community (bankers, attorneys, insurance people), as to their knowledge of the other firm and of its individual partners. All responses should be directed to the one partner who is in charge of the merger program.

Another excellent technique, with the consent of the other firm, would be for a partner from each of the two firms to visit with the major clients of both firms and to notify them of your intention, soliciting their responses. This should not be done, however, until the merger appears to be imminent because of the possibility of unsettling long-standing client relationships.

Rule 4. Put the Understanding in Writing

Before any resources are expended in a review of the other firm, the terms of the merger and the projected structure of the combined organization should be set forth in a written memorandum, to be signed by all partners. Among the points to be covered in such a document are:

1. The name of the new firm.
2. The duties and responsibilities of each partner, including:
     a. Naming the managing partner
     b. Executive board, if any
     c. Heads of departments
     d. Specialists
     e. Managers of offices
3. The effective date of the merger.
4. An agreement as to the components of a partnership agreement, which could be attached as a separate document. The partnership agreement

must set forth all the details as to setting partnership compensation, management of the firm, withdrawal of partners, disability, retirement and death provisions, and all other matters normally included in such an agreement.

5. An agreement, in generalities, as to the purpose of merger, what is to be accomplished, the goals and plans of the combined organization.

6. Stipulation of what is to happen should the merger not work out. For example, it might be stipulated that for a period of two years either party has the right to withdraw and resume prior practice without any penalty and with best efforts to restore to prior position.

7. The capital commitment of each of the parties and how that commitment is to be fulfilled (cash, receivables, valuation of assets, and the like).

Rule 5. Designate a Partner in Charge of Merger

One partner should be designated by your firm as the person responsible for handling the merger discussion and investigation. The partner should have the right to call upon others in the firm to assist in whatever manner is necessary in order to effect the merger. He should maintain files on each of the merger candidates so that the firm can build a history of policies and procedures in this area.

Once the partner in charge has completed his evaluation and obtained the input from the other partners who have polled the community, the partner in charge should then make a report to all of the partners with his recommendations as to whether to proceed and how to proceed, incorporating in the report a timetable leading up to the effective merger date.

It is important that this person in charge work closely with an attorney who is familiar with your firm and who will be of importance to your firm at the time it becomes necessary to draw up the documents, such as the merger memorandum and the articles of partnership.

In spite of all the rules and admonitions, and the extreme care and caution utilized in potential mergers, mistakes can always occur. In combining so many different personalities—both partners and employees—there is probably no such thing as a problem-free merger. Therefore, the levels of expectation, while enthusiastic, should be modest. At one time our firm merged with a firm that had 15 employees. In a little more than a year, all 15 employees of the other firm, professional and administrative, were gone—a result of most of them being either unwilling or unable to live up to the standards of performance which our firm expected. This was a matter we had not discovered during our period of review of the potential merger firm. Another item which our "audit" failed to uncover was that many of the professional staff members were on a commission basis with the firm because, apparently, they had brought the accounts into the firm. After payment of these commissions to staff members, in addition to their salaries, there was little if any margin for profit for the firm. In addition to a screening-out process of staff, there was an additional screening out of clients which were determined to be unprofitable for us to service.

One of the difficulties in making any merger work is convincing the partners of the original firm that the old loyalties must now be transferred to the new entity. This is a goal which all the partners must not only subscribe to, but also practice. Their attitude toward the new firm will be a strong influence on the professional and administrative staff. They must be positive in expressing the loyalty and dedication to the firm philosophy, and in exhibiting the expected performance intrinsic to a successful practice. In this regard, all the partners must be united.

10

Building the Long-Range Plan

The following story about George W. Jefferson and Stanley L. Kaminski will both introduce and illustrate the importance of planning. They had been employed for several years as senior accountants by the firm of Ashley, Butler and O'Hara, a local firm in a community with a population of about 10,000. They had both grown up in the town. About five years ago, George and Stan left the firm and started their own company, Jefferson and Kaminski. Their agreement consisted of a solemn handshake, a promise of hard work, and a sharing of everything on an equal basis—both profits and problems.

True to their words, they both worked very hard at building the practice, having little time for their families, outside activities, or even each other. Their contact with each other was limited mostly to hasty consultations on accounting or tax questions regarding jobs in progress. Their incomes grew beyond their strongest expectations.

At midnight on April 15, George and Stan bumped into each other at the post office, mailing their personal tax returns. George said, "What a season! I must have added at least a dozen 1040s, and all at more than our $35 minimum rate. And that doesn't even include the gas station and barber shop owners that one of my clients referred to me last week."

Stanly replied sadly, "Yeah, but I'm getting tired of working so hard. We *never* get any time off."

"But look at all the money we're making," said George. "Besides, if you could get your billing rate up on your clients, you wouldn't have to put in as many hours. Which reminds me, *I'm* doing more billing than you are, and we're still dividing profits equally."

Whether it was the late hour or the postseason fatigue, this discussion led to a furious argument about their practice. The bitter words finally ended in a decision that they would sell or split the practice and each would go his separate way.

The following week George and Stanley approached you, as their friend and as one of the larger and more stable practitioners in the community, and offered you their practice for $275,000. The price is based on their income statement which appears as Exhibit K-1. As a friend and colleague, what would you say to them?

Please give it some serious consideration and thoughtful evaluation *before* you proceed to the discussion which follows.

Would You Buy This Practice?

You might consider their practice a good buy at that price. But if you are truly their friend, should you be advising them to sell? Haven't they built something of value which they should protect and nurture?

There is a very basic answer to George and Stan's situation, an answer which in fact could not only save their practice (and their friendship), but also enable them to continue growing toward even greater levels of professional and financial achievement. That answer is in the development of a long-range plan for their practice. By taking the time to sit down with each other and set forth in both broad and detailed terms the kind of practice they are interested in evolving and the directions suitable for both of them in achieving this, they should be able to continue working profitably with each other on a more realistic and amenable basis.

Specifically, this means spelling out precise philosophies, setting forth goals that are ambitious but attainable, putting the plan in writing, and providing for systematic implementation of the plan as well as for future modifications.

In planning and working together, George and Stanley will discover, they can realize far greater results than the broken partnership that would result from their present attitude. Together they can learn about practice management and plan to correct the mistakes they have been making—inadequate fee structure, inadequate training, too many hours, lack of firm planning, lack of image, no managing partner, and no practice development program, to name a few. From what they have already achieved, it appears that they would be capable of reorganizing the practice they already have and building for the future on a sounder base.

As a friend, you wish them the best. Unfortunately, the unhappy fact is that George and Stanley are hardly the exceptions among smaller firm practices. By far the greater percentage of smaller firms in the country have not understood the crucial value of developing a long-range plan for themselves. There is also a sizable number of larger firms which have overlooked its significance. Surveys taken in practice management seminars have shown that the percentage of firms having a long-range plan increased with the size (gross volume) of the firms in the group. The indication, therefore, is that there is a correlation between long-range planning and firm size. Of course, it can be argued that firms with larger practices got that way for reasons other than long-range planning. But, nonetheless, a long-range plan is a vital element in promoting a firm's growth because it alone serves to set the psychological stage for practice development activities, unite the partners in a common philosophy and goal, and develop the realization that their individual futures are best served in working together as part of a firm.

Such measurable effects of long-range planning were made evident in the early history of our firm. Our growth rate averaged about 34 percent a year with a cumulative growth of 480 percent in a six-year period. Then, in the following year our size doubled, primarily as the result of a successful merger. Before adopting our growth plan, our practice was routine, growing slowly and lacking in goals. Partners spent all of their time handling *their own* group of clients, running on treadmills to meet clients' demands and deadlines. There was no time to attend professional education programs or to be active in professional societies. Occasionally we had crisis-motivated meetings of the partners, but the purpose of these meetings was to resolve emergency situations (such as, today is payday and there's no money in the bank, or why is the statistical typist planning to leave?). Although each of the partners had a vague notion of personal goals and those of the firm, they were seldom more concretely expressed than "to make more money." It seemed like a typical local firm practice.

When I began reflecting on this situation, a single theme kept running through my mind: *the practice is running us—we are not running the practice.* Though we were by no means in the same critical state of conflict as George Jefferson and Stanley Kaminski, we shared the same nebulous lack of concretely expressed mutual goals. It became obvious to me that, just as the practice management surveys had indicated, successful firms don't just happen. *They are planned.*

Developing the Long-Range Plan

The original long-range plan for our firm was developed at a three-day retreat. Some people consider "retreat" a negative term and prefer that these meetings be called "advances" or "planning sessions." Our meetings were held at a resort far from the firm's offices. All the firm's partners and principals participated. We started out with a pile of blank sheets of paper. Initially each person present was asked two questions: (1) How big do you want this firm to be in five years? (2) What part do you want to play in that growth? That got the ball rolling and the blank pages started to fill up. As our ultimate, quantitative goal, we projected that at the end of five years we would have seven offices and a total personnel of 100, of which 20 percent would be partners.

In developing our long-range plan, we relied heavily on practice management material published by the AICPA. This material contained a comprehensive blueprint for a "long-range plan," based on a case study of a full five-year plan for a hypothetical CPA firm. In this case study, there were specific conclusions as to the growth in the firm's gross fees, types of services, and net income.

The AICPA practice management publication included a number of forms useful in practice development and provided specific programs on how the firm could become better acquainted with bankers and lawyers in its practice area. It stated that as many goals as possible should be *quantified,* and it set forth some hypothetical projections for a growth plan, as in the following examples:

1. Gross auditing fees are to increase at the rate of 10 percent per year for the next ten years.
2. The minimum annual net income for a partner should be $50,000.
3. Staff personnel should increase at the rate of 5 percent per year.
4. A ratio of one partner to every four staff members should be attained.
5. Management services engagements should account for 15 percent of the firm's fees in three years and 25 percent in five years.
6. The average productive time should be 1,500 hours annually for a partner and 1,750 hours annually for a staff member.

These guidelines were helpful in the development of our first five-year plan and could provide effective guidelines for the preparation of yours. Although the material we used is now out of print, much of it has been updated and expanded in the "Management of an Accounting Practice Handbook" published by AICPA. (This three-volume set is a profitable investment—not a cost—for a growing, local firm.)

In the course of developing our growth plan, we decided to define and write down our firm's philosophies and to spell out the specific steps we would take in implementing these philosophies. We felt that, while some of our philosophies seemed obvious, we wouldn't really know the actual parameters until we sat down and attempted to define them *specifically.* We recognized that, like many firms, we might be giving lip service to philosophies that we didn't really practice. For example, many accountants will claim that they try to employ the highest quality staff personnel, but their compensation and recruiting practices belie this claim. So we attempted to define our philosophies in the following areas: (1) personnel, (2) administration, (3) professional development, (4) partners, (5) practice, (6) client relations, (7) public relations, and (8) growth.

YOUR FIRM'S PHILOSOPHY

Develop a philosophical statement which is expressive of your firm's concerns. The following is an example:

> We recognize that the profession of accounting, by a technical definition,
> includes the recording, summarizing, and analyzing of economic transactions.

However, we also recognize that these economic transactions are created by human interchanges. It might then be said that a balance sheet or profit and loss statement is a formalized numeric presentation of the results of many human interactions. It is the recognition of and dedication to such humanistic aspects which have been the foundation of the firm's growth.

We are organized as a firm to provide service to our clients. As a CPA firm we deal with countless equations. The most important one to us, however, is the human equation. Adding our skills—professional, technical and humanistic—to the needs of our clients, renders a plus on both sides of that equation.

If any one concept epitomizes the attitude of the firm, it is that each client is special, and his needs and concerns—so important to him—are also important to us. Regardless of size, each client receives the personalized service that has become the guiding philosophy of this firm.

PERSONALIZED SERVICE

The human equation needs to be emphasized in your firm because a professional service is a personalized service. While different members of your firm, with varying degrees of skills and experience, may work on an engagement, there is still one person to contact, one person who is responsible. In our firm that person is called a PIC—person in charge.

The mission of the PIC is to communicate, coordinate, and make sure the firm is responsive to its client's needs. The rest of the firm is there to support the PIC in the fulfillment of this mission.

While professionalism is critical, an entrepreneurial attitude is important in understanding the problems of conducting a business in today's environment. Our business requires us to understand the client's business, and to approach it in a professional manner. That takes a special approach to the client's practice. Be among those professionals who believe in this special approach of humanistic accounting.

PERSONNEL

To render the quality of service which will meet your standards and satisfy your clients, you must hire, train, and retain the best personnel available at various levels of experience and specialization. Your personnel are your most important asset, and the investment you make in them yields the best dividends for your clients.

Academic training is not enough. Emphasize on-the-job training and education in communication skills.

INVOLVEMENT

Believe in involvement. In addition to the total involvement with your clients, be involved in community and professional affairs. Community involvement includes service by your firm members with civic, charitable, fraternal, athletic, and academic organizations. Members of your firm can serve in positions of importance in local, state, and national professional organizations. And they can write articles and deliver speeches for both business and professional organizations.

Members of your firm who specialize in a particular area can be continuously involved in keeping up to date in their fields: data processing, utilities, transportation, government, real estate, manufacturing, wholesaling, retailing, or other fields.

QUALITY OF SERVICE

Recognize that your most important product is service, and be dedicated to the highest standards of quality in your product. To this end, you need to develop a quality control program. Your quality control program should include standards, policies, and procedures regarding:

· **Independence**
· **Personnel:** Hiring, training, advancement, continuing professional education.
· **Conduct of engagements:** Planning, field work, supervision, and review.
· **Acceptance and continuation of clients:** Be as careful in selecting potential clients as they are in selecting their CPA firm. Potential clients should be approved by a partner and the managing partner. In special circumstances approval should be required of a quality control committee. Similar procedures are followed for continuation of clients.
· **Inspection:** Internal inspection of your quality control system should be conducted each year by experienced people who are not members of your firm's management. An outside inspection (peer review) should be conducted every three years in accordance with your membership in the AICPA Division of Firms. You can become actively involved in peer reviews of other CPA firms throughout the country.

Using a Long-Range Plan

Our original long-range plan was distributed to all members of our firm—with great success. It developed a feeling of working together toward achieving the goals we all have in common. The staff saw a firm which has a direction and a destiny, and they wanted to be part of it. We have also used our plan very effectively in discussing mergers with other firms and in recruiting personnel. (To a potential staff member, for example, there is no part of the plan that is more effective than the objective 20 partners within five years when at the time there are only six.)

The completion of a five-year plan does not mean that growth planning is laid to rest for five years. The plan must be continually reviewed and, if necessary, modified, as illustrated by the following example.

At one of our annual retreats, during which we were reviewing our growth plan, some of the partners in our firm suggested that we make a substantial investment in the hiring of someone to head our MAS department and in the purchasing or leasing of a computer to replace the service bureaus we were using. Although there was no question that our firm should ultimately head in those directions, one partner kept insisting that instead of moving forward with new programs we'd better get our present programs in order. He made a strong case for the resolution of a problem that we didn't notice—or perhaps didn't want to face. He forced our attention to the fact that our emphasis on growth had caused our service to clients to be less prompt, that financial statements and management letters were getting to clients behind schedule and that we had to get an unprecedented number of filing extensions on tax returns. The more the subject was discussed, the more the other partners became convinced; and the MAS head and the in-house computer were deferred. We therefore modified our plan somewhat to "get back to basics" and to adapt our growth plan to rectify the problems of client service.

The goals expressed in a long-range plan and the means of accomplishing these goals can change with the passage of time. Unless specific procedures are set up for updating the plan, a firm may fail to achieve its goals. Often, this updating process may even entail scrapping the original plan and starting from scratch. A good approach is to update the plan each year. Updating requires some discipline, but it is essential to the success of the plan.

HOW TO GET STARTED

If you decide to develop your own long-range plan, here are some suggestions on how to get started. Select a meeting place for a retreat (planning session) away from your office and allocate two to three consecutive days to working on the plan. Be sure to plan the program well in advance. Adopt a theme, such as "What Should Our Firm Look Like Five Years from Now?"

Materials for the retreat should be distributed well in advance of the meeting. This gives each participant a chance to review and consider the concept and saves much time at the meeting. The advance material should contain a history of the firm, financial statements, operating statistics, budgets, and information about your present practice area. It should also include articles on the current state of the profession and on the future prospects of the profession. Articles on long-range planning and the long-range plans of others are also helpful. You might include questionnaires similar to those in Exhibits K-2 and K-3, which will stimulate thinking about where you are and where you should be.

An agenda for the meeting is helpful, but discussion must be free and open. As noted earlier, the AICPA's "Management of an Accounting Practice Handbook" can serve as an excellent catalyst for discussion. Be prepared for some problems, however. The discussion will force each partner to verbalize his ambitions for himself as well as for the firm. This may uncover divergent objectives and perhaps bring to the surface concealed animosities between partners, which can put a severe strain on the partnership. Yet, the discovery of divergent objectives and the revelation of concealed animosities are among the important elements of the long-range plan. It is the resolution of these conditions that will give the firm the strength and cohesion to successfully implement the plan and to face the challenges of the future.

The role of the discussion leader is critical here. Not only must the leader maintain the dignity of the meeting but, more important, must direct the discussion toward the best interests of the firm.

If necessary, the leader may have to "interpret" comments that stem from a hostile attitude against one individual into a question of concern for the group. Positions may well have to be compromised. The overriding theme should be that the interests of the firm must come before the interests of any one individual. No proposal should be allowed to be put to a voting test if there is a possibility that the partner being voted against will carry a grudge. If consent does not appear to be unanimous, the topic should be deferred.

Although every firm has a different set of goals, philosophies, and capabilities, there are certain essential elements common to all successful growth plans. Therefore, your plan should include the following elements:

1. It should spell out specific philosophies.
2. It should set forth goals in a quantified fashion which are ambitious but attainable.
3. It should be in writing.
4. It should provide for methodical implementation.
5. It should provide for future modifications.

During the planning session, one of the partners should be assigned the task of taking minutes or notes. (For convenience, these can be taken on a tape recorder.) The notes should then be typed in rough and distributed to the participants. A draft of the full report should then be distributed, reviewed at a special meeting, and edited for final publication.

As a firm grows, it soon passes the stage where day-to-day contact is sufficient for effective management. To initiate and maintain an effective management plan which suitably applies to the management aspects of the firm, a partners' retreat or planning session serves as an excellent technique. It provides for communication, management decisions, and continual updating of the firm's long-range thinking. In fact, for many firms which have instituted the partners' retreat, it has become the single most important activity of the year, providing a specific opportunity to put the firm's orientation, productivity, and expectations into perspective. The concerns, as one CPA expressed them, are:

> Once in a while we (need to) consider what else is going on around us. What's going on in the community? What's happened to our families in the last year? What's happened to our health? What's happened in the profession? In the

next three to five years do we still want to be where we thought we wanted to be a year ago? Are things that we're doing now going to get us there?[1]

A retreat helps a firm's members to individually and collectively address these questions.

Planning Your Planning Session

One of the critical factors in planning a retreat is choosing a location that is physically and emotionally removed from the office, and therefore away from ringing telephones, staff interruptions, and client pressures. A resort setting can be most relaxing and still appropriate as long as the atmosphere is both confortable and businesslike.

Because creative thinking, which is what the retreat is intended to nurture, is not a process that can be forced, the time span for the retreat should be ample—two- and three-day retreats generally work very well. If you are in charge of organizing the event, arrive the day before and check to be sure that all materials and arrangements for the planning session have been taken care of. The first day can begin a little later than normal business hours to underscore the unhurried atmosphere. Some firms devote about two-thirds of the day to business sessions and set aside the remainder for recreation and leisure. A social hour and dinner gathering easily provide an informal opportunity for partners to exchange ideas that have been stimulated during the day's session.

To make most effective use of your planning session, every partner should be provided with as many pertinent facts and as much relevant statistical information and comparative data as possible. To accomplish this, the managing partner often coordinates the preparation of a document in which financial, statistical, and operational data are presented. The process of compiling this data through the firm's accounting and reporting systems and then organizing such a document can in itself reveal a great deal about the condition and quality of the data base on which you are managing your firm. It may even motivate you to employ time study and value analysis techniques to discern adequate resources necessary for handling your current workloads and to forecast.

The presentation document or "planning book" can further function as a guide to the firm's operations for the next year. In addition to the broad information developed by the managing partner, the partner in charge of each department can contribute an analysis of that department's operations for the previous year. This also serves the greater purpose of ensuring that each person has taken the time and attention necessary to specifically examine his

---

[1]Charles B. Larson, CPA, "Partners' Retreat," *Journal of Accountancy*; December 1977, p. 67.

responsibilities and to communicate them to his partners. It would be highly disadvantageous for the managing partner to develop all the materials for this meeting since one of the keys to the planning session's success is the involvement of *every* partner, beginning with advance preparation and extending throughout the actual meeting.

Since the underlying purpose of the partners' planning session is *planning for the future*, this perspective should be emphasized by a well-composed agenda. While it is necessary to review past facts, it should be approached as a basis for discussing the firm's future. Specific topics would include:

1. Client relations and a review of clients gained and lost
2. Firm budget for the coming year and the establishing of financial goals
3. Economic, social and professional changes
4. Individual goals
5. The long-range plan
6. Concluding specific objectives for the coming year and assigning responsibility for their implementation

Since the first agenda will probably be composed by the managing partner (perhaps with the administrative manager), it is a good idea for all the partners and staff who will attend the planning session to review the proposed topics and make further suggestions and additions. Once these modifications have been reviewed, a final version can be prepared. As the firm becomes more experienced in its planning sessions, the responsibility for planning and conducting them should be assigned to partners other than the managing partner. Strive for that balance between not encumbering the agenda with more topics than can possibly be undertaken in the time allotted for the entire session and not omitting any subjects which are pertinent to the development of the firm. The sample agenda in Exhibit K-4 will give you an idea of how a planning session can be effectively structured. Similarly, Exhibit K-5 contains a comprehensive checklist of topics which may be included in a planning session.

Follow-Up

The follow-up to your planning session is critical to its success. Simply put, without that conscientious follow-up, the effectiveness of your planning session can be reduced to little more than that of a diversionary exercise. A system for putting into action the decisions and plans which have evolved out of the planning session will increase the effectiveness of the time and effort the partners have spent together. This action system can easily be shared by reviewing your agenda and assigning specific partners and staff members to follow through on various topics. Either their reports can be distributed individually at the time of completion, or you can arrange for a special meeting to cover those topics of a timely or particular interest. Some subjects undertaken in the planning session will be of a more ongoing nature. Be sure that someone has been appointed to monitor them consistently so that next year the subject can properly be reviewed.

It is inevitable that the planning session, if it generated any degree of enthusiasm, will develop more ideas than can possibly be accomplished in a year's time. This, in fact, is healthy and will help keep the partners motivated. You must be careful, however, to establish priorities and specific timetables so that the most important ideas are addressed first. The least important ones may have to be carried over to another time.

Your Personal Long-Range Planning Session

Just as your firm benefits from regular sessions of questioning, reaffirming, taking stock of itself, and monitoring its plans, so do you benefit individually. As the introduction to this book emphasized, knowing yourself is a lifelong process, and it is therefore important to regularly take the time to analyze and reevaluate your own goals. Keeping a written record of your *personal* planning sessions can be as helpful to you as the firm's plan is to your practice. It will enable you to see just how close you have come or are coming to your expectations. You might even have superceded your own goals far earlier than you'd anticipated and without even realizing it. Conversely, you may see that you are far behind where you wish to be, and therefore need to make the effort to discover why. Undertaking your personal planning session prior to the partners' retreat may enable you to approach the group session with greater personal clarity, though you must be willing to remain open to the ideas and exchanges that the partners' session is designed to evoke. And just as in the partners' session, aiming for goals that are broader than what you might realistically reach can be healthy as long as you establish priorities and a timetable that will be satisfying for yourself.

One impressive illustration of a man who set out a long-range plan for himself is the story of Lee Iacocca, now the president of Chrysler Corporation. Iacocca became a vice president of Ford Motor Company at the precocious age of 36. But as one of his professional goals, that vice presidency was not a total triumph for him. He had planned to be there by the time he reached 35!

When Iacocca left Ford many years later, he was a millionaire several times over. Since the beginning of his career, he had kept a schedule for himself—both of positions he expected to attain and of projected future earnings—"on a little scrap of paper," as his wife, Mary, once described it.

Do you have a little scrap of paper in your pocket or in your wallet? Does it show: volume in 3 years, $300,000; 5 years, $500,000; 7 years, $750,000; 9 years, $1,000,000? Lee Iacocca's scrap of paper never let him forget his goals. What do you have to remind you?

The Long·Range Plan: Training a Successor and Developing the Retirement Plans

Two frequently overlooked elements of long-range planning are training a successor to the managing partner and developing equitable retirement plans for the firm. The successor problem will be illustrated by two hypothetical CPA firms: Avery, Brown and Cahill, and Xavier, Young and Zane.

TRAINING THE SUCCESSOR TO THE MANAGING PARTNER

The Story of Avery, Brown, and Cahill

Solomon Avery had maintained control over the firm he founded throughout its 15 years of growth. He looked forward to the excellent education his work would soon enable him to provide for his three children and to build a dream house for his family. Avery ran his firm on a day-to-day basis and dictated his partnership policies as he went along. Over the course of those 15 years, many CPAs joined the firm only to subsequently leave. Finally, only Sam Brown and Burt Cahill managed to tolerate Avery's style of practice and his complete domination of the firm.

Suddenly and unexpectedly, Sol Avery died. He had never initiated any plans for the firm's continuance nor had he specified any death benefits in writing. Brown and Cahill divided the practice between them and went their separate ways. Not only did Avery's wife and children fail to receive their dream house or their college educations, but they gained nothing from the practice.

The Story of Xavier, Young, and Zane

Edward Xavier founded the highly successful firm of Xavier, Young, and Zane 30 years ago. He was an excellent managing partner in giving ample direction to all elements of the firm's operation. Unfortunately, though, he was hesitant to train a successor, fearing that an heir might maneuver him out of his position before he was ready to retire. Thus, he kept all management decisions and prerogatives to himself.

After completing lavish preparations for his personal retirement plan, Xavier finally stepped down and moved out of the firm. The firm, by this time, was a very substantial one and required the attention of a managing partner familiar with the complexities of its operation and the peculiarities of its staff. Young did not have the human relations skills necessary for such a position even though he was a superb technician, and Zane, a dedicated family man, did not want to assume the additional responsibilities and pressures that would involve any more time than he already spent away from his family.

After Xavier's retirement, the firm's volume began to decline rapidly. In desperation, Young and Zane pleaded with Ed Xavier to return. Ed saw this necessity, if only to protect his retirement income. Unfortunately, his health had become precarious and the added pressures of the firm's reorganization proved too much for him. Xavier, Young, and Zane were finally forced to merge with a national firm, if only to provide some semblance of a retirement program for Ed Xavier.

These stories are only two examples of how imperative the training of a successor to the managing partner should be in the development of a firm's long-range plan. Since the management of a practice is a specialty which requires priority in the firm activities and a unique combination of talents, it can never be assumed that simply any willing partner in the firm would be capable of taking over that position effectively.

The requirements for a suitable successor are as specific and unique as those for the managing partner. Assuming that the professional characteristics of honesty, competency, and loyalty are intrinsic, the successor must also be:[2]

1. Self-confident enough to take risks (and accept the responsibility for their possible failure), yet not overconfident to the point of not seeking and heeding advice.
2. Willing to make many sacrifices, both personal and financial, for the sake of the firm.
3. Able to withstand discouragements and turn disappointments into something positive.
4. Innovative and receptive to new methods and directions for the firm. If a managing partner closes his mind to change and fails to think ahead, the firm will not not grow.
5. Able to motivate and inspire the staff at all levels. The managing partner's character, enthusiasm, and vision will be the sustaining elements in holding together an existing organization.
6. Appreciative and knowledgeable of the firm's history so that the firm will be guided in a manner that is in keeping with its evolution.

Perhaps the hardest task of all for a managing partner, particularly a founding one, is to stand aside and allow that person for whom he has become a mentor to take the reins of responsibility and act according to his own intuitions. It is important to recognize a person's right to fail:

> You must grit your teeth and let some younger member of the organization try something you are convinced will not work. You must not stand by expecting that he is going to fail. If you give him permission to go ahead, you must get behind him and give him all the support you can. If his idea does not work he

[2]Rea, Richard C., "Some Observations on the Continuation of a Firm," *Journal of Accountancy*, March 1973, p. 89.

will end up with an increased respect for your judgement. Strangely enough, every once in a while he will try something you are convinced won't work. But it does![3]

Equally important in the development of a successor is the acceptance by the other partners and the staff of his position. If others will not accept his direction when you are not there, no matter how well qualified he is, his effectiveness will be crippled. One way to test both his performance and the acceptance of the firm is to take a long vacation and see what happens while you are gone.

If necessary, when choosing the sucessor to the managing partner, you may also choose to elect a deputy managing partner. He will have the same relationship to the managing partner as the vice president of the United States has to the president. The deputy managing partner will be involved and familiarized with all the important aspects of the practice.

THE RETIREMENT PLAN

Because accounting firms vary so greatly in terms of profitability, capability of the younger partners, and financial resources of their retiring partners, there can be no universal formula for the proportioning of retirement plans. In determining a formula that will work for your firm, you should strive to develop one that will not be burdensome to the remaining partners of the firm as the years pass and more partners retire. Very often healthy firms make the mistake of establishing payout provisions which are tolerable only as long as the firm grows. But several years after the first retirement, when other partners are ready to receive their payout and the firm is no longer experiencing a strong growth momentum, the burden of such a liability could easily cause the firm to break apart. The following studies illustrate the need for well-planned retirement programs.

Tong and Oshira

Take, for example, the firm of Tong and Oshira. Tong, the founding partner, retired and had been paid off according to a formula established 20 years earlier when Oshira joined the firm. Now Oshira was ready for her retirement, but at this point the formula produced such a large figure that the remaining partners told her they would abrogate the partnership agreement rather than meet the terms of payment. As a result, the firm broke up. Obviously, a plan that will work well for the founder and for one or two partners who soon follow will often not work at all when younger partners reach retirement age.

[3]Ibid., p. 44.

The Demise of Peterson and Fleming

The firm of Peterson and Fleming had developed a long-range plan and had been in business for many years when George Peterson retired. He received a substantial payout spread over five years. Frank Fleming succeeded him as managing partner and worked on until the age of 67. The partnership agreement, which had been worked out by Peterson and Fleming and partners subsequently taken in, provided voluntary, but not compulsory, retirement at age 65. The younger partners in the firm, two of whom were reaching the age of 60, pressed Fleming to decide upon his plans. Feeling he was still competent and effective and wanting to remain involved with the business into which he had put so much of his life, he was reluctant to give them an answer.

The partners, however, perceived Fleming's competency declining and notified him that they wanted the partnership agreement amended to permit voluntary retirement at age 60. Fleming realized that if they elected to retire within the year, he would be compelled to stay in the firm or to accept less generous terms, since the firm could not affort the payout of three partners in accordance with the terms of the partnership agreement. In fact, he was not sure how well it would endure his own payout. After all the years of working, planning, and building a growing business, the firm of Peterson and Fleming stood in jeopardy because they had neglected to properly consider their retirement structure. A few months later, Peterson and Fleming merged with a large local firm.

It is important to be farsighted in developing your retirement plans and be sure its proportions will neither place an undue financial burden on the remaining partners nor establish a pattern which cannot be continued in the future. An unrealistic retirement program, which places a heavy financial burden on the active partners, is doomed to failure. Inability to develop retirement plans may be the reason for the mortality of local CPA firms. Check your own community—most likely you will find very, very few second-generation local firms (founding partner or partners retired), and even fewer third-generation local firms. Their scarcity is probably because of failure to plan in advance to solve two critical problems: (1) the successor to the managing partner, and (2) a viable retirement program.

Some retirement packages consist of the total of two amounts: the capital account on the accrual basis and the percentage (expressed in units) of the average gross annual revenues. The total amount can be paid in monthly installments. For the safety of the firm it is recommended that the payments not exceed the rate of 50 percent of the retired partner's average monthly salary of the past three years. The 50 percent will be considered as a safety factor.

In the event of death, the partnership agreement might provide that the partner's heirs receive 75 percent of the total which would have been due on retirement. This amount is funded by insurance. Programs of today may not be suitable to some future generations of the firm. That's why they should be reviewed and evaluated at your planning sessions. It is hoped that these dynamic and recurring introspections will give your firm the viability to provide continuity to the second and even third generations.

A CASE STUDY IN LONG-RANGE PLANNING FOR FIRM AND SELF

This is the story of Jerome Goldsmith, CPA, a local practitioner. Parts of Jerry's story may seem familiar to you; you may even feel they are quite pertinent, if not to yourself, at least to some of your colleagues. Consider the directions you feel Jerry should take, and try to determine some concrete suggestions as to what he might do to improve his situation.

Jerry started his own practice about six years ago and has attained some degree of success. He has a fairly stable list of clients, many of whom have been with him since the inception of his practice. His firm has grown from what originally began as just himself to now include a typist and two professional staff members. One staff member is a senior accountant who has been with him for four years, the other is an entry-level person who has been employed less than a year.

Jerry's office facilities are modest, with a limited library. He does not participate in professional societies and he manages to cram in just enough CPE hours each year to maintain his certificate. Since neither staff person is certified, and they are not required by state law to attain CPE standards, he does not pay for any courses for them, nor does he encourage their voluntary attendance.

Although Jerry makes a living out of the practice, he and his family never feel satisfied with their income. It seems as if he is spending too much on the office, with nothing left for the house or a newer model car. The Goldsmiths also think that it is about time to move to a better neighborhood.

Jerry has become concerned lately because neither his staff nor his gross fees have materially increased during the last few years. He does not feel enthusiastic about the future, especially considering the demands of new professional standards, government regulations, and increased costs. He is becoming increasingly alarmed by continually mounting administrative and personnel problems. He finds that immediately after April 15, he has a mental slump lasting two to three weeks. He is not interested in any of his professional challenges or opportunities and feels apathetic about the practice. Another slump occurs after the heavy September 30 closings have been completed early in December. And he usually loses a couple of weeks in sluggish inactivity through the holiday season, which is always a bitter disappointment to his family. His employees are not too happy with their meager bonuses at Christmas time, either.

Life away from the office has also become rather dull for Jerry. Other than some interest in professional football, his outside activities are pretty much confined to going to church once a week and keeping up with a "couples" bridge club, composed mostly of his wife's friends. The rest of his time is largely spent watching television, at least whenever he manages to stay awake. Other than a rare game of golf with a former business associate, he participates in no physical activities.

What do you think about Jerry Goldsmith? His practice? His quality of life? How would you consel him to improve his situation?

An Evaluation

Probably the first thing Jerry needs is a thorough medical checkup to make sure that none of his problems are being caused by something physical. While at the doctor's office, it would be extemely helpful to him to have a diet and exercise regimen prescribed that would be appropriate for his age and physical condition. It is highly advisable for Jerry to follow the doctor's advice.

Having addressed and passed these fundamentals, Jerry can then examine his emotional and professional problems. It is obvious that his general lack of enthusiasm has had pervasive effects on both his business life and his personal life. He has indulged in a great many apathetic attitudes and has failed to remain young, enthusiastic, and ready for change. To begin to overcome this financially and emotionally defeating ennui, Jerry needs to scrutinize himself and put considerable energy into changing the areas of his own makeup that call for self-improvement.

The balance sheet test. Jerry Goldsmith is a prime candidate for taking the mirror balance sheet test which has been advocated in the introduction. It is certainly not too late in his career to allocate some personal time *alone* in order to consider the self-evaluation processes described in the various exercises of Appendix A. Getting away from both his home and work contexts may help him to see things with more objectivity, but if this is not practical (or if the thought of going away by himself is in any way intimidating), just spending some quiet hours in the office after everyone has gone for the day will serve his purpose. He needs reflective time for himself through which he can refine his character to effectively incorporate viable plans for his professional life and his personal life.

If Jerry's period of reflection is successful, it will result in his reestablishing in his mind that managing a CPA practice is the kind of life's work that will yield him the most personal satisfaction. If, on the other hand, he realizes that it is not, he can address alternatives, such as working in a private business as a controller or financial officer or, simply, keeping his own practice a small one, yet making it the *best* small practice possible.

Implementing the decisions. Once he has made his decisions, Jerry can direct himself toward some of the professional, business, and personal aspects of his practice, such as (and this is not meant to be all-inclusive):

1. Becoming active in professional associations
2. Attending practice management conferences
3. Setting up short-range and long-range plans for the firm (and sharing them with his family and staff)
4. Improving his staff members' capabilities by sending them to appropriate CPE programs, spending time in personal training and communications, and encouraging them to advance and to assume more responsibilities
5. Getting involved in the community and soliciting referral sources, such as attorneys and bankers
6. Working to develop a speciality
7. Expanding his horizon of friends through his practice development activities
8. Setting aside "quality" time for his family and personal life
9. Constantly reexamining the level of his billing rates and the quality of service to clients
10. Accepting problems as a challenge
11. Doing whatever is necessary to regenerate enthusiasm for both his work and his personal time

Think about all the things discussed in this chapter. Isn't a long-range plan, reviewed annually, just as important to your practice as your audit manual? When it comes to your own personal long-range plan, it could very well be even more important than that.

Building for The Future

During the 1970s the problems and changes within the public accounting profession accelerated at a pace accurately predicted by such books as *Future Shock.* Among the numerous new developments in the field were:

1. Establishment of the Financial Accounting Standards Board (to replace the Accounting Principles Board)
2. Issuance of statements on auditing procedures (as many issued in the last decade as in the entire thirty years prior)
3. Issuance of "Statements on Standards for Accounting and Review Services" (SSARS) 1 and 2, relating to the compilation and review services, tolling the departure of unaudited financial statements
4. Elimination of constraints on advertising, solicitation, and encroachment
5. Action in most states to require continuing professional education on the part of CPAs
6. Legislation permitting accountants to practice as professional corporations
7. Establishment of the Division for Firms within the American Institute of Certified Public Accountants (marking the first time firms were enrolled as members rather than only individual CPAs)
8. Evolution of self-regulation within the profession, as a result of which CPA firms are required to submit to a peer review every three years

Government influence in the profession during the 1970s also grew markedly. The SEC required more reporting and more emphasis on disclosures to the public. Changes in tax legislation continued and the Foreign Corrupt Practices Act was introduced. The Metcalf Committee, a U.S. Senate subcommittee, submitted a 1,760-page report on *The Accounting Establishment,* illustrating government's desire to increase supervision, and a subcommittee of the Ninety-fifth Congress published a report called *Accounting and Auditing Practices and Procedures,* a report which ran to 2,176 pages.

Because of this unusual scrutiny and the litigation in which the profession was involved, public accounting appeared to suffer a loss of public confidence. Cases such as the Continental Vending case; *1126 Tenants Corpora-*

tion v. Max Rothenberg & Co.; and *Equity Funding, National Student Marketing,* and *Hochfelder v. Ernst & Ernst* may have encouraged public skepticism toward the profession. The deathly black cover of *Forbes* magazine on March 15, 1977, read:

Accountant's Report

To the Directors and Stockholders:

We have examined the Consolidated Balance Sheet of the company and consolidated subsidiaries as of December 31, 1976 and 1975. In our opinion, these financial statements present fairly the financial position of the companies, in conformity with the generally accepted accounting principles consistently applied.

On the other hand, there is a growing body of opinion that holds that our opinion is not worth a damn.

S/Hoskins, Anderman & Waterson
Certified Public Accountants

As a result of these changes within the profession and changes in the mood of Congress and the public, it became painfully obvious to many practitioners that it was no longer possible to hide behind file-piled desks, running our adding machines and balancing our books in obscurity. The spotlight was aimed in our direction and as professionals we had to mature and respond.

Despite this unaccustomed turmoil, the public accounting field advanced in significant respects. According to AICPA statistics, membership doubled during the 1970s; the number of members in public practice grew from 42,765 to 85,171 and the number of firms grew from 13,997 to 28,288.[1] The average net income of partners in CPA firms also rose in important proportions, as Table 11-1 shows.

Growing technology, computerization, consumerism, and competition, all are key words for our present environment. World events come to us—and affect us—instantaneously, computers are constantly outdating traditional functions and even themselves, capabilities have expanded in field after field beyond imaginable limits, and yet recession, double-digit inflation, and acceleration of changes in the quality of life pressure us relentlessly. The marketplace result of many of these changes is that smaller firms have become interested in smaller clients while the bigger and national firms are also strenuously competing for so-called "small business" clients.

I recently performed a very revealing investigation. It was very simple: I tried to list all the leading local firms which were in practice at the time I opened my first office and that are still in business. I came up with *not one.* How many second- or third-generation local firms are there in your com-

---

[1]"Report of the Special Committee on Small and Medium Sized Firms," AICPA booklet published Oct. 1980, p. 7. (Author served as member of the committee.)

TABLE 11-1   **Average Net Income per Partner***

Year	Individual	Small Firm	Medium Firm	Large Firm	National Firm
1972	$24,342	$26,048	$31,047	$36,311	$ 50,915
1973	25,641	25,987	30,496	30,084	76,926
1974	28,784	26,245	33,446	42,991	84,711
1975	27,441	29,027	38,708	45,423	86,784
1976	29,598	28,565	41,002	49,890	96,370
1977	32,603	30,159	41,577	52,310	88,596
1978	33,567	33,900	48,294	59,298	96,154
1979	36,907	35,536	52,583	63,339	103,592
1980	39,816	39,354	55,462	70,349	120,646

*Statistics published by the Texas Society of CPAs.

munity? What does this say to you about the future of local firms in practice today?

Prevailing Advantages of the Local CPA Firm

Local CPA firms offer advantages to the public which can be appreciated and emphasized, and are, in fact, the reasons that today's successful local firms are flourishing. Usually, they establish a closer and more personal relationship with the client, the result of which is better communication. In many instances, fees are lower since local practice does not have the same large overhead costs attributable to a regional or national operation. Frequently, local firms have less turnover of personnel servicing the clients (often national firm clients are confronted by new people each year doing their audits and thus complain of having to make the same explanations to new people every year).

In the local firm the staff person is offered a more varied professional experience, is involved in more of the accounting functions of a public accounting practice, and works on a great variety of businesses and industries. The staff also usually has direct contact with the partners of the firm and its clients; a member of the staff does have a chance to reach the partner level sooner in a local firm than in a national organization.

Challenges of the Future

Richard Rea, editor of "The Practitioners' Forum" in *The Journal of Accountancy*, spelled out the challenge to local CPA firms thus:[2]

[2] Richard Rea, "A Small Practitioner Looks to the Future," *The Journal of Accountancy*, June 1974, pp. 75–79.

1. Clients will increasingly rely on you for advice in management decisions.
2. You will be called upon to give current values in financial statements.
3. You will be asked to give opinions on management effectiveness as well as on the financial statements.
4. You will have to take the lead in forecasting financial results before others, perhaps less qualified, become recognized in the field.
5. You will be challenged to reflect the value of human resources on the balance sheet of the future.
6. You will be faced with the question of how to capitalize the cost of personnel development.
7. You will be challenged in the field of socioeconomic accounting. (How will you portray a private firm's role in and contribution to society? This may be your biggest challenge!)
8. Your role in the future will include increased activities in politics and government.
9. You will have to use your expertise in the development of the methods and techniques to measure the gross national product.
10. You will be challenged to convince the public and the law-makers that our tax structure must be redesigned to encourage the generation of new capital by business.

Written about seven years ago, it appears now to be a mixed bag of prophecies. My own list of projections for local firms ten years from now is somewhat different but no more clairvoyant. It includes:

1. Computer services. In the 30 years since the first computer was introduced, no modern industry has changed more dramatically than the computer industry. In the past five or six years alone, technological innovations have proliferated with explosive impact, making it possible for the first time for the small business and the family to acquire a computer. It is estimated that the sales of small business computers will double in the next two years. A computer costing $50,000 today equals the capacity of a computer costing $2.5 million 15 years ago. It has been said that if the auto industry had made the same advances in cost performance as the computer industry in the past 35 years, you could probably buy a brand new car for less than $5 and it would probably run ten years on one gallon of gasoline.

   Handwritten or manually prepared bookkeeping records will become virtually extinct within the next ten years. In 1969 there were 50,000 computers installed in the United States; in 1979 there were approximately 500,000. The numbers will probably double every three to four years. By 1991 you will be living in the age of the automated CPA office, with computers, terminals, CRTs, word processors and video tapes as standard equipment. You are going to have to do much to prepare for it—technically, financially, educationally, and emotionally.

2. Firm size. By the end of the 1980s firm sizes will have grouped into three

major segments: the multinational giants, state and regional firms with 100 to 150 professional members, and the local firms. The state and regional firms will result from mergers and from growth of large locals. They will be having a difficult time with management and a supply of adequate capital. The very small local firms will continue serving individuals and local businesses, but they will be facing increasingly heavy competition from service bureaus and other nonlicensed groups.

3. International business and taxation. The influx of foreign capital into the United States will continue. We, as professional groups, should become skilled in international taxation, foreign exchange, fund float between countries, and the like.

4. Minority group participation. At least 50 percent of the new members of the profession within the present decade are going to be women, blacks, hispanics, and members of other minority groups. They will become more prevalent at partner and manager levels.

5. Partner-in-charge of marketing. The intense competition and the new nonrules as to advertising and promotion will cause firms to expend more and more of their resources in the area of marketing. Each firm, except the very smallest local practices, should have a partner in charge of marketing who would be skilled in marketing, public relations, and advertising.

6. Specialization. The trend toward specialization will increase and specialists will become professionally recognized within the next ten years. There will be demands for new services, such as more compliance in operational auditing, more forecasting and projections, and more management services. There will be greater need for specialists in EDP auditing. The local firms with any growth in mind should look upon specialization not as a burden, but as a challenge to develop a specialization to be their particular niche in the market place.

7. Political involvement. The accounting profession will become more actively participatory on the political scene by expressing opinions on issues, moving toward public offices, and being active in the community.

8. Professional standards. Standards for smaller businesses will become minimized so that we reach an effective cost-benefit ratio as far as reporting for small business ventures. A universal standardization of rules will develop for required inflation accounting. By 1990, peer reviews may become mandatory within the profession.

9. Consultation. The consultation aspect of the CPA service will increase in demand. There will be increased emphasis on what should be done next, rather than on what has already been done.

10. Education. Yesterday's training will not handle tomorrow's practice. There are topics that must be added to achieve the capability sufficient to handle the practice of the future, such as computer sciences, behavioral

sciences, management, marketing, economics, international taxation, and political science.

(*A reassuring postscript:* In the 1990s, quality professional and administrative staff will still be hard to find and clients will still be saying that the fees they are billed for are too high.)

How to Proceed in the Coming Decade

The survival and future success of your local firm will depend on your dedication to sound management and quality service. You will have to learn to consider yourself as your most important client and always take the time to give your very best management consulting services and advice to your own firm. Just as you would want clients and potential clients to come to you with their tax problems and management problems, you should be willing to seek outside professional help in the growth and development of your firm. Consultation with experts concerning the marketing of your services, management of your practice, and implementation of the computer sciences into your practice can be measurably significant. You should also join and be active in professional societies. You might also consider joining an association of firms, thus being able to share in the management materials which such associations provide.

Consider mergers with other firms. As has been pointed out in prior chapters, one plus one can frequently equal a great deal more than two where firms which are being merged have complementary skills to offer each other.

Be sure you know what your market really is. You can't go after every potential piece of business you see available. Inventory your capability of service and seek that market which you can service effectively. Once you have determined your field, pursue it in an ethically aggressive manner.

You cannot distribute all of your profits to the partners every year and build for the future. The allocation of resources between current distribution and investment in the future involves reaching a very difficult and delicate balance for your firm. But be reassured that investment in the future can ensure growth of the firm and provide room for the future partners who will carry on the work that will finance your retirement and that of your outgoing partners.

Plan for the future and bring together all the elements of the firm toward a common direction. This provides for the most effective utilization of your firm's resources and sets a course which it can follow.

Continue to maintain your technical skills and capability in all areas of public practice, yet be adaptable. Expanding a practice does not depend so much on how pretty your financial statements look, or how neatly your tax returns are prepared, as it does on your ability to adapt to the recurring changes in our contemporary world, in the economy, in our society, in the profession, and, equally important, in ourselves. These changes must be recognized, accepted, and acted upon. Just as the profession is different today from ten or twenty years ago, so it will continue to change. Be prepared for these changes.

Finally, have confidence in yourself and in your firm. Know yourself and your firm's direction and operation intimately. Your confidence will carry you through the difficult, uncharted future of the profession.

APPENDIX A

The Nature of Self-Exploration

Exhibit	Title
A-1	Do You Have a Multidimensional Personality?
A-2	Are Your Goals Compatible with Your Personality?
A-3	How Do You Rate Your Nontechnical Skills?
A-4	Are You Ready Now?

The following exercises are designed to help you reach a better understanding of yourself and a clearer perception of your personal and career goals. This is by no means a pass-or-fail type of examination. For in self-examination, there is no passing and failing, there is only *knowing*. These exercises help you to think about yourself in a very internal way—not as you feel other people see you, or even as you *would like* to see yourself. By probing as objectively as possible, you can begin realistically to build a self-confident approach to the development of viable goals. Your only score will be the measure of how accurately *you regard yourself* after you have gone through this phase of self-recognition and self-appraisal.

The exercise in Exhibit A-1 was intended to stimulate you to consider yourself as a multidimensional being. Though career development may be of paramount interest to you as a professional, it is crucial to remember that all the other aspects of your life come into play in your ultimate success. For that ultimate success will not be measured strictly in terms of the positive data on your balance sheet but rather will be determined by your own feelings about yourself, in all of the various aspects with which your life is involved. Even though a high level of professional achievement may be overwhelmingly attractive, if your goals indicate perpetual family, emotional or personal conflicts, they may not be realistic.

The next exercise, Exhibit A-2, is designed to make even clearer for you how realistic your goals are for yourself. It should indicate the kinds of demands that will be made upon you as a managing executive and help you

153

154

EXHIBIT A-1. Do You Have a Multidimensional Personality?

1. What kind of work do you enjoy doing?_____

   How great a proportion of your general workload is this?_____

2. What personal and leisure activities do you really enjoy?_____

   How much time do you get to spend at them?_____

3. What kind of tasks do you dislike?_____
   How much of your time do they take up?_____

4. How do you feel about working under pressure?_____

5. How do you handle personal confrontations?_____

6. What makes you happiest in life?_____

7. What have you been required to do that you don't particularly enjoy doing?____

8. If you were not an accountant, what jobs or positions would you like to have?____

9. What would you like to be doing five years from now?_____

10. What would you like to be doing 20 years from now?_____

11. What would like to be doing right now?_____

12. What do you expect to get out of life, not only in terms of career?_____

13. Are your career goals compatible with this expectation and the long-range hopes you described in 11 and 12?_____

14. How do you feel others see you? (Go into detail, relating to close personal and casual friends, family and professional colleagues.)

15. How do you see yourself (emotionally, professionally, spiritually, physically, creatively; as a friend, a competitor, a mentor, a student, an innovator, a technician; whatever terms best describe your character as you yourself perceive it)?_____

EXHIBIT A-2.   Are Your Goals Compatible with Your Personality?

	I enjoy	I am indifferent to	I am resistant to
1. Attending to details			
2. Being precise			
3. Discerning between fact and nonfact			
4. Doing research			
5. Clarifying disorganized material			
6. Learning from clients and others			
7. Being expressive			
8. Developing perspective			
9. Seeking causes of change			
10. Presenting complex things in an understandable way			
11. Contending with fuzzy problems			
12. Being realistic			
13. Taking pride in my own performance			
14. Having varied interests			
15. Being imaginative			
16. Being patient with others			
17. Being in a position of ultimate responsibility			
18. Being in charge			
19. Being in the middle			
20. Challenges			
21. Demonstrating warmth			
22. Being involved in the process, as much as seeing the product			
23. Recognizing, accepting, and coping with disorder			
24. Delegating to others			
25. Working with people			
26. Understanding people			
27. Thinking in the abstract			

to see your own propensity for dealing with them. Check the choices which most accurately indicate your responses.

The point of Exhibit A-2 was to demonstrate what kinds of attitudes and interest are required of a managerial person and to show you the kinds of demands that will be made upon you. Did you feel you enjoyed most of the listed activities? Or were you indifferent or resistant to many, yet nevertheless proficient at them? Managing a very large local practice requires both the skill at and a measure of enjoyment of many of the areas in this exercise, though certainly not *all*. If you are not skilled in many of these situations, but feel you have the capability and desire to become so, then you are headed in the right direction. If you are not so inclined, then it may be time to reconsider your goal. Likewise, if you are proficient in most of these situations, but dislike being involved in them, think about what would be required to change your attitudes and if the effort is worth it to you.

EXHIBIT A-3. How Do You Rate Your Nontechnical Skills?

	Strong	Moderate	Weak
1. Respect for superiors			
2. Ability to organize			
3. Ability to make firm decisions and willingness to accept responsibility for their outcome			
4. Self-confidence			
5. Fear of failing			
6. Loyalty to the overall goals of the organization			
7. Ability to inspire cooperation			
8. Ability to delegate authority rather than making every decision myself			
9. Ability to ignore the occasional barbs of unkind critics			
10. Ability to stay calm when dealing with subordinates			
11. Ability to forget the job in favor of family or friends when the day is over			
12. Ability to make friends other than professional colleagues			

Because a host of nontechnical skills plays as vitally important a part as technical proficiency in the CPA's success, evaluating yourself in these terms is implicit in projecting your ability to function as a managing executive. In Exhibit A-3, check the responses which most accurately indicate the degree of your feeling:

Consider what this exercise revealed about your willingness to give of yourself to the development of your practice. Most people are content to work for others and collect a regular paycheck. It is quite easy to leave decisions to others and complain about them afterwards. When you run your own practice, you make the decisions and you have to meet the payrolls and the bills. The characteristics of the entrepreneur are indeed different from those of the employee. The traits of the successful practitioner include the strong desire for success, the proprietory instinct (being your own boss), and a sincere attitude of cooperation. Though every person is made up of a unique combination of personal and professional characteristics, these traits are fundamental. Analyze how successfully your own combination lends itself to managerial success. For example, you may be strong in self-confidence yet have a high degree of fear of failing. This may, in fact, be beneficial if it stimulates you as a manager to plan in ways that will prevent failure. Or you may be exceedingly high in motivation and managerial skills yet unable to let go of the problems and pressures of your job at the end of your work day. An obsessive devotion to your work may indicate a lack of personal balance in other aspects of your life.

The purpose of the exercise in Exhibit A-4 is to help you recognize one more level of preparedness for undertaking the development of a large practice.

EXHIBIT A-4. Are You Ready Now?

	Yes	No	Maybe
1. If you had your college career to do over again, would you still become a CPA?			
2. Do you keep current on the reading of professional publications?			
3. Are you able to convince others of your technical abilities and of your competence to perform?			
4. Are you eager, anxious, and excited about developing your practice?			
5. Are you active in professional organizations?			
6. Are you thoroughly familiar with generally accepted standards and accounting principles?			
7. Have you discussed your plans with experienced practitioners in your area?			
8. Has the concept of "being your own boss" been a strong desire of yours?			
9. Is it more important to you to see your name on the letterhead than it is to see it on a salary check?			
10. Have you had direct client contact and management responsibilities in your present and prior activities?			
11. Are you comfortable with the prospect of *not* receiving a regular paycheck?			
12. Do you have the ability to supervise and motivate others?			
13. Does your spouse and/or family support your decision to develop your own practice?			
14. Is the feeling of independence important to you?			
15. Is dealing with people one of your stronger qualities?			
16. Are you willing to dedicate the time to keeping up to date with intellectual, technical, and professional developments?			
17. Are you knowledgeable in the fields of psychology and interpersonal relations?			
18. Do you have capabilities in both written and spoken communication?			
19. Do you have sufficient *diversified* experience in accounting, auditing, tax, and management advisory services?			
20. Are you aware of the high rate of failure in new businesses in general?			
21. Do you have a financial plan?			
22. Are you willing to compromise your standard of living to develop and expand your practice?			
23. Are you willing to go into debt to accomplish it, if necessary?			

One purpose of Exhibit A-4 is to help you recognize the level of your own preparedness for building a large local practice. Perhaps you are not financially ready to risk some of the monetary sacrifices that may be called for. Or you may have begun to realize that you need a broader background in facets of the practice with which you may not be well acquainted. Since good managers are highly skilled in human relations, you may see that you need to undertake a program in improving your ability to work with both groups *and* individuals. These human relations skills will be consistently called upon in your dealings with associates and staff as well as with clients.

Though all of these exercises were intended to cause you to probe many aspects of your self and your goals, they should also have enabled you to confirm intuitions about yourself which you may now be able to regard with greater certainty.

Timing is an essential determinant in the fulfillment of any goal. Recognizing to what degree your preparedness is immediate or potential is equally as important as discerning your various levels of capabilities. Perhaps these exercises have caused you not only to reevaluate your objectives as an accounting practitioner, but also to more realistically estimate your projections as to when you will be able to fulfill them.

APPENDIX B

Matrix for a Successful Firm

Exhibit	Title
B-1	Income Report for Firm AB
B-2	Income Report for Firm YZ
B-3	Statistics for the Two Firms

This appendix relates to several chapters of the book (especially STEPS 1, 2, 3, and 4) and compares the potential income of a partner in a poorly managed firm (AB) to that of one in a well-managed firm (YZ). These modules can be expanded from the single partner in the examples to any number of firm partners.

Notice the following major differences in firm YZ:

- Higher utilization (chargeable hours)
- Higher billing rates through application of a different billing formula
- The high ratio of staff to partner, 4 to 1 versus 2 to 1 (while retaining the level one clerical person per partner).

EXHIBIT B-1. Income Report for Firm AB

	Compensation	Rate*	Utilization	Billing
Partner	?††	$60,00	1,000	$ 60,000
Senior	$20,000	29.00	1,500	43,500
Associate	12,000	17.00	1,500	25,500
Total	$32,000	$32.25†	4,000	$129,000
Clerical (1)	10,000			
Overhead (equals payroll)	42,000			
Costs	$84,000			84,000
Profit				$ 45,000††
Percent				35

*Formula: Compensation ÷ 2,080 × 3

†Average rate

††Maximum partner's earnings

EXHIBIT B-2. Income Report for Firm YZ

	Compensation	Rate*	Utilization	Billing
Partner	?‡	$75.00	1,400	$105,000
Manager	$30,000	53.00	1,800	95,400
Senior	20,000	35.00	1,900	66,500
Associate	14,000	25.00	1,900	47,500
Associate	12,000	21.00	1,900	39,900
Total	$76,000	$39.80†	8,900	$354,300
Clerical(1)	10,000			
Overhead (equals payroll)	86,000			
Costs	$172,000			172,000
				$182,300††
Profit				
Percent				51.5

*Formula: Compensation ÷ 1,700 × 3
†Average rate
‡Maximum partner's earnings

EXHIBIT B-3. Statistics for the Two Firms

	AB	YZ
Billing total	$129,000	$354,300
Per partner	129,000	354,300
Per person	32,250	59,050
Per clerical	129,000	354,300
Per staff	34,500	62,325
Average hourly billing rate—firm	32.63	39.80
Average hourly billing rate—staff	23.00	33.24
Profits:		
Per partner (and this is the key item)	$ 46,500	$182,300
Percent of gross	35.6	51.5
Per hour	$ 11.63	$ 20.48

Organization Structure[1]

Exhibit	Title
C-1	Checklist 1: Assigned Responsibilities
	Managing Partner
	Department Director
	Practice Partner
	Partner in Charge of Office
C-2	Checklist 2: Committees
	Administration
	Financial
	Personnel
	Practice Development
	Quality Control
	Steering

The following lists of assigned responsibilities (job descriptions) were found effective for firms with a staff of 25 to 100.

---

[1]See discussion in STEP 1.

EXHIBIT C-1. **Checklist 1: Assigned Responsibilities**

Managing partner

The managing partner is elected annually by the partners and is responsible to them. Two specific major functions are:

- To implement firm policies, similar to a president of a company in relation to the board of directors (the partners)
- To assume responsibility for the day-to-day operation of the firm

Just as MP stands for managing partner, the initials stand also for the two general functions of this partner:

- Motivation
- Planning

The job responsibilities include the following (some of which may be delegated to others):

1. Establishes partners' annual compensation, subject to acceptance by partners
2. Calls and conducts partners' meetings, including necessary agendas and minutes
3. Serves on all committees, and serves as chairman of the steering committee
4. Coordinates the efforts of departments, committees, and functions, and is supportive of their efforts
5. Reviews firm correspondence and reports
6. Supervises all administrative functions
7. Represents the firm in all areas, from merely receiving mail addressed to the firm to handling legal matters on behalf of the firm
8. Initiates, coordinates, and reviews partners evaluations
9. Maintains official partnership records, such as the partnership agreement
10. Evaluates expansion and growth possibilities for the firm and makes appropriate recommendations
11. Subject to the approval of the partners, selects:
    a. department heads
    b. committee chairmen and members
    c. partners in charge of offices
12. Appoints an inspection team on an annual basis in compliance with firm's quality control system
13. Makes recommendations of new partners and any change in status of partners
14. Authorizes and executes such contracts, commitments, and other legal documents as may be required by the partnership agreement, or as specifically authorized by the partners, or as deemed necessary in the ordinary conduct of the firm's affairs
15. Disseminates and implements firm policies and procedures
16. Approves firm publications, public seminars, and other public representations of the firm
17. Resolves internal conflicts as between departments, committees, or partners
18. Directs and administers compliance with regulations under which the firm operates

No better summation of the responsibilities can be made than the immortal four words on the desk of the late Harry S. Truman: "The buck stops here."

Department director (accounting and auditing, tax, management consulting services)

1. Develops expertise in departmental discipline
2. Available for consultation in specialty
3. Develops departmental manuals

4. Has authorization to sign the firm name (reports, tax returns, letters, etc.)
5. Has the following responsibilities to personnel in department:
   a. Attentive to them as individuals and sympathetic to personal matters
   b. Involved in scheduling
   c. Supervises training in specialty
   d. Communicates firm policies
   e. Supervises, directs, and motivates
   f. Makes periodic evaluations
   g. Encourages specialization
   h. Reviews continuing professional education requirements
6. Distributes technical and current information to appropriate personnel
7. Develops all personnel in the department, particularly a potential successor to the director
8. Initiates departmental participation and contact with firm management
9. Anticipates number of people required in department on a timely basis
10. Directs continuing professional education in specialty
11. Maintains quality controls in department
12. Develops speaking and writing opportunities
13. Participates in professional activities related to specialty
14. Develops and implements practice development techniques

Practice partner (engagement partner, partner in charge)

Each client of the firm has a designated *practice partner*. In the case of some of the larger engagements, there is to be a backup practice partner. The practice partner makes effective use of the principals and managers in the supervision of engagements, thus expanding the partner's (and the firm's) capabilities to render quality service to a multitude of clients. The practice partner's responsibilities to each client are:

1. The direct contact and the ultimate responsibility for the firm's relationship with the client, with a goal of making each one an *enthusiastic* client
2. Responsibility for setting fees, billing and collecting
3. Responsibility for on-the-job training of staff personnel, including behavioral matters as well as technical requirements
4. Approval of time budgets and audit plans
5. Return of reports, tax returns, management letters, and correspondence before processing
6. Signing of items listed in 5
7. Training of principals and managers who have the potential to become practice partners
8. Evaluation of staff personnel
9. Extension of services to existing clients
10. Responsibility to provide staff with experience in various areas of engagements, in various industries, and with different supervisory personnel
11. Periodic evaluation of whether or not firm should continue relationship with client
12. Preservation of the firm's independence (in fact and in appearance), when, for example, accounts receivable reach the status of loans

The practice partner should participate in all areas of practice development, including:

1. Community affairs and organizational activities
2. Contacts with bankers and lawyers
3. Speaking and writing engagements
4. Seminars

EXHIBIT C-1. **Checklist 1: Assigned Responsibilities** (*Cont.*)

Partner in charge of office

1. Security of the office (doors locked, files protected, etc.)
2. Housekeeping matters (cleanliness, light bulbs, etc.)
3. Favorable relationship with landlord
4. Reception of visitors
5. Use of conference rooms and library
6. Mail (incoming and outgoing)
7. Interoffice transfers
8. Adequacy of support personnel
9. Close liaison with managing partner
10. Resolution of personnel conflicts
11. Professional atmosphere in the office (voice levels, appearance of desks, etc.)
12. Telephone
    a. Service and adequacy
    b. General inquiries and calls
13. Protection of firm assets
14. Space needs, maintenance, and decor of office
15. Authority to sign firm name to reports, tax returns, letters, etc., in the absence of departmental director
16. Authority to release files or to release copies from files

EXHIBIT C-2. **Checklist 2: Committees**

Six committees are suggested with general responsibilities that are listed below. The responsibilities are not listed in any order of importance. There may be some overlap, but these matters can be readily resolved in operation. The committees are listed alphabetically.

Administration

 1. Administrative personnel
 2. Production of firm reports
 3. Files
 4. Purchasing procedures
 5. Adequacy and control of firm's supplies
 6. Adequacy and control of firm's equipment
 7. Telephone services
 8. Mail services
 9. Security of offices
10. Housekeeping
11. Reception of visitors
12. Conference rooms and libraries

Financial

 1. Cash flow and cash requirements
 2. Monthly financial reports
 3. Firm's annual report and tax returns
 4. Budgets
 5. Accounts receivable and collections
 6. Internal controls
 7. Banking relationships
 8. Billing
 9. Fee standards
10. Financial manuals (billing procedures, collection procedures, etc.)
11. Financial analysis and recommendations

Personnel

 1. Staff level guidelines
 2. Staff reviews
 3. Levels of compensation
 4. Staff training
 5. Scheduling
 6. Recruiting
 7. Continuing professional education
 8. Employee files
 9. Advancement
10. Personnel manual (office manual)
11. Personnel policies—holidays, work hours, etc.

Practice development

 1. Creation of the best possible image for the firm
 2. Relationship with attorneys, bankers, brokers, and other spheres of influence
 3. Development of new areas of practice
 4. Expansion of present areas of practice
 5. Firm seminars
 6. Firm publications
 7. Speaking and writing opportunities for firm members

EXHIBIT C-2. **Checklist 2: Committees** *(Cont.)*

Quality control
1. Compliance with the firm's quality control document
2. Development of expertise in the field of quality control review of other CPA firms, publicizing of such expertise, and generation of revenues from such practice

Steering (in some firms designated as the executive committee)
1. Partnership philosophies and policies
2. Long-range planning
3. New partners
4. Changes in partner's status or compensation
5. Development of principals into partners
6. Partnership agreement
7. Partners' compensation
8. Partners' retirement
9. Contingency planning
10. Locations
11. Capital improvements or investments
12. New departments
13. Participation in professional and community activities
14. Mergers and acquisitions

APPENDIX D

Forms For Practice Management[1]

Exhibit	Title	Usage
D-1	Change in Status	Notifies the necessary functions of the firm of a client change, such as a new address or the loss of a client (with the reasons stated).
D-2	Mailing List Additions	Controls who gets on the mailing list (for newsletter and the like). Note "Mailing Codes" for names sought for the list.
D-3	Time Report	Probably the most important form of all, this form captures the time and charges that form the basis for billing to clients.
D-4	Retainer and/or Fee Projection	A guideline for projecting fees, normally for a client on general ledger services.
D-5	Billing Draft	Used by partners to draft a bill that will go to a client.
D-6	Receipt of Cash	When mail is opened all checks received are listed on this report, a copy of which goes to each partner.
D-7	Credit or Adjustment Authorization	To be completed and processed before a credit may be issued to a client. Requires managing partner approval.
D-8	Report Control	This form accompanies financial statements through the firm and is "signed off" as each step is completed
D-9	Engagement Status Report	Prepared weekly during the course of an extended engagement.
D-10	Continuing Professional Education Attendance and Evaluation Form	To monitor compliance with CPE standards.
D-11	Request to the Management Consulting Department	To generate and monitor engagements for a specialized department.
D-12	Notice of Partner's Absence	Advance notice of when a partner will be away, and who is responsible for costs incurred.

[1]This appendix relates especially to STEP 2 and STEP 5.

Exhibit	Title	Usage
D-13	Record of Conversation	To make an immediate record of phone conversations, creating simultaneously an action document in and of itself. A pad of these forms is kept handy at all telephones.
D-14	Record of Conference	To manually record a conference, using the same document for follow-up.
D-15	Profitability Impact Report	Goes to a partner when a staff person is working on an engagement for which there is no engagement letter or the client's balance is over 120 days.

CHANGE IN STATUS

CLIENT NO. ☐☐☐☐ ☐☐☐   **OFFICE** _____ CHANGE **EFFECTIVE** AS OF _____

CLIENT _____

☐ NEW ADDRESS: _____   ☐ NEW PHONE: _____
_____   OFFICE _____
_____   HOME _____

☐ **ADD** or ☐ **CHANGE** THE FOLLOWING:
SIC # _____ F.Y.E. _____ STAFF _____

☐ CHANGE IN PIC:
   ☐ FROM _____ ☐ TO* _____
   APPROVED BY NEW PIC: _____
                                           (SIGNED)
   (*IF CHANGED TO NOTE RECEIVABLE OR LITIGATION, TO BE SIGNED BY M.P. OR D.M.P.)

☐ CHANGE IN SERVICE: _____

☐ CHANGE IN FEES: _____

☐ CHANGE IN RETAINER:
   ☐ MONTHLY, IN ADVANCE $_____ ☐ SPECIAL (_____) $ _____
   ☐ QUARTERLY $ _____ ☐ DISCONTINUE $ _____

☐ **NEWSLETTER:** ☐ **ADD TO MAILING LIST** ☐ **DELETE FROM MAILING LIST**

☐ OTHER CHANGES: _____

☐ **NO LONGER CLIENTS**

   ☐ **DELETE** FROM RUN, INACTIVATE FILES, REMOVE FROM MAILING LIST (**ZERO** BALANCE IN ACCOUNTS RECEIVABLE)

   STATE IN DETAIL REASON(S) FOR LOSS (THIS SECTION MUST BE COMPLETED)

   _____
   _____
   _____
   _____
   _____

AUTHORIZED BY: _____
(TO BE SIGNED BY PARTNER, PRINCIPAL OR MANAGER)   DATE SIGNED

**ALL FORMS RECEIVED AFTER THE 25th OF THE MONTH
WILL BE PROCESSED IN THE MONTH FOLLOWING.**

DISTRIBUTION OF COPIES
FORWARD **ALL** COPIES TO EDP. RETAIN PHOTOSTAT IF DESIRED.
WHITE — EDP DEPT.   **CANARY** — FILE ROOM
PINK — P.I.C. A/C BOOK   **GOLD** — WORD PROCESSING

EDP DEPT.
REC'D DATE _____
PROCESSED _____
BY _____

MAILING LIST ADDITIONS

☐ CLIENT RELATED:

CLIENT NAME _____ NUMBER ☐☐ ☐☐-☐☐☐ ☐☐☐

☐ NOT CLIENT RELATED

MAILING CODES

NAME _____

STREET _____

CITY/STATE/ZIP _____

(OPTIONAL) C/O _____   ☐☐☐☐

NAME _____

STREET _____

CITY/STATE/ZIP _____

(OPTIONAL) C/O _____   ☐☐☐☐

NAME _____

STREET _____

CITY/STATE/ZIP _____

(OPTIONAL) C/O _____   ☐☐☐☐

NAME _____

STREET _____

CITY/STATE/ZIP _____

(OPTIONAL) C/O _____   ☐☐☐☐

── MAILING CODES ──

CLIENT RELATED	NON CLIENT RELATED			
9100 BOARD MEMBER OF CLIENT	0100 ATTORNEY	0700 C.P.A.	1200 INSURANCE	1800 SECURITIES (DEALERS/BROKERS)
9200 EMPLOYEE OF CLIENT	0200 ACCOUNTANT	0800 CONSULTANTS	1300 MEDIA (TV, RADIO, ETC.)	1900 SPORTS
9300 PARTNER OR COVENTURER	OR BOOKKEEPER	0900 EDUCATOR	1400 MEDICAL	9900 RELATIVE, FIRM MEMBER
WITH CLIENT	0300 ADVERTISING	1000 ENTERTAINMENT	1500 MORTGAGE	9910 FORMER FIRM MEMBER
9400 RELATIVE OF CLIENT	0400 BANKER	1050 FINANCIAL, OTHER	1600 PUBLIC RELATIONS	9999 OTHER (MISC.)
9500 STOCKHOLDER OF CLIENT	0500 BUSINESS BROKER	THAN BANK	1700 REAL ESTATE	
9600 OFFICER OF CLIENT	0600 BUILDING TRADES	1100 GOVERNMENT		

BY _____   DATE _____

FORWARD TO EDP DEPARTMENT

170

TIME REPORT

Print Name _____ Initials _____

Function _____

Period Ending _____

Reviewer _____

Chargeable Time _____
Non-Chargeable Time _____
Total Time _____

CLIENT NAMES	CLIENT NUMBERS	ENGAGE NUMBER	FUNCTION CODE	TOTAL HOURS	DATE	PERIOD ENDING	REMARKS & COMMENTS (20 characters ONLY)

PG ____ OF ____

TOTAL HOURS (Must Crossfoot)

SIGNATURE: _____

INSTRUCTIONS:

Client Name
Record client name as in the client book and accounting file.

Client Number / Engagement Number
Record 5 digit client no. and 3 digit engagement suffix exactly as shown in Client Book.

Function (Billing) Code
Record the number from the billing time code sheets (100-999). These are detailed in the manual TIME REPORTS AND BILLING CODES.

Date
Record the dates that are covered by the time sheet.

Hours
Record the nearest 1/10 hour all time expended (1/10 = 6 min. = 0.10).
Total across to the total hours column.
Summarize chargeable and non-chargeable time in upper right hand corner.

Period Ending
Record the date representing the period covered by the work performed

Remarks and Comments
Record all comments or other information that will help explain the work performed and time expended.
Must be done for ____ 48 (misc.) codes.

900 Codes
Record and circle on bottom lines of time sheet.

171

EXPENSE REPORT

Print Name _____ Initials _____

Period Ending _____

CLIENT NAME	FUNCTION CODE	EXP. DATE	CLIENT NUMBER	ENGAGE NUMBER	EXPENSES	G/L—FIRM USE ONLY		REMARKS & COMMENTS
						ACCOUNT	SUB A/C	
					$			
TOTAL EXPENSES					$			

SIGNATURE: _____

Advances, Tickets & Adjustments

Date	Description	Amount
		$
TOTAL		$

Internal Accounting

Balance Forward Due To (From)	$
Add: Advances	
Subtotal	
Deduct: Expenses	
Closing Balance Due To (From)	$
Date Settled	CHK #
SIGNATURE	

INSTRUCTIONS:

Function Code
There are specific categories related ot the various expense categories.
800 Series — Chargeable to Client
900 Series — Non-chargeable to Client

Exp. Date
The day or period expenses were incurred.

Expenses
List the total expenses for the respective function code. Also list items prepaid by the firm that are to be charged to the client (i.e. Airline Tickets, etc.) ATTACH ORIGINAL RECEIPTS.

Advances, Tickets and Adjustments
List, describe and total all advances and expense items prepaid by the firm. (i.e. Cash, Airline Tickets, Rent-A-Car, etc.)

Internal Accounting
For bookkeeping use only.

172

EXHIBIT D-4. Retainer and/or Fee Projection

RETAINER CALCULATIONS

CLIENT:_____ NUMBER ☐ ☐ ☐ ☐ ☐ ☐ ☐ ☐ ☐

PERIOD ENDING:_____ PREPARED BY:_____

MONTH RETAINER WILL START:_____ APPROVED BY:_____

ON NUMBERED LINES, INSERT NAME OR LEVEL

	NUMBER OF HRS. (Annually)	RATE	SUB-TOTALS	TOTAL
A. WRITE-UP (FREQUENCY:_____)				
1)_____			$	
2)_____				
3) COMPUTER CHARGES	....			
TOTAL WRITE-UP				$ (A)
B. YEAR END TAX RETURNS:				
1)_____				
2)_____				
3) A & A REVIEW				
4) TAX REVIEW				
5) COMPUTER CHARGE (1065 & 1120S)	....			
TOTAL YEAR END TAX				$ (B)
C. FINANCIAL STATEMENTS: (FREQUENCY:_____)				
1)_____				
2)_____				
3)_____				
4) A & A REVIEW				
TOTAL FINANCIAL STATEMENTS				$ (C)
D. PROPERTY TAXES:				
1)_____				
2)_____				
TOTAL PROPERTY TAX				$ (D)
E. 1040's (HOW MANY_____)				
1) NAME OR LEVEL_____				
2) TAX REVIEW				
3) COMPUTER CHARGES	....			
TOTAL 1040				$ (E)
F. CONFERENCES:				
1)_____				
2)_____				
3)_____				
TOTAL CONFERENCES				$ (F)
G. OTHER_____				$ (G)

TOTAL HOURS ☐

TOTAL PROJECTED ANNUAL BILLING @ STANDARD ...... $_____

DIVIDED BY 12 .... $_____

MONTHLY RETAINER .... $_____

173

BILLING DRAFT

AS OF
CHECK ONE

☐ JAN. ☐ FEB. ☐ MARCH
☐ APRIL ☐ MAY ☐ JUNE
☐ JULY ☐ AUG. ☐ SEPT.
☐ OCT. ☐ NOV. ☐ DEC.
☐

A. BILLING CODE NUMBER   PERIOD

AMOUNT

$ _____ .
_____ .
_____ .
_____ .

B. OTHER BILLING DESCRIPTION

_____ .
_____ .
_____ .
_____ .
_____ .
_____ .

C.

NAME	HOURS	BILLING RATE	TOTAL

D. TOTAL BILLING

$

E. CLIENT LABEL

BILL TO

OR

NAME: _____

ADDRESS: _____

_____

_____

ATTN.: _____

F. TYPED BY:_____ DATE _____ INV. NO._____

G. ☐ SEE SPECIAL HANDLING INSTRUCTIONS ON REVERSE SIDE.

174

SPECIAL HANDLING

*Please check the applicable code and, where necessary,
write in the comments needed.*

CODE

☐ 1. Special Request, one time only, Instructions:_____
_____
_____
_____
_____
_____

☐ 2. Analysis Request — needed by:_____
Time period to be covered, from:_____ to:_____
Standard Time:_____
Billed vs. Standard:_____
Other:_____
_____
_____
_____

NOTE: Will be prepared before next BILLING CYCLE, not during this one.

☐ 3. PIC to review final typed invoice before mailing. (Turn-around must be same day to C&C.) (C&C must handle the actual mailing for control purposes.)

☐ 4. Client requests copy of WIP run, please attach copy to invoice.

☐ 5. Copy of invoice mailed per client request. (C&C applies this code on duplicated invoices mailed to clients tying in collection controls, i.e. "I never received a copy of the invoice, etc.").

☐ 6. Detail employee name/rate/hours/totals as indicated on front of billing draft.

☐ 7. Detail only employee name and rate as indicated on front.

☐ 8. DO NOT MAIL — Give typed invoice to PIC for direct handling. PIC is responsible for mail or delivery to client.

☐ 9. Internal Billing — no copy to be mailed or given to client.

EXHIBIT D-6. **Receipt of Cash**

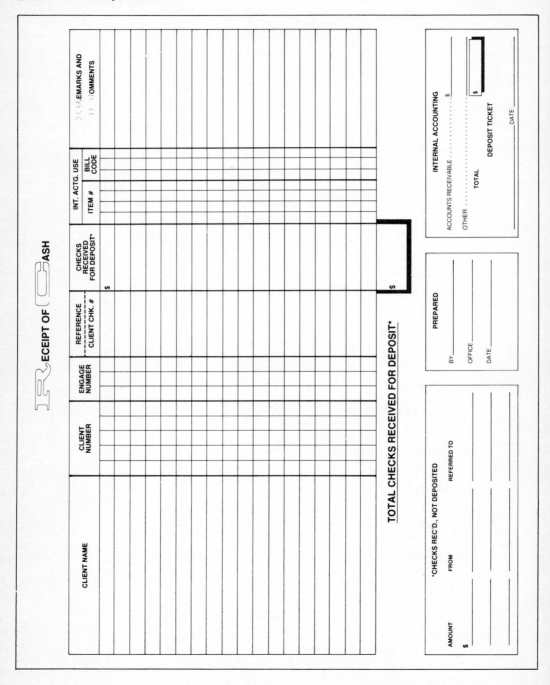

176

CREDIT OR ADJUSTMENT AUTHORIZATION

CLIENT NO.

NAME _____

Part 1. P.I.C. Request

DEBIT (Charge)		CREDIT	
Reserve for Bad Debts	$ _____	Accounts Receivable*	$ _____
Discounts and Allowances	_____	Other: _____	
Fee Income _____	_____		
Capital Account _____	_____		
Other: _____ (PIC)	_____		

*APPLY TO INVOICE
IF NOT STATED, APPLIES TO
OLDEST ONES FIRST.

DATE	NO.	AMOUNT
___	__	$ ___
___	__	___
___	__	___

TOTAL $ _____ $ _____

☐ Send Credit Memo to Client   ☐ Other Instructions: _____

☐ Do **NOT** Send; Internal Only

Reason for credit or adjustment, include names of personnel involved. (Use additional sheet if necessary):

INTERNAL INFORMATION	TO APPEAR ON CLIENT'S CREDIT MEMO

(Signed) _____   (Date) _____

Part 2. Managing Partner

☐ Approved to process.   ☐ Additional action. _____

_____

(Signed) _____   (Date) _____

Part 3. Credit and Collection

Credit Memo Issued:

Credit Memo No. _____ Date _____ By _____

Apply to Item Numbers: _____

DISTRIBUTION OF COPIES:
GOLD-RETAINED BY PIC, FORWARD FIRST 3 TO MANAGING PARTNER
PINK-ACCOUNTABILITY OR PERSONNEL FILE — **WHITE & CANARY**-CREDIT AND COLLECTION

REPORT CONTROL

CLIENT NUMBER ☐☐ ☐☐☐ ☐☐☐☐ ☐☐☐

OFFICE:

CLIENT NAME _____

DUE DATE:

(GIVE REASON IN SPECIAL COMMENTS AREA BELOW FOR OTHER THAN NORMAL ONE WEEK PROCESSING)

ADDRESS _____

NO. OF COPIES:

_____ (ZIP CODE)

Client (Bound)	
Accounting File	
PIC ( )	
Managing Partner	
Quality Control Partner	
Other	
TOTAL	

Principal _____

MAIL TO: (IF DIFFERENT)

☐ **STATEMENT FORMAT INFORMATION:**

_____ { Name (only if different than above)

☐ **FINANCIAL STATEMENTS**
☐
YEARS ENDED

ENDED

☐ See Accountants' Review Report
☐ See Accountants' Compilation Report

☐ **LETTER FORMAT**

CLIENT'S LOGO

☐ Attached

☐ N/A (Reason)

SPECIAL REQUIREMENTS
CHECK AS APPLICABLE

☐ Audited engagement – a secondary A&A dept. review (and sign-off) is required.

☐ Company is subject to SEC reporting requirements.

☐ Other regulatory requirements: _____

☐ The following is to appear at bottom of each basic statement page (Pages to):

THE ACCOMPANYING NOTES ARE AN INTEGRAL PART OF THIS STATEMENT.

SPECIAL COMMENTS (IF ANY):

QUALITY CONTROL PROCEDURES
(PROCESSING)

	NAME	DATE	NOTES, QUESTIONS, RECOMMENDATIONS
1. Prepared			
2. PIC			
3. Acctg. & Audit			
4. Typed			
5. Proofread			
6. Signed			
7. Printed			
8. Mail/Del'd/Pickup			

Forward attached Yellow copy to word processing after Item 8 is completed

ENGAGEMENT STATUS REPORT

OFFICE: _____

CLIENT NAME: _____ NUMBER: [ ][ ][ ]

REPORT AS OF (FRIDAY): _____ PIC: _____

RELIABLE ESTIMATES ARE **CRUCIAL**. THEY IMPACT ON SCHEDULING AND PROFITABILITY. THEREFORE, THERE IS A HEAVY RESPONSIBILITY ON THE IN-CHARGE ACCOUNTANT, AND HOW THIS RESPONSIBILITY IS IMPLEMENTED REFLECTS ON THAT PERSON'S PERFORMANCE. THIS REPORT IS DUE MONDAY MORNING AS TO THE STATUS AT THE END OF THE PRECEDING WEEK.

=== BUDGET COMPARISON ===
(IN HOURS)

UNEXPENDED TIME:

TOTAL BUDGETED TIME .... _____

TIME EXPENDED TO DATE .... _____

(A) UNEXPENDED BUDGETED TIME _____

*ESTIMATED TIME TO COMPLETE ENGAGEMENT:

PARTNER...................... _____

MANAGER/PRINCIPAL .... _____

SUPERVISOR/ADVANCED SENIOR... _____

OTHER STAFF................... _____

(B) TOTAL TO COMPLETE .... _____

▶ PROJECTED FAVORABLE (UNFAVORABLE) VARIANCE (A) – (B) .... [ ]

*ESTIMATED TIME TO COMPLETE ENGAGEMENT SHOULD BE DIRECTLY RELATED TO SCHEDULING/STAFF OF ENGAGEMENT.

REASONS FOR MAJOR VARIANCES (OVER 10%)

_____
_____
_____
_____
_____
_____

=== REVIEW DATE ===

ESTIMATED REVIEW DATES FOR A & A DEPARTMENT:

PRELIMINARY .... _____

YEAR END .... _____

IF CHANGED, REASONS:

_____
_____
_____

_____   _____
ACCOUNTANT IN CHARGE   DATE PREPARED

** ACTION LINE **

MAJOR VARIANCES REVIEWED BY A & A DEPT. AND PIC. – RESULTS OF REVIEW (IF APPLICABLE):

_____
_____
_____

COPIES
WHITE: A & A (DEPUTY DIRECTOR**   **PINK:** PRINCIPAL OR MANAGER
YELLOW: PIC   **CANARY:** WORKPAPER FILE COPY
If **Action Line Is Used, Forward A Copy Of Completed Form To Managing Partner**

CONTINUING PROFESSIONAL EDUCATION ATTENDANCE AND EVALUATION FORM

(WRITE FIRMLY, THIS IS AN ORIGINAL AND THREE COPIES)

NAME (PRINT, LAST NAME FIRST) _____

FLORIDA CPA CERTIFICATE NUMBER [ ][ ][ ][ ][ ][ ]

AFFILIATION (IF OTHER THAN RACHLIN & COHEN) _____

CPE COURSE, PROGRAM OR SEMINAR ATTENDED

TITLE _____

DATE _____ LOCATION _____

SPONSOR _____ SPONSOR NO. _____

DISCUSSION LEADERS _____

OTHER NOTES: _____

NUMBER OF CREDIT HOURS:

		THIS COURSE	YEAR TO DATE (OPTIONAL)
CONTACT TIME OF 50 MIN. = 1 CREDIT HOUR	A & A CREDIT		
	OTHER CREDIT		

I HEREBY CERTIFY THAT I ATTENDED THE FULL CPE SESSION AS DESCRIBED.

_____   _____
SIGNATURE   DATE

PROGRAM EVALUATION

	OUTSTANDING	GOOD	AVERAGE	NEEDS IMPROVEMENT
1. COURSE CONTENT	☐	☐	☐	☐
2. DISCUSSION LEADERS:				
a. _____ (NAME)				
• KNOWLEDGE OF SUBJECT MATTER	☐	☐	☐	☐
• PRESENTATION SKILLS	☐	☐	☐	☐
b. _____ (NAME)				
• KNOWLEDGE OF SUBJECT MATTER	☐	☐	☐	☐
• PRESENTATION SKILLS	☐	☐	☐	☐
c. _____ (NAME)				
• KNOWLEDGE OF SUBJECT MATTER	☐	☐	☐	☐
• PRESENTATION SKILLS	☐	☐	☐	☐
d. _____ (NAME)				
• KNOWLEDGE OF SUBJECT MATTER	☐	☐	☐	☐
• PRESENTATION SKILLS	☐	☐	☐	☐
(If more than 4 Discussion Leaders, use additional form.)				
3. OVERALL SATISFACTION WITH COURSE	☐	☐	☐	☐

4. COMMENTS AND SUGGESTIONS FOR IMPROVEMENTS: _____

_____

_____

DISTRIBUTION OF COPIES

WHITE – PROGRAM CHAIRMAN   **PINK** – PERSONNEL FILE
CANARY – CPE PARTNER   **GOLD** – RETAIN FOR PERSONAL CPE RECORDS

EXHIBIT D-11. **Request to the Management Consulting Department**

REQUEST TO THE MANAGEMENT CONSULTING DEPARTMENT
(PLEASE TYPE OR WRITE FIRMLY, THIS IS AN ORIGINAL AND THREE COPIES)

This form is to be used for *all* requests to the MC Department.

FROM _____ DATE _____

CLIENT _____ CLIENT NO. [ ][ ][ ]

☐ Internal Memo Only ☐ Draft Engagement Letter to Client (To be signed by _____) ☐ Letter or Report for Client ☐ Other _____

Type of Assignment:

☐ Systems & Procedures EDP ☐ Engagement Planning Audit ☐ Operations Review EDP ☐ Inventory Control

☐ Systems & Procedures Manual ☐ EDP Review Audit ☐ Operations Review Mfg. ☐ Cost Accounting

☐ Feasibility Study ☐ Management Letter Review ☐ General Management ☐ Internal Control

☐ Other: _____

Nature of Client Business: _____

Client Contact (Name and Title): _____

Details of Assignment (or Attach Information as Necessary): _____

_____

_____

_____

_____

_____

_____

_____

_____

_____

_____

_____

MC DEPT. USE ONLY
Assigned To: _____
MCD Engagement #: _____
Service Code: _____
COMPLETED
Date: _____ Signed: _____

Estimated Time Budget _____ Due Date _____

Copies To _____

DISTRIBUTION OF FORM
WHITE: RETAINED BY PREPARER   **OTHER COPIES:** DIRECTOR, MC DEPT.

EXHIBIT D-12. **Notice of Partner's Absence**

NOTICE OF PARTNER'S ABSENCE

PARTNER'S NAME: _____

PERIOD FROM: _____ THROUGH _____

DESTINATION: _____

REASON:	#	DESCRIPTION

(   )   904   PROFESSIONAL MEETINGS (AICPA, FICPA, DADE CHAPTER, ETC.)

Describe:
_____
_____
_____

(   )   907   SEMINARS (CPE, ETC.)

(   )   910   JURY DUTY

(   )   913   VACATION

(   )   ...   CLIENT RELATED (CLIENT: _____)

(   )   948   OTHER:
_____
_____

↑
Please check Billing Codes.

EXPENSES:

(   )   PERSONAL

(   )   BILL TO CLIENT

(   )   FIRM TO BE REIMBURSED BY: _____
_____

(   )   OTHER _____

COMMENTS:
_____
_____

_____   _____
SIGNATURE   DATE

Attach copy of Itinerary, if available.

DISTRIBUTION OF COPIES:
WHITE - Managing Partner   CANARY - Adm. Asst. (Partner's File)
PINK - Bookkeeping   GOLD - Copy Retained

EXHIBIT D-13. Record of Conversation

RECORD OF CONVERSATION

PREPARED BY:_____

DATE:_____TIME:_____

☐ CALL FROM:_____☐ CALL TO:_____

☐ CONVERSATION WITH: _____AT:_____

☐ OTHER:_____

RELATES TO

CLIENT:_____

SUBJECT:_____

CLIENT NO.
(IF APPLICABLE)

WHAT THEY (HE/SHE) SAID	WHAT I SAID

ACTION LINE

ACTION TAKEN:_____

FOLLOW-UP REQUIRED:_____

COPIES OF THIS RC: ☐ CLIENT FILE; ☐ P.I.C. _____; ☐ _____; ☐ _____; ☐ _____

183

EXHIBIT D-14. Record of Conference

RECORD OF CONFERENCE

CLIENT NO.
(IF APPLICABLE)

PREPARED BY: _____

DATE: _____ LOCATION: _____

TIME FROM: _____ TO: _____

CLIENT: _____

SUBJECT: _____

IN ATTENDANCE: CLIENT   R & C   OTHER
_____   _____   _____
_____   _____   _____
_____   _____   _____

DISCUSSIONS	DECISIONS

ACTION TAKEN

FOLLOW-UP REQUIRED: _____

▶ COPIES OF THIS RC: ☐ CLIENT FILE; ☐ P.I.C. _____ ; ☐ _____ ; ☐ _____ ; ☐ _____

PROFITABILITY IMPACT REPORT

DATE: _____

FOR IMMEDIATE ATTENTION OF (PIC): _____

CLIENT: NAME _____ **NO.**

STAFF WORKING ON ENGAGEMENT: _____

_____

Firm policy is that we do **not** work on engagements when:
1. There is no current engagement letter.
2. The balance due exceeds 120 days.
3. Quality Control Committee, under special conditions, has not approved engagement.

The above information indicates apparent violation of this rule as follows:
- ☐ 1. No current engagement letter.
- ☐ 2. Balance over 120 days $_____ .
- ☐ 3. Requires approval by Quality Control Committee.

Please explain to the Managing Partner whether (a) you do not agree with information, or (b) why you permitted this work contrary to firm policy.

DATE   BY

RESPONSE BY P.I.C. TO MANAGING PARTNER
(DUE WITHIN **ONE** WORKING DAY)

DATE   BY

Forms For Partners[1]

Exhibit	Title	Usage
E-1	ASR—Accountability Statistical Report	These statistics are compiled monthly and are reviewed with the partners on an individual basis by the managing partner.
E-2	Report Card for Partners, Principals, and Managers	On an annual basis this form is prepared by all partners, principals, and managers, evaluating themselves as well as all other partners, principals, and managers. The forms are summarized by the managing partner and then discussed with each individual. In addition to the constructive approach to the results, the annual process complies with a firm's quality control system.

[1]See STEP 3.

Pic:_____

Month Ending:_____

Items Covered: 1. Billing and profitability 3. Work in process
                    2. Receivables   4. Utilization

Purpose of ASR: To determine whether the PIC is meeting established goals and to use such statistics in providing for constructive direction in achieving and surpassing the standards

Use of ASR: The Administrative Partner will review our monthly computer reports with each PIC and complete the ASR (which summarizes the information and highlights variances, favorable and unfavorable). The ASR will then become part of the bimonthly accountability meeting.

	By	**Date**
Prepared	_____	_____
Accountability	_____	_____

1. Billing

	Current Month	(To Date Months)
Billing goal	$	$
Actual billing	$	$
Percent	%	%
Total write-ups	$	$
Total write-downs	$	$
Percent (actual billing to fees at standard)	%	%

Material Variances (with Comments)

Client		$ Favorable ($ Unfavorable)	Comments
Number	**Name**		

187

Accountability Meeting

2. Receivables

Total outstanding . . . . $

Over 120 days . . . . $

   Percent . . . . %

Write-offs:

   Month . . . . $

   Year to date . . . . $

Material Items

| Client | | Dollar | |
Number	Name	Value	Comments

Accountability Meeting

3. Work in Process

Total . . . . $
More than 60 days . . . . $
   Percent . . . . %

Material Items

| Client | | Dollar | |
Number	Name	Value	Comments

Accountability Meeting

---

4. Utilization

	Month	Year to Date (Months)
Chargeable Hours:		
Goal (standard)		
Actual		
Percent		

Comments

Accountability Meeting

EXHIBIT E-2. **Report Card for Partners, Principals, and Managers**

Report Card for PARTNERS, PRINCIPALS, MANAGERS

EVALUATION OF ______________________ PERIOD COVERED:

FROM ______________________

RETURN TO MANAGING PARTNER BY ____________ TO ______________________

INSTRUCTIONS: Report Card is to be completed and returned to Managing Partner on a **confidential** basis. Evaluate others as you would want to be evaluated yourself, taking into consideration partners' standards. If you have no basis for judgment, check the first box. Data may be obtained from the Managing Partner or Administrative Partner.
If either of the last two boxes is checked (ERRATIC, DISAPPOINTING), please list specific examples (as Item 3, Page 3) so that such matters may be dealt with on a constructive basis with the party reviewed.
You may evaluate by checking the 28 boxes, by written comments in the GRAY areas of each section (A through E), or by doing both or a combination of both.
In evaluating **yourself,** complete pages 1, 2 and 4. In evaluating others, use pages 1, 2 and 3.
A summary of the evaluations about you will be reviewed with you by the Managing Partner.
While this form is used to comply with our Partnership Agreement and Quality Control Document, its main use has always been to keep all of us on the "right track" on a constructive basis.

	No basis for judgment	Outstanding, rarely equaled	Excellent, unusually well done	Satisfactory, normal expectancy	Erratic, less than expected	Disappointing, needs improvement
A Workload and production — COMMENTARY:						
1. Fees produced by person's client responsibility (Billing Run)	☐	☐	☐	☐	☐	☐
2. **Profitability** of service to clients (considering hourly rates, markdowns, mark-ups, etc.)	☐	☐	☐	☐	☐	☐
3. Fees produced individually (Chargeable Hours)	☐	☐	☐	☐	☐	☐
4. Effectiveness in collecting receivables	☐	☐	☐	☐	☐	☐
5. Performance and up-to-date knowledge in basic areas of practice (what every P.I.C. is expected to know)	☐	☐	☐	☐	☐	☐
6. Performance and up-to-date knowledge in specialized area	☐	☐	☐	☐	☐	☐
B Client relations — COMMENTARY:						
7. Reputation for "attentive" service	☐	☐	☐	☐	☐	☐
8. Ability to complete work promptly	☐	☐	☐	☐	☐	☐
9. Availability to clients when needed	☐	☐	☐	☐	☐	☐
10. Confidence in person and satisfaction with work	☐	☐	☐	☐	☐	☐
11. Expansion of service to existing clients, using TIC Program, Management Consulting and Special Services	☐	☐	☐	☐	☐	☐

1

	No basis for judgment	Outstanding, rarely equaled	Excellent, unusually well done	Satisfactory, normal expectancy	Erratic, less than expected	Disappointing, needs improvement

C Personnel development

COMMENTARY:

12. Participation in recruitment and/or training programs	□	□	□	□	□	□
13. Efforts to bring along subordinates	□	□	□	□	□	□
14. Attitude toward employees	□	□	□	□	□	□
15. Employee attitude toward person evaluated	□	□	□	□	□	□
16. Effectiveness as RAP Partner	□	□	□	□	□	□

D Standing in the community and profession

COMMENTARY:

17. Image in the community as a top-level citizen and professional person	□	□	□	□	□	□
18. Positions of leadership in community organizations	□	□	□	□	□	□
19. New clients brought in through individual contacts and efforts	□	□	□	□	□	□
20. Standing within the profession (positions of leadership, etc.)	□	□	□	□	□	□
21. Participation in professional activities	□	□	□	□	□	□

E General

COMMENTARY:

22. Self-motivation (initiative, drive, energy)	□	□	□	□	□	□
23. Leadership (ability to motivate others)	□	□	□	□	□	□
24. Stability and maturity (discerning what is important, reliability in crisis)	□	□	□	□	□	□
25. Judgment (when to decide and when to consult)	□	□	□	□	□	□
26. Contribution to Management of Firm	□	□	□	□	□	□
27. Cooperativeness and team play	□	□	□	□	□	□
28. Promotion of firm's standing	□	□	□	□	□	□

TOTALS Number of ✓'s in each column	□	□	□	□	□	□

Prepared by: _____ Date _____

2

CONSTRUCTIVE COMMENTARY

Prepare this side about the person you are evaluating.

1. What do you consider this person's outstanding contributions to the firm or for the firm?

   _____

   _____

   _____

2. How can this person improve?

   _____

   _____

3. List specific instances causing ERRATIC or DISAPPOINTING ratings (or any instances indicating sub-standard performance)

   _____

   _____

   _____

   _____

4. Other comments

   _____

   _____

5. BOTTOM LINE: In introducing this person as my partner, I presently feel:

   ☐ PROUD   ☐ Indifferent   ☐ uneasy   ☐ _____

   (If Indifferent or Uneasy, why?)

   _____

   _____

3

SELF EVALUATION

1. **Past Performance**
   What I have accomplished during the past year:

   _____
   _____
   _____

2. **Short Range Goals**
   What I hope to achieve during the next 12 months:

   _____
   _____
   _____

3. **Long Range Goals**
   A. **Self** — What I would like to be doing 5 years from now:

   _____
   _____
   _____
   _____
   _____

   B. **Firm** — what should the firm be doing 5 years from now:

   _____
   _____
   _____
   _____
   _____

4. **Contingency Planning**
   If I were no longer here, my firm responsibilities should be handled:

   _____
   _____
   _____
   _____
   _____

4

APPENDIX F

Forms for Personnel[1]

Exhibit	Title	Usage
F-1	Review Procedures	To review a staff person at any one of the following times—within 90 days of employment, quarterly, after an engagement of 40 hours or more.
F-2	Performance Review and Discussion	Can be prepared by any senior staff member or partner at any time to recognize performance better than anticipated, or performance which indicates need for improvement.
F-3	Exit Interview	Prepared at the time an employee leaves. It captures important information, recovers firm property, and is invaluable in unemployment compensation claims.
F-4	Awards Nomination	To nominate individuals for the employee recognition award.
F-5	Referral Commendation	To recognize employees who have referred new business to the firm.

[1]See discussion in Chapter 4.

195

EXHIBIT F-1. Review Procedures

The objective of our review procedures are to communicate present status in the firm, prospects for the future, and how the individual and the firm might work together to attain the career objectives of the individual consistent with the policies and procedures of the firm.

PERSON EVALUATED: _____ | C.P.A.? YES ☐ NO ☐ |

STATISTICS: Date Employed_____Present Level _____Since_____

 Years in Public Practice _____

FUNCTION _____RAP PARTNER_____

THIS REVIEW COVERS THE FOLLOWING (CHECK APPLICABLE BOX):

	PERIOD OF ENGAGEMENT	WHEN CONDUCTED	TOPICS COVERED
☐ 1.	July, August, September	October	Career Progress
☐ 2.	October, November, December	January	Compensation, Career Progress
☐ 3.	January, February, March	April	Career Progress
☐ 4.	April, May, June	July	Advancement, Career Progress
☐ 5.	Engagement of 40 Hours or More	Immediately After Engagement	Performance on Engagement

Client: _____Engagement:_____Hours:_____

CONSTRUCTIVE COMMENTS

Weak points noted: *Strong points noted:*

_____   _____

_____   _____

Suggested positive action: Effective use by individual and firm:

_____   _____

_____   _____

_____   _____

_____   _____

Complete Both Sides

Reviewer	Date
Reviewee (For Item 5, Engagement, Only)	Date

ATTRIBUTES	RATINGS & COMMENTS
A. Technical Ability; Including Knowledge of Theory, Workpaper Techniques, etc.	☐
B. Capacity to Learn, Creativity and Imagination	☐
C. Attitude Towards Work, Sense of Responsibility, Maturity, Dependability	☐
D. Ability to Communicate With Client; Client Confidence in Staff-Person	☐
E. Sensitivity To Clients' Needs, Sense of Urgency	☐
F. Ability to Understand Instructions, Make Decisions and Complete Assignments Without Excessive Supervision	☐
G. Ability to Relate to Other Staff Members Including Communication, Supervision, Training, etc.	☐
H. Professional Development, CPE Participation, Educational Pursuits, Professional Societies, Professional Bearing and Appearance	☐
I. Practice Development Appropriate for Level, Community Activities, Referral Sources, Speaking, Writing, Organization Activity	☐

CHECK LIST FOR REVIEW	**CONCLUSIONS (Ratings 1 to 5)**
The Rating Scale is as follows: 5 EXCELLENT 2 BELOW AVERAGE 4 ABOVE AVERAGE 1 POOR 3 AVERAGE N/B NO BASIS FOR JUDGMENT Any comments which may be helpful to the individual's professional growth should be made in the space provided to the right of the rating. Interviewee's responses should be similarly recorded.	**PRESENT LEVEL** (1 equals not fulfilling present requirements; 5 equals promotion potential) ☐ **FUTURE PROSPECTS** (1 equals probably not suited for future plans of firm; 5 equals potential partner material) ☐

PERFORMANCE REVIEW AND DISCUSSION

This form may be used at such times as indicated in staff level guidelines or whenever a review and discussion would be constructive in the career of a staff person.

The reviewer and reviewee should sign the form and forward to department head; then to be placed in personnel file.

STAFF PERSON | LEVEL

ENGAGEMENT

☐ Financial Statement
☐ Tax Return
☐ _____

AS OF

☐ Performance Better Than Anticipated:

☐ Performance Indicates Need For Improvement (Include, where applicable, recommendations as to additional training and professional education):

REVIEWER | DATE

☐ Comments By Staff Person (Optional):

(SIGNED)

☐ Positive Action By Department Head:

(SIGNED)

198

Instructions

This form should be completed for all terminating personnel by function head as indicated by circumstances. Internal accounting will complete all statistical information necessary and forward to exit interviewer for review and recommendations. It is then to be forwarded to the managing partner for approval before an interview is conducted with any terminating personnel.

Employee Name:_____

S.S.#_____**Position:**_____

Function:_____**Date Hired:**_____

Termination Date:_____

Forwarding Address: (Must be completed for W-2 purposes, if different from address on file)

_____

_____

1. Is employee leaving on a voluntary basis? ☐ YES ☐ NO
2. If yes, what are his or her reasons? (If written resignation, please attach)_____

_____

3. What are our reasons?_____

_____

_____

4. What did employee enjoy most while in the Firm?_____

_____

5. What did employee enjoy least while in the Firm?_____

_____

6. Have we been contacted for a reference by new employer? ☐ YES ☐ NO
   If yes, what was our response?

   (If possible, identify firm and compensation)

_____

_____

7. Determine that the following Firm items have been returned: (No final check will be released until all Firm items have been returned)

Item	Serial No.	Returned	N/A
MANUALS:			
Accounting and auditing	_____	_____	☐
Administrative	_____	_____	☐
EDP	_____	_____	☐
Tax	_____	_____	☐
EQUIPMENT			
Calculator	_____	_____	☐
Carrying case	_____	_____	☐
Keys	_____	_____	☐
Parking card/ decal	_____	_____	☐
Insurance I.D. card	_____	_____	☐

Financial Information

1. **Earned Income:**

   Semimonthly rate $_____
   Hourly $_____

   Final salary determination:

	Time	Money
ATC hours available	_____	$_____
Hours worked since last paid	_____	$_____
Unused vacation time balance granted last May 31		
Total Earned Pay	_____	$_____

2. **Optional Considerations:**

   NOTE: For information purposes only:

   Unused sick leave hours   _____

   Unused bonus days   _____

   Additional amount, if any, to be paid:

   Reason:_____

   Recommended by:_____
   Signature
   Date:_____ $_____

   APPROVAL OF ABOVE:

   Total earned pay $_____

   Additional amount$_____

   Total to be paid $_____

   _____   _____
   Managing partner   *Date*

3. I have reviewed and understand the determination of my final salary and verify the accuracy of the comments:

   _____   _____
   Employee signature   *Date*

4. Final check presented at the time of interview: ☐ YES ☐ NO
   Final check to be mailed on the next regular date: ☐ YES ☐ NO

CONCLUSION

Synopsis of termination situation and Firm attitude about this individual:

_____

_____

_____

_____

_____

_____

_____

_____

_____

_____   _____
Interviewer   *Date*

REVIEWED:

_____   _____
Managing partner   *Date*

Note: Please forward to personnel file upon completion

EXHIBIT F-4. **Really Cares Awards Nomination**

The RC Award is to give special recognition to those members of the Firm who demonstrate that they REALLY CARE—about our clients, about other members of the Firm, and about the Firm. It indicates that, in so doing, they Really Care about themselves as *professional* men and women. The RC Award is our Distinguished Service Medal awarded to those people who make that *extra effort* in giving service to a client, in helping another person, and in promoting the Firm.

Those so honored are selected by the Firm's operations committee. Anyone can be nominated, and any one can make a nomination.

The award includes: name engraved on the Plaque in the Reception area, Company Certificate (copy to the personnel file), the RC pin, lunch with the Managing Partner, and a stash of cash.

If you would like to nominate someone in the firm for the RC award, complete the following and submit it to the managing partner:

I nominate_____

for the RC award because_____

_____

_____

_____

_____

_____

_____

_____   _____
       Date   *Signed (optional)*

Operation Committee: Reviewed _____
                                                  Date

Forward Copies to: Managing partner
                       Personnel file

EXHIBIT F-5. Referral Commendation

Name of referring person: _____

Name of client: _____

Client number: _____

Type of business: _____

How obtained: _____

Submitted by:

_____
Name   *Date*

Forward to PIC for completion

Date of acceptance by Quality Control Committee: _____

Compensation payments based on collections only for two years and only if referring person is a
fellow employee effective:

_____
Date

Approved by:

PIC signature _____ Date _____

MP signature _____ Date _____

When form is completed, copies to be made and distributed:
☐ Referring person ☐ Bookkeeping ☐ PIC
Original to Personnel file

202

APPENDIX G

Practice Development Materials[1]

Exhibit	Title	Usage
G-1	Letter	Follow-up letter after client conference in office
G-2	1040 Control Sheet	Page 3 of processing form captures additional service ideas for after the tax season
G-3	1040–ES Instructions	Mailed to client with Vouchers 2, 3, and 4 as they fall due
G-4	Welcome Letter	Sent to all new clients by the managing partner
G-5	Your Fiscal Year End	Sent to clients at the month beginning their fiscal year end
G-6	Year End Checklist	Allocation of responsibilities as between client and accounting firm
G-7	Management Letter	A sample management letter incorporating some innovative ideas
G-8	General Ledger Referral System	Forms used to implement a general ledger type of referral system
G-9	1921 Ads	Sample of CPA ads *before* they were prohibited
G-10	Advertising—Proper or Improper?	Testing your knowledge of present ethical standards for advertising
G-11	Practice Retention and Development Program	A comprehensive outline for developing a written plan for your firm

[1]See discussion of practice development in Step 5.

Dear John Client:

I just wanted to follow up on our meeting of January 4, 19XX, at your office with you, Barbara Staffperson, Larry Taxperson, and me. The highlights of the meeting are:

1. **19XX Personal income tax return, Form 1040 (late filing).**   In order to complete this return, we need many items that we have not yet received. Barbara put together a complete list of the items which she and I delivered to you. We tried to follow up subsequent to that delivery date and you were not in. The list is now with you, and we must have these items in order to complete the return. In addition, we have to complete the corporation subchapter-S return for the year ending October 31, 19XX. As soon as we receive all of the data, we should be able to complete the return.

2. **Client Products Corp. return, Form 1129.**   There are four returns to bring this corporation current, which are from the years July 31, 19XX, through July 31, 19XX. The net effect is that for the first three of those years there will be no tax due. However, there will be a tax due for the year ending July 31, 19XX, which is presently on extension. You should have taxable income of approximately $8,400. The tax on that, for both federal and state, will be approximately $2,000. If we get the information that we were missing, we should be able to deliver those returns to you by January 9, 19XX.

3. **International Industries Corp.**   As we discussed, there was a $5,000 plus loss in International and this loss appears to have been pursuant to Code Section 1244, and, therefore, we are going to take the loss pursuant to that Code section. This will come off on your 19XX tax return, the year in which you lost the month.

4. **Client Industries Inc.**   For the year ending October 31, 19XX, the company showed a $8,900 loss. We are still waiting for information from your bookkeeper regarding the fiscal year ending October 31, 19XX, which we also need in order to finish your personal return for 19XX. As soon as we get that information we will move forward to close out that year.

5. **Keogh Plan.**   Barbara will follow through in checking with the pension plan consultant to determine whether or not they ever filed regarding the 5500 Forms. In addition, she will check with the bank to find out if any forms have ever been filed and what the status of the plan is. After she has checked it out we will be able to make our recommendations.

6. **Quarterly Form 942—household employee.**   On a quarterly basis, beginning with the period ending March 31, 19XX, please give the payroll information such as social security number, name and salary amount to Jan Para so that she can prepare the quarterly household payroll form, Form 942. This should occur quarterly, and once you have filed, you will be getting the preprinted form.

7. **Client Industries, Inc. pension and/or profit sharing plans.**   You were going to discuss with Mike Agent and our Tax Department the setting up of a pension and/or profit sharing plan. This was going to be done as quickly as possible since it ties in with other tax planning we discussed. Please let me know when such a meeting is to be arranged so that I can make sure that the appropriate people are there.

8. **Outstanding balances due.**   Based on our conversation, I am going to have our bookkeeping department do a complete analysis on all of the accounts we've been involved with as to standard time, amount billed, payments and balances to date. We received your check of $4,000. We estimate the remaining balance to be approximately $3,500 through November billing. We want to resolve those outstanding balances as quickly as possible. You mentioned that for a couple of years you were on a monthly retainer and we'll have to see how this fits in as far as what we did for those retainers. As soon as I get all the information, I'll call you and we can discuss it.

9. **Copies of notes.**   When all of the open corporations are completed, Barbara will give you a complete list of all intercompany debts. As we discussed, we would like to have copies of notes (representing these debts) for our files.

10. **Trade Association.**   You mentioned to me that Ms. Anne Executive would be contacting us from the Trade Association to discuss the possibility of our doing accounting work for them. To date, I have not heard from her and if you would follow up, I would be most appreciative.

Well, it seems like we're finally getting on the right track and everything will soon be current. I hope we can keep it that way. Although we haven't gotten everything filed yet, I'm looking forward to winding everything up very quickly.

Cordially yours,

Harvey Partner

January 11, 19XX

HP: cs

    cc: Barbara Staffperson

        Larry Taxperson

        Jan Para

CONTROL SHEET

Form **1040** U.S. Individual Income Tax Return

CLIENT CODE NO. [   ] [   ] [   ]   NAME

ALERT! — FOLLOW UP FOR NEXT YEAR
(To be completed by Reviewer)

☐ Net Operating Loss _____   ☐ Installment Sale _____

☐ Investment Tax Credit _____   ☐ Residence Sale _____

☐ Capital Loss _____   ☐ Adjust Income Averaging,

☐ Contributions _____   Per RAR _____

☐ Other_____   ☐ Condemnation Award _____

Part 1. General Instructions
(To be completed by person in charge)

Person in Charge _____

Billing: ☐ With Return (see Part 4)

    ☐ From Billing Runs

Client Records:

    ☐ None

    ☐ Retain in Office

    ☐ Return to Client

Disposition of Completed Return:

☐ Normal Mailing

☐ Call Client to Notify:

    — Pick up

    — Delivery

    — Mail

☐ **Contact with Client by Partner Only**

Special Instructions:

_____

_____

_____

_____

_____

_____

Part 2. Concurrent Time Record

	*Interview	*Preparation	*Preparation	Review	
				Technical	Final
Acct. ➡					
Date/Hrs.					
Date/Hrs.					
Date/Hrs.					
Date/Hrs.					
Date/Hrs.					
Total Hours					

Total Time

*Indicate reason(s) for time in excess of normal time anticipated, such as: additional work this year (explain), inadequate instruction, client records inadequate, had to wait for additional information, changes requested by client, etc.

_____
_____
_____
_____
_____
_____
_____

Part 3.   Computer Processing

	First Run	Second Run	Third Run
To Data Center (date)			
From Data Center (date)			
Data Charges	$	$	$
Indicate Name and Date: Reviewed*			
Processing Completed			
Control Forms Completed			
1040 Reviewed and Signed			

*Reviewer is to complete ALERT! (Follow Up for Next Year) at top of Page 1.

Part 4.   Billing With Return (Optional)
(Use Separate 1040 Invoice Series)

☐ Bill to: (If other than client). ⎫ Code No. _____

⎰ Name _____

☐ Services rendered in connection with preparation of Individual Income Tax Returns.

☐ _____

☐ $ _____ Invoice No. _____ Prepared by _____

- -

Part 5.   Completion

	Date	By		Date	By
			Call for		
Mailed			Pick up		
Delivered			Picked up		

SUPPLEMENTAL SERVICE NOTICE

Form **1040** U.S. Individual Income Tax Return

LOG
Number_____
Date _____

CLIENT CODE NO. [ ] [ ] [ ]   Name _____

Every one who handles a client's tax return (Form 1040) should have an **awareness** of additional services which could be of value to the client. This awareness can come about in talking to the client or in reviewing the return and supporting documents. Place an "X" in the box for each item which should be followed up. Add your initials, suggested implementation date, and comments (if any). When the 1040 is completed, this notice is to be forwarded to the PIC.

Service Items	By (Initials/Date)	Suggested Implementation Date	Comments
☐ Estate planning, gifts, trusts or updating Wills.			
☐ Income tax planning (including Tax Reform Act aspects).			
☐ Tax entity change — incorporation, small business corporation.			
☐ Newsletter mailing list.			
☐ Tax shelter investments.			
☐ Tax free bond investments. ·			
☐ Amend prior year returns — additions, deductions, net operating loss carrybacks, etc.			
☐ New Florida resident—Homestead exemption reminder.			
☐ Intagible tax follow-up.			
☐ Professional Corporation.			
☐ KEOGH Plan.			
☐ I.R.A.			
☐ Set up accounting books or system of recording tax data.			
☐ Looking for investments.			
☐ Other (Describe) _____			

Additional Notes:

_____

_____

_____

PIC FOLLOW UP:

_____

_____

_____

1. **Instructions for filing your estimated tax by September 15, 19XX.**   It is tax payment time again. The next Voucher Form 1040-ES for 19XX Estimated Taxes is due by September 15.
2. **The following instructions apply to the enclosed Voucher No. 3:**
   a. Payment is to be made for the amount shown on *line 3*. Make your check or money order payable to **Internal Revenue Service.** For positive identification, you should put your social security number on the check.
   b. Mail the payment, along with this Voucher No. 3, to:

   Internal Revenue Service Center

   [Address]

   c. *Must be mailed on or before September 15, 19XX.*
   d. If line 3 shows a zero balance please disregard these instructions, which are being forwarded only to consider the possibility of an amended declaration.
3. **Questions or Changes.**   If you have any questions regarding these procedures, or should you care to amend your estimated tax on account of significant changes in anticipated income, please get in touch with us *at once.* We have held your vouchers in safekeeping to forward them to you at the appropriate due dates.
4. **New Tax Law.**   The recently passed tax laws provide for some of the most sweeping changes in the past 25 years! Rates have gone down—you might need to amend your estimated tax. The estate tax area has been so radically changed that you undoubtedly need a new will and new estate planning. There are great new tax savings opportunities for businesses and investors. Call us so that we can help you with these opportunities.

We welcome you as a client.

That means a great deal to us. As managing partner, I want to assure you that we are going to do everything we can to justify your confidence in us.

I am taking the liberty of enclosing a copy of our monthly newsletter. The calendar of due dates is on a perforated page which can be removed and forwarded to someone in your organization who might be responsible for the follow-up of the items listed. You will now be receiving this newsletter on a regular basis.

The purpose of the newsletter is to stimulate your interest in tax and accounting subjects in a general way. Occasionally, we use this newsletter as a means to readily convey important decisions, changes in tax law, or accounting procedures before we are able to contact each client individually.

We hope that you will find this additional service a valuable one. Incidently, if you have any associates or professional contacts that you think should receive this newsletter, please let us know.

Other literature about the firm, its partners, and its departments is available. A call to my office would get you this information. Should you have any questions regarding your account with us or with proper names, addresses, listings, or whatever, please feel free to contact our bookkeeping department at 555-0412.

We welcome you as a client, and hope we will fulfill your expectations. Do not hesitate to contact me directly should you find we are falling short of the mark. Or, call me if we can be of any additional service to you.

Cordially yours,
John Partner
Managing Partner

RE: Your Fiscal Year End

Dear _____:

This letter is sent at the beginning of the last month of your fiscal year as a reminder that the **year end** is **approaching** and it is time for consideration of **tax planning** and scheduling of mutual requirements.

The deadlines to be considered are:

· End of Fiscal Year _____
· Due date of Federal Income Tax Return _____
· Due date of State Income Tax Return _____
· (In most cases federal and state *estimated* income tax returns are also required.)
· Due date of pension and/or profit sharing returns _____

We have available a **checklist** which details items normally required for a year-end closing. Not all of them will be applicable to your business. Many of them can be completed by your personnel, and if properly executed could save the accountants' time. We would be pleased to send you the **checklist,** or review it with you.

One other important point! To preclude any possible misunderstanding of what our services include or do not include, or of what each of us is responsible for, we now have a policy of preparing an annual engagement letter for our mutual signing. We trust you will understand and approve of these procedures.

Should you have any questions regarding the fiscal year closing, tax planning, or any other problems for which we can be of service, do not hesitate to call. Thank you for your courtesy and cooperation.

Date _____   Partner _____

Exhibit G-6. Year End Checklist

Please complete the following items which are checked. All schedules should be current as of the closing date (unless otherwise noted) and agree with the adjusted totals as shown in the general ledger.

	To Be Completed by		
	Company	CPA	N/A
1. Review *old* outstanding checks on all checking accounts and write off as necessary.	( )	( )	( )
2. Make all journal entries which you feel are necessary prior to closing books. Review all prior year's adjustments for possible entries.	( )	( )	( )
3. A general ledger trial balance on wide analysis paper. Double-space all items. Put balance sheet accounts and profit and loss accounts on separate sheets. Group accounts as they were grouped for last year's report. Total the trial balance after the balance sheet accounts and after the profit and loss accounts.	( )	( )	( )
4. A copy of the bank reconciliation on *each* checking account.	( )	( )	( )
5. A schedule of investments showing the details of the investment and any income for the year and accrued income.	( )	( )	( )
6. A schedule of notes receivable by name, date, amount, collateral, any interest income for the year and accrued interest.	( )	( )	( )
7. A schedule showing the composition of the balance in accrued interest receivable and interest income. If practicable, this should be consolidated in the schedule of notes receivable.	( )	( )	( )
8. A schedule of trade accounts receivable including age and indicating uncollectible items.	( )	( )	( )
9. A schedule of the balance in customers' deposits, by name, date, and amount.	( )	( )	( )
10. A schedule of accounts with officers, employees, partners, and/or stockholders showing names, dates, and amounts.	( )	( )	( )
11. A complete physical inventory of all merchandise held for sale as of the last day of the fiscal year. The inventory should be priced and totaled. Be sure to indicate marked-down and obsolete items.	( )	( )	( )
12. A copy of your prepaid insurance schedule register for the year showing policies, coverage, amortization of expense, accruals, and unexpired balances.	( )	( )	( )
13. A schedule of officers' life insurance listing insurance company, policy number, annual premium, due date, insured, cash surrender value, and policy loans.	( )	( )	( )

		Company	CPA	N/A
14.	An analysis of the balance in any prepaid expense accounts, describing the items by date, vendor, and amortization taken, if any.	( )	( )	( )
15.	A detailed schedule of the balance of utility deposits, showing deposit receipt numbers.	( )	( )	( )
16.	A schedule listing all additions to property accounts during the year by vendor, date, and description of asset.	( )	( )	( )
17.	A schedule of gain or loss on sale of assets, showing the purchase price, the sales price, the dates bought and sold, the accumulated depreciation to date of sale, and the gain or loss on the sale.	( )	( )	( )
18.	A schedule of contracts and/or notes payable, showing the payee, the amount, the terms, the collateral, the interest rate, interest expense, and any accrued or deferred interest on each note in the schedule.	( )	( )	( )
19.	A schedule of trade accounts payable showing vendor and amount.	( )	( )	( )
20.	A detailed schedule of any accrued expenses or liabilities showing the calculation of such items (accrued salaries, fees, interest, real estate or other taxes, commissions, etc.).	( )	( )	( )
21.	A detailed analysis of any changes in capital accounts since the last balance sheet date.	( )	( )	( )
22.	A schedule of the following accounts, showing date paid, vendor, and amount:			
	Miscellaneous income—individual amounts over $_____ only.	( )	( )	( )
	Miscellaneous expense—individual accounts over $_____ only.	( )	( )	( )
	Taxes	( )	( )	( )
	Donations	( )	( )	( )
	Rent (income and/or expense)	( )	( )	( )
	Repairs and maintenance—individual amounts over $_____only.	( )	( )	( )
	_____	( )	( )	( )
	_____	( )	( )	( )
23.	*We shall wish to know details of all leases, contracts, agreements, and any important corporate papers.*	( )	( )	( )

	To Be Completed by		
	Company	**CPA**	**N/A**
24. Reconcile and balance all intercompany accounts.	( )	( )	( )
25. Other:			
_____	( )	( )	( )
_____	( )	( )	( )
_____	( )	( )	( )
_____	( )	( )	( )
_____	( )	( )	( )

Checklist completed on _____ (Date)

By: _____ for company

_____ for accountants

Notes:

Exhibit G-7. **Management Letter: (a) Transmittal Letter; (b) Analysis of Material Weakness in Internal Accounting Controls; (c) Other Constructive Suggestions; (d) Appendix—Objective of Internal Accounting Control**

Exhibit G-7. **(a) Transmittal Letter**

In connection with our examination of the financial statements of RC Enterprises, Ltd. as of February 18, 19XX we have made a review of accounting procedures and internal control. While the primary objective of such a review is to afford us a basis of determining the scope of our audit procedures, it nevertheless presents us with an opportunity to submit, for management's consideration, suggestions for changes in procedures which, in our opinion, would strengthen internal control or contribute to the improvement of operating efficiency.

The comments in this letter are based upon observations made in the course of such a review. The review was not designed for the purpose of expressing an opinion on internal accounting control, and it would not necessarily disclose all weaknesses in the system. The matters discussed herein were considered during our examination of the above mentioned financial statements, and they did not modify the opinion expressed in our report on those financial statements. However, we offer for your review the internal control weaknesses, as noted on the following page and our proposed solution thereto.

Weaknesses marked with an asterisk reflect comments that are uncorrected items repeated from last year's management letter. The Company should be aware that failure to correct these weaknesses has a direct impact on the operating efficiency of the company and the timeliness and cost of performing an audit.

Please indicate in the "Action Taken" column of the letter, what corrective measures the Company intends to implement with regard to each comment, and return an annotated copy of the letter to us.

If you have any questions regarding these or any other matters, please feel free to contact us.

Exhibit G-7. **(b) Analysis of Material Weaknesses in Internal Accounting Controls (Matters Requiring Corrective Action)**

Action Taken

Cash Receipts
1. Deposits are not being made daily. All cash received should be deposited intact daily to insure proper controls over cash.
2. The mail is opened by persons having access to cash receipts records. The mail should be opened by a person not having access to cash or accounting records. All mail receipts should be listed by this person, and subsequently compared with the cash receipts records by another person not having access to cash.

Cash Disbursements
1. The Company's controller is an authorized check signer with access to cash receipts and accounting records. This person should be relieved from duties as an authorized signer.
2. Supporting documents are not effectively cancelled to prevent subsequent misuse. All invoices should be marked "Paid" with the paying check number noted. This procedure should particularly be followed when a group of invoices are paid with one check, each individual invoice should be cancelled.

Action Taken

Accounts Receivable

The duties of the accounts receivable bookkeeper should be completely separate from any cash functions.

Payroll

Again, the controller should not be allowed to sign payroll checks since this person participates in the maintenance of accounting records.

General

We observed that certain personnel had duties and responsibilities that appeared to conflict with sound internal control procedures. We hope the company will develop the framework, by reviewing and making whatever changes are necessary to its present accounting and procedures manual, to insure proper segregation of duties and responsibilities in order to safeguard the company's assets and minimize the possibility of loss.

Exhibit G-7. (*c*) Other Constructive Suggestions for Improvement of Operational Efficiency and Internal Accounting Control

Action Taken

Cash Receipts

1. Deposits for daily mail receipts should be prepared by a person not responsible for recording cash receipts and not having access to customers' ledgers.
2. The company's bank should be instructed not to cash checks payable to the company.

Cash Disbursements

1. Invoices should be approved by a responsible official before payment, and such authorization should be indicated on the face of the invoice.
2. The company does not appear to have adequate control over the supply of unused checks. All unused checks should be kept in a safe and secure location.

Accounts Receivable

1. All accounts receivable sales should be reviewed for customer's credit outstanding prior to completing the order.
2. All monthly customers' statements should be independently checked to the accounts, controlled, and mailed by someone other than the accounts receivable bookkeeper.

Payroll

The company does not appear to have adequate control over the maintenance of employee files. All employee files should be reviewed periodically to insure that each file contains a current W-4 signed by the employee, and all documents authorizing the employee's wage rate and any changes therein.

216

Action Taken

Property and Equipment

1. There is not a policy as to the dollar amount for capitalizing fixed assets. There should be a written description stating when an expenditure should be capitalized as a fixed asset or recorded as repairs and maintenance.

2. Detailed subsidiary records of assets and the applicable reserve for depreciation should be maintained currently and periodically compared with a physical inventory of the property on hand. This might be an application for your EDP system.

Purchases

The company does not use prenumbered purchase orders. All purchases should be made using prenumbered purchase orders. These purchase orders should be prepared in triplicate. One copy goes to the vendor, one copy with the invoice in the paid bill file, and one copy for a numerical sequence file.

Sales

1. The company has accepted bad checks for the sale of merchandise while bad checks previously received from the same customer remain uncollected. The company should prepare and circulate, to its various store locations, a list of bad check issuers on a regular and timely basis.

2. The company is using sales invoices in place of credit memos as needed. Prenumbered credit memos should be used. Such credit memos should be initialed by an authorized individual indicating approval before the credit memo is processed.

General

1. Paid invoices occasionally are filed in incorrect files. The filing of invoices should be delegated to a responsible person so the chances of misfiling invoices will be reduced.

2. The company's general accounting office appears to be in a state of disorganization. Paperwork does not appear to flow in an efficient manner. The company should consider evaluating its present system to determine alternatives available that would facilitate the flow of paperwork and insure that all such paperwork is safeguarded.

3. The company's general journal does not provide sufficient explanations for journal entries therein. Every journal entry should be followed by a brief explanation.

4. We noted that the controller was not informed of various transactions when they occurred. It is extremely important that the Company's controller be knowledgeable of all transactions of the company so the accounting records can be correctly maintained.

5. The company's controller does not appear to possess a strong enough background in financial accounting to keep pace with the company's size. This individual, however, does appear very

Action Taken

General (*Cont.*)

knowledgeable of the company's present system of internal control. This knowledge might best be put to use in an "office manager" position. The company should consider refilling the controller position with someone possessing a strong understanding of and background in financial accounting.

6. The company appears to lack adequate insurance coverage to protect its assets. The newly acquired computer equipment is not insured. The company should review its existing policies with a responsible official and increase its coverage to limits that would protect the company from loss.

7. The company does not maintain paid and unpaid invoices in one location. Invoices are filed in the general accounting office and in the company secretary's office. All invoices should be filed in one location to facilitate the record keeping function.

8. The company's computer room appears to reach temperatures that are understood to possibly cause mechanical difficulties with such equipment. The company should consider whatever measures are necessary to insure that such equipment is maintained at acceptable temperature levels.

EXHIBIT G-7. *(d)* Appendix—Objective of Internal Accounting Control

The objective of internal accounting control is to provide reasonable. but not absolute, assurance that the company's assets will be safeguarded against loss from unauthorized use or disposition, and that the reliability of financial records for preparing financial statements and maintaining accountability for assets will be preserved. The concept of reasonable assurance recognizes that the cost of a system of internal accounting control should not exceed the benefits derived and also recognizes that the evaluation of these factors necessarily requires estimates and judgments by management.

There are inherent limitations that should be recognized in considering the potential effectiveness of any system of internal accounting control. In the performance of most control procedures, errors can result from misunderstanding of instructions, mistakes of judgment, carelessness, or other personal factors. Control procedures whose effectiveness depends upon segregation of duties can be circumvented by collusion. Similarly, control procedures can be circumvented intentionally by management either with respect to the execution and recording of transactions or with respect to the estimates and judgments required in the preparation of financial statements. Further, projection of any evaluation of internal accounting control to future periods is subject to the risk that the procedures may become inadequate because of changes in conditions, and that the degree of compliance with the procedures may deteriorate.

EXHIBIT G-8. General Ledger Referral System

A General Ledger Sheet For Referrals

Ben Barrister - Wills,
Trusts, Probate

Sam Solicitor -
Corporate Law, Divorce, Litigation

NAME   BARRISTER & SOLICITOR, P.A.

ADDRESS 123 Justice Way, Miami, Fla. 33199 (305) 555-0412

Account No. _____

DATE 19__	ITEMS	FOLIO			DEBITS	DATE 19__	ITEMS	FOLIO			CREDITS
May 3	S.S. Form Corp.					July 7	B.B. Unavd. Statements,				
	for ADAMS family						Tax Returns,				
	(10-26-377) *						FONZ Distributors,				
18	S.S. CARSON divorce						Inc. (12-26-239) *				
	(12-18-297)					Oct 3	B.B. Tax Examination,				
June 20	B.B. Probate						MR. + MRS. BIONIC				
	HUGHES estate						(12-15-284)				
	(72-19-803)										
Sep 30	S.S. MORK vs.										
	MINDY (15-16-800)										
Sep. 31	B.B. Prepare wills										
	for OSMONDS										
	(12-26-792)										
	* = Client No. and partner Code.										

219

A Referral Memorandum

INTER-OFFICE REFERRAL FORM

TO: _H. MILLER_

FROM: _N.S. RACHLIN_

DATE: _9-30_

REGARDING CLIENT:

_15-16-800_

MORK, MR. and

MRS. M.

SUBJECT MATTER: _MINDY MORK is bringing divorce action against MR. MORK. He has been our client for 6 years, and based on your recommendation I referred him to Sam Solicitor. I have already called Sam to alert him._

[X] Attorney   [ ] Banking   [ ] Insurance   [ ] Other

[X] Referred To

SAM SOLICITOR

BARRISTER & SOLICITOR, P.A.

Miami

[ ] Referred From

_____

_____

_____

[ ] Referred To

(Decided on one

referral for this

case)

[ ] Referred From

_____

_____

_____

OTHER COMMENTS:

To date no business from Sam. We have rec'd. one referral from Ben.

221

Assume that all of the statements below about you or your firm are substantially accurate. Indicate which statements, under professional standards would be proper to include in an ad and which would not.

	Proper	Improper
1. I have had seven years experience in preparing income tax returns for local taxpayers.	_____	_____
2. When it comes to taxes, I specialize in *refunds*, not payments.	_____	_____
3. I know the local IRS agents and can get your return accepted quickly.	_____	_____
4. I worked as a field auditor for the IRS for four years.	_____	_____
5. I know all of the latest loopholes that big business uses and can apply them to your return.	_____	_____
6. Have your return prepared by a licensed CPA.	_____	_____
7. Our percent of tax refunds is greater than any CPA in town.	_____	_____
8. "In my 10 years in business, this CPA firm got me to pay the lowest taxes," says John Businessman, another satisfied client.	_____	_____
9. I specialize in compilation reports which the local banks will accept just like a certified audit, and they cost a heck of a lot less.	_____	_____
10. You'll get a bigger loan with less interest costs by taking my reports to your bank.	_____	_____
11. I always accompany my clients when they go to the bank for a loan. I have the experience to explain the financial statements to the banker.	_____	_____
12. Mary Q. Banker says, "This CPA firm prepares the best financials in town."	_____	_____
13. During the months of August and September we are giving a 20 percent discount on all audits for small and medium size businesses.	_____	_____
14. Our firm has the best reputation in town for getting reports and tax returns out accurately and on time.	_____	_____
15. Our firm's membership in the AICPA requires us to have a quality control review every three years.	_____	_____
16. We specialize in tax planning and tax preparation for business executives.	_____	_____
17. I have served as an officer or director of the Junior Chamber of Commerce, Red Cross, Kiwanis, Rotary, and Scouting Council.	_____	_____
18. We know all the adjustments and other intricacies for making your financial statements come out the way you want them.	_____	_____
19. Before opening my own practice I had eight years experience in the small business department of a large national accounting firm.	_____	_____
20. As a management counsultant specialist I can save you thousands of dollars in the operation of your business.	_____	_____
21. Our office has people who are fluent in Spanish and French, and one who can communicate (in sign language) with the deaf.	_____	_____
22. We accept American Express, Visa, and Master Charge.	_____	_____

Exhibit G-11. Practice Retention and Development Program

Item	To be Done (Use Supplemental Pages as Necessary)	Assigned to	Target Date	Remarks
I. Retention of clients				
A. Service factors:				
1. Quality:				
a. Financial statements				
b. Tax returns				
c. Other reports, writings				
d. Understanding and application				
2. Timeliness:				
a. Quality control				
b. Pressure "bombs"				
(1) Tax returns				
(a) Due dates				
(b) Payments				
(2) Tax research projects				
(3) Year end planning				
(4) Regulatory agency reports				
(5) Financials for credit grantors				
c. Paper and work flow				
3. Other				
a. Client correspondence and maximum utilization of it				
b. Internal memos to and from staff concerning client				
c. Year end checklist				

223

EXHIBIT G-11. Practice Retention and Development Program (*Cont.*)

Item	To be Done (Use Supplemental Pages as Necessary)	Assigned to	Target Date	Remarks
d. Deferred compensation area				
e. Audited or unaudited				
f. "Full service" CPA firm				
g. Small business department				
h. EDP service (including internal flow)				
i. Client education				
4. Engagement and other letters and dictation				
5. Potential litigation				
B. Human factors:				
1. Single assignments for personnel versus rotation				
2. Maximum staff productivity				
3. Client-staff-partner syndrome				
4. Communications				
5. Education				
6. Concern about client, staff, etc.				
7. Visitations				
8. Image:				
a. Switchboard				
b. Reports, etc. (Section 1–A–1)				
c. Other firm members				
9. Staff participation at client meetings				

10. "Salesmanship" training
11. Attitude
    a. Staff motivation and retention
    b. Staff meetings; availability of partners, principals and managers
    c. Compensation
    d. Professionalism
    e. "One firm" concept (including integration of speciality departments)
    f. Upgrading of staff
12. Standardization of scheduling and client assignments
13. Effective time management:
    a. Partners
    b. Staff

C. Fees and Billing:
    1. Retainers
    2. Extras
    3. Billings:
        a. Setting
        b. Selling
        c. Clarity
        d. Timeliness
        e. Collection
        f. Telephone calls
        g. Travel time
    4. Possible shift from quarter hours to tenths of an hour

D. Expansion of services:
    1. Tax planning:
        a. Business
        b. Personal
            (1) Income
            (2) Family

EXHIBIT G-11. **Practice Retention and Development Program** (*Cont.*)

Item	To be Done (Use Supplemental Pages as Necessary)	Assigned to	Target Date	Remarks
2. Financial counsulting:				
a. Cash flow				
b. Personal retirement				
3. MAS:				
a. EDP				
b. Operation manuals				
4. Referral source:				
a. Successful relationship				
b. Poor relationship				
5. Other:				
a. Public speaking engagements				
b. Business contacts				
c. Audited or unaudited				
d. Speciality				
6. Seminars for clients				
II. Third party consideration				
A. Referrals by firm:				
1. Quality of professionals (lawyers, insurance representatives, etc.)				
2. Fees charged				
3. Overkill				
4. Communications				

     5. Monitoring

     6. Reciprocity

  B. Interaction with other disciplines:

     1. We are CPAs, not attorneys

        a. Writings

        b. Conferences

     2. When other professional is wrong

        a. Determination

        b. Verification

        c. Communication

        d. Dictation

III. Loss of clients

  A. Analysis

     1. Investigation

     2. Report to the steering committee

  B. Contact lost client:

     1. Orally or by letter

     2. Visitation

  C. Codification:

     1. Individual involved:

        a. Staff

        b. Partner

     2. Cause

IV. Other

  A. Organizational flow chart—pyramid

  B. "Audit" of practice retention and development program

227

APPENDIX H

Forms for Tax Practice[1]

Exhibit	Title	Usage
H-1	Productive Planning	Return postcard, mailed with tax workbook
H-2	Quality Control Verification	Follow-up mailer after Form 1040 is mailed
H-3	Financial Planning	Return postcard which is mailed with business returns
H-4	Tax Department Control Report	Semimonthly report to the partner in charge (PIC)
H-5	Request to Tax Department	Form which generates request for tax research
H-6	Instructions—Form 1040	Sample instruction form for a 1040 return
H-7	Instructions—Form 1065	Sample instruction form for a partnership return
H-8	Instructions—Form F1120	Sample instructions for a state corporate return

[1]See tax practice discussion in STEP 6.

EXHIBIT H-1. Productive Planning

PRODUCTIVE PLANNING

The following are a few of the RACHLIN & COHEN services available for more productive planning. We would welcome the opportunity to consult with you about available services. By indicating your interest below, we will contact you at a convenient time.

FINANCIAL PLANNING

☐ CASH MANAGEMENT — A review of the effectiveness and profit impact of your company's cash management policies, including receivables and collections, short term investments, payables, borrowings and bank relations.

☐ CASH FORECASTING AND PROJECTIONS — A formal estimate of your company's cash flow for a specified period of time.

☐ PRICING STRATEGY — A review of your company's operations and the establishment of pricing policies based upon production and general and administrative expenses.

☐ INVENTORY REDUCTION — A review to help your company identify opportunities for inventory reduction.

☐ EDP REVIEW — A review of your company's computer facilities to determine its operational effectiveness and efficiency

☐ EDP FEASIBILITY — A review of your company's operations and growth plans to determine the cost effectiveness of a computer system to improve efficiency and management information.

☐ OTHER — (Such as Business Forecasts, Tax Carrybacks and Rebates, Family Financial Planning, Estate Planning, Tax Planning in Projected Business or Property Sales, etc.)

TAX PLANNING

☐ Estate planning, gifts, trusts or updating Wills.
☐ Income tax planning for next year.
☐ Tax entity change — incorporation, small business corporation.
☐ Tax favored investments.
☐ Tax free bond investments.
☐ New Florida resident — need Homestead exemption and other Florida tax information.
☐ Retirement Plans, KEOGH Plan, I R A , etc.
☐ Set up accounting books or system of recording tax data.
☐ Other (Describe)
   Some of these concepts may also require the services of an attorney.

NAME

ADDRESS

PHONE NUMBER

BEST TIME TO CONTACT

229

☐ Return was received⎯⎯⎯⎯⎯⎯⎯⎯⎯⎯⎯⎯⎯⎯⎯⎯⎯⎯⎯⎯⎯⎯⎯⎯⎯⎯⎯⎯⎯

☐ Help — have not yet received return.
Please call

TAX PLANNING

After the hustle and bustle of the tax season we would welcome the opportunity to discuss various tax services available to you. Indicate your interest below and we will contact you at a time convenient for you.

☐ Estate planning, gifts, trusts or updating Wills.

☐ Income tax planning for next year.

☐ Tax entity change — incorporation, small business corporation.

☐ Tax favored investments.

☐ Tax free bond investments.

☐ New Florida resident — need Homestead exemption and other Florida tax information.

☐ Retirement Plans, KEOGH Plan, I.R.A., Etc.

☐ Set up accounting books or system of recording tax data.

☐ Other (Describe) . . . .

Some of these concepts may also require the services of an attorney.

The best time to contact me⎯⎯⎯⎯⎯⎯⎯⎯⎯⎯⎯⎯⎯⎯⎯⎯⎯⎯⎯⎯⎯⎯⎯⎯

From: ⎯⎯⎯⎯⎯⎯⎯⎯⎯⎯⎯⎯⎯⎯⎯⎯⎯⎯⎯⎯⎯⎯⎯⎯⎯⎯

QUALITY CONTROL VERIFICATION

Your Income Tax Return was mailed to you recently.

In providing a full service to our clients, we are concerned that the return reached you in good order, on a timely basis.

We can verify our Quality Control Procedures if you would kindly complete the attached pre-addressed card which requires no postage.

Thank you,

FINANCIAL PLANNING

The following are a few of the RACHLIN & COHEN services available for more productive financial planning. We would welcome the opportunity to consult with you about available services. By indicating your interest below, we will contact you at a convenient time.

☐ **CASH MANAGEMENT** — A review of the effectiveness and profit impact of your company's cash management policies, including receivables and collections, short term investments, payables, borrowings and bank relations.

☐ **CASH FORECASTING AND PROJECTIONS** — A formal estimate of your company's cash flow for a specified period of time.

☐ **PRICING STRATEGY** — A review of your company's operations and the establishment of pricing policies based upon production and general and administrative expenses.

☐ **INVENTORY REDUCTION** — A review to help your company identify opportunities for inventory reduction.

☐ **EDP REVIEW** — A review of your company's computer facilities to determine its operational effectiveness and efficiency.

☐ **EDP FEASIBILITY** — A review of your company's operations and growth plans to determine the cost effectiveness of a computer system to improve efficiency and management information.

☐ **OTHER** — (Such as: Business Forecasts, Tax Carrybacks and Rebates, Family Financial Planning, Estate Planning, Tax Planning in Projected Business or Property Sales, Etc.)

NAME _____   PHONE NUMBER _____

COMPANY _____   BEST TIME TO CONTACT _____

231

To: _____

As of: _____

To provide reasonable assurance that deadlines are not missed, that our clients receive timely service, and that you are kept posted on all tax activities where you have PIC responsibility, we provide you with this semimonthly report, consisting of:

1. Tax return log. All tax returns (except 1040s) submitted to the tax department, with the status of each.

2. Tax examination update sheet. All current activity on tax examinations.

3. Research summary sheet. The status of projects which are in process or have been completed by the tax department. The managing partner has set a standard of one tax project per month from each PIC. How is your list doing?

4. Tax extension control. All tax return extensions (except 1040s) which have been submitted to the department.

   A copy of these logs, particularly the projects log (item 3), is available for discussion at PIC accountability sessions.

   In maintaining these logs we have done our job. Here is how you can cooperate in doing your job:

1. Check each log carefully and promptly notify tax department of any errors, additions, or correcitons.

2. Communicate with clients, as necessary.

3. Communicate with department heads and staff members, as necessary.

4. Let us know of any ideas or suggestions to further improve our service to our clients.

Prepared By: _____

Date: _____

EXHIBIT H-5. Request to Tax Department

REQUEST TO TAX DEPARTMENT

(PLEASE TYPE OR WRITE FIRMLY, THIS IS AN ORIGINAL AND THREE COPIES)

This form is to be used for *all* requests to the Tax Department, *except* for **income** tax returns.

FROM _____   DATE _____

CLIENT _____   CLIENT NO. ☐☐☐

☐ Internal Memo Only   ☐ Draft Letter to Client   ☐ Internal Memo For Client,   ☐ Other _____
                            (To be signed by _____)   with Cover Letter

Type of Assignment:

☐ Research Project   ☐ Form 706   ☐ Form 709   ☐ Tax Projection

☐ Tax Examination   ☐ Correspondence   ☐ Estate Planning   ☐ Other _____

Description of Assignment (or Attach Memo in Detail and Summarize Below):

_____

_____

_____

_____

_____

_____

_____

_____

_____

_____

_____

_____

_____

_____

Time Budget _____ Due Date _____

Copies To _____

| TAX DEPT. USE ONLY |
| Assigned To: _____ |
| T.D. Control #: _____ Date: _____ |
| COMPLETED |
| Date: _____ T.D.M.#: _____ |

DISTRIBUTION OF FORM
WHITE: RETAINED BY PREPARER   **OTHER COPIES:** MANAGER, TAX DEPT.

TAX RETURN

1040
U.S. INDIVIDUAL INCOME TAX RETURN

Date _____

Name	SSN: _____
Period Ending	This number should be indicated on all checks regarding this return.

General

The following procedures are applicable to the tax return which is with the enclosed pre-addressed envelope. Attached to this Instruction Sheet is the **COPY** for your files and records. If there are any questions do not hesitate to contact us.

Signature

SIGNATURE. The Form 1040 is to be signed by:
( ) Both husband and wife   ( ) Taxpayer only   ( ) Other _____
Fill in the date after each signature.
If Voucher 1 of Form 1040ES (Estimated Tax) is enclosed, it is to be signed in a similar manner.

Due Date

Mail on or before _____

Payment

Enclose **separate** checks payable to "Internal Revenue Service" for the following:

	DATE	CHECK NO.
$ _____ Balance Due, Current Year		
$ _____ Voucher 1; Estimated Tax		

NOTE: Your Social Security Number (SSN) should be indicated on all checks

Estimated Taxes

Estimated taxes have been computed based on the current year's taxes unless we have been advised to the contrary. Payment schedule:

Voucher	Due		Amount		DATE	CHECK NO.
	Credit Carry-over	$ _____				
1	April 15	$ _____				
2	June 15	$ _____				
3	Sept. 15	$ _____				
4	January 15	$ _____				

The IRS does NOT send notices of these payments. Keep the vouchers in a secure place and note payment dates.

Overpayment

There has been an overpayment amounting to $ _____ which has been applied as

$ _____ Refund Requested

$ _____ Applied to Estimated tax

Other Notes

All clients are advised to maintain a current **will**, reflecting present family and financial circumstances. **Florida Residents:** Homestead exemptions are to be claimed annually. Intangible Tax Returns and Personal Property Returns may be required.

TAX RETURN

1065
U.S. PARTNERSHIP
RETURN OF INCOME

Date _____

Name		I.D. No. _____
Period Ending		

General

The following procedures are applicable to the tax return which is with the enclosed pre-addressed envelope. Attached to this Instruction Sheet is the **COPY** for your files and records. If there are any questions do not hesitate to contact us.

Signature

The return must be signed and dated by one of the Partners.

Date Due

Mail on or before _____

Payment

Send **no** payment with this return.

Information For Personal Returns

Form 1065 is an information return. Partners are to report their share of gain or loss, together with other items such as the investment tax credit, on their Individual Income Tax Returns. This information is included on **FORM K-1.**

The partner's share of a loss is limited to the *tax basis* which includes the investment and adjustments for profits, losses, distributions, and share of the partnership liabilities.

Please distribute the Forms K-1 enclosed to the partners.

Other Notes

TAX RETURN

F1120
FLORIDA CORPORATION
INCOME TAX RETURN

Date ....

Name	FLA. I.D. NO. ....
Period Ending	This number should be indicated on all checks regarding this return.

General

The following procedures are applicable to the tax return which is with the enclosed pre-addressed envelope. Attached to this Instruction Sheet is the **COPY** for your files and records. If there are any questions do not hesitate to contact us.

Signature

The return must be signed by an Officer of the Corporation at the bottom of Page 1. Complete Title and Date.

Other page(s) to be signed: ....

Due Date

Mail on or before ....

Payment

Enclose checks payable to FLORIDA DEPARTMENT OF REVENUE for the following:

ON OR BEFORE	AMOUNT	DATE PAID	CHECK NO.
....	$	....	....
....	$	....	....

Estimated Taxes

Estimated Taxes have been computed based on current year's tax unless we have been advised to the contrary. Payments due with Form F-1120—ES are:

DUE	AMOUNT	DATE PAID	CHECK NO.
....	$	....	....
....	$	....	....
....	$	....	....
....	$		

Overpayment

There has been an overpayment of $ .... , which will be applied as follows:

$ .... Refund Requested

$ .... Credited to Estimated Tax

Other Notes

> *Copies of Pages from Federal Income Tax Return are required, and are attached.*

INFORMATION FOR FOLLOW-UP

Items to Carry Forward

1. Operating Loss ....
2. Capital Loss ....
3. Contributions ....
4. Other ....

236

APPENDIX I

Forms for Estate Planning[1]

Exhibit	Title	Usage
I-1	Estate Planning Questionnaire	To gather the information needed for estate planning and to guide the client in "getting the house in order"
I-2	Procedures in Estate Planning	Allocates responsibilities to the members of the estate planning team and serves as a checklist to completion
I-3	Projected Cash Requirements and Sources	Two worksheets to project the cash needs for the widow or widower and heirs and to measure the sources of funds with which to meet the needs
I-4	The Will Quiz	A brief quiz to highlight the reasons a person should have a will and a current one, at that

[1]See Chapter 7.

EXHIBIT I-1. **Estate Planning Questionnaire**

1. Family Information
2. Important Contacts
3. Real Estate
4. Cash
5. Stocks and Bonds
6. Life Insurance
7. Miscellaneous Assets
8. Personal Liabilities
9. Business Interests

PART 1: Family Information

1. HUSBAND AND WIFE:	Husband	Wife (indicate "same" where applicable)
a. Full name	_____	_____
b. Date of birth	_____	_____
c. Place of birth	_____	_____
d. Present permanent address	_____	_____
e. Other present address(es)	_____	_____
f. Have you every been divorced?	☐ Yes ☐ No	☐ Yes ☐ No

(If yes, submit all pertinent information, such as date, where divorced, former spouse, children, financial obligations to children and/or former spouse)

g. Have you every been a widow or widower before?	☐ Yes ☐ No	☐ Yes ☐ No

(If yes, submit all pertinent information)

h. Have you ever created a trust?	☐ Yes ☐ No	☐ Yes ☐ No
i. Have you ever opened a joint account (check or savings)?	☐ Yes ☐ No	☐ Yes ☐ No
j. Have you ever opened an account (check or savings) in trust for another?	☐ Yes ☐ No	☐ Yes ☐ No
k. Have you ever purchased property in joint ownership with unequal contribution towards cost?	☐ Yes ☐ No	☐ Yes ☐ No
l. Have you ever been named as trustee by someone else or administered assets of others or for others?	☐ Yes ☐ No	☐ Yes ☐ No

(If yes, submit all pertinent information, i.e., documents, trust agreements, trust returns, etc.)

EXHIBIT I-1. **Estate Planning Questionnaire** (*Cont.*)

PART 1: Family Information (*Cont.*)

1. HUSBAND AND WIFE: (*Cont.*)	Husband	Wife (indicate "same" where applicable)
m. Date of marriage	_____	_____
n. Place of marriage	_____	_____
Social Security information:		
o. Social Security number	_____	_____
p. Years paid (if known)	_____	_____
q. Present monthly benefits	_____	_____
r. Last time Social Security account credits were verified with Social Security administration	_____	_____

2. CHILDREN *(Indicate by (P) after name if by previous marriage of husband or wife):*

Name and Address:	By Previous Marriage	Date of Birth (Mo Day Yr)	Is Child Married?	Is Child a Dependent?
	(H)(W)		Yes No	Yes No
	( )( )	/ /	☐ ☐	☐ ☐
	( )( )	/ /	☐ ☐	☐ ☐
	( )( )	/ /	☐ ☐	☐ ☐
	( )( )	/ /	☐ ☐	☐ ☐

3. GRANDCHILDREN:

Name and Address:	Date of Birth (Mo Day Yr)	Is Grandchild Dependent?
		Yes No
_____	/ /	☐ ☐
_____	/ /	☐ ☐
_____	/ /	☐ ☐

EXHIBIT I-1. **Estate Planning Questionnaire (*Cont.*)**

4. OTHERS FOR WHOM THERE IS ONGOING FINANCIAL OBLIGATION:

Name and Address:	Date of Birth (Mo Day Yr)	Relationship
_____	/ /	_____
_____	/ /	_____
_____	/ /	_____

5. SPECIAL FAMILY PROBLEMS, IF ANY:

a.   Previous marriages and commitments therefrom _____

_____

_____

b. Other_____

_____

_____

PART 2:   Important Contacts:

	Name (Including Firms, As Applicable)	Address and Telephone Number
Accountant	_____	_____
	_____	_____
	_____	_____
	_____	_____
Attorney	_____	_____
	_____	_____
	_____	_____
	_____	_____

EXHIBIT I-1. **Estate Planning Questionnaire** (*Cont.*)

PART 2: Important Contacts: (*Cont.*)

	Name (Including Firms, As Applicable)	Address and Telephone Number
Banker	_____	_____
	_____	_____
	_____	_____
	_____	_____
Trust officer	_____	_____
	_____	_____
	_____	_____
	_____	_____
Stock broker	_____	_____
	_____	_____
	_____	_____
	_____	_____
Investment advisor	_____	_____
	_____	_____
	_____	_____
	_____	_____
Life insurance advisor	_____	_____
	_____	_____
	_____	_____
	_____	_____
Casualty insurance agent	_____	_____
	_____	_____
	_____	_____

EXHIBIT I-1. **Estate Planning Questionnaire (*Cont.*)**

PART 2:   Important Contacts: (*Cont.*)

	Name (Including Firms, As Applicable)	Address and Telephone Number
	_____	_____
	_____	_____
Trustees	_____	_____
	_____	_____
	_____	_____
	_____	_____
Executors	_____	_____
	_____	_____
	_____	_____
	_____	_____
Designated guardian for children	_____	_____
	_____	_____
	_____	_____
	_____	_____
Physician	_____	_____
	_____	_____
	_____	_____
	_____	_____
Clergyman	_____	_____
	_____	_____
	_____	_____
	_____	_____

EXHIBIT I-1. **Estate Planning Questionnaire** (*Cont.*)

PART 3: Real Estate (Other Than Residence)

Date _____

Description and Location	Cost	Balance of Mortgage*	Current Fair Market Value		
			Husband	Wife	Joint
_____	$ _____	$ _____	$ _____	$ _____	$ _____
_____					
_____	_____	_____	_____	_____	_____
_____					
_____	_____	_____	_____	_____	_____
_____					
_____					

(For rental property prepare supplemental schedule of annual gross rents, real estate taxes, operating expenses, depreciation, annual net income)

Personal Residences

Description and location _____

_____

Form of ownership_____

Owners and percentage of ownership_____

_____

Date of acquisition __/__/__ Cost basis_____
             (Month Day Year)

Current value $_____

Mortgage balance* $_____

   *Submit mortgage details in Part 6.

PART 4: Cash Includes: Checking account, savings, certificate of deposit, money market certificates, savings bonds

Institution	Type of Account	Owned (H, W, J)	Amount
_____	_____	_____	$ _____
_____	_____	_____	_____

243

EXHIBIT I-1. **Estate Planning Questionnaire (*Cont.*)**

PART 4: Cash Includes: Checking account, savings, certificate of deposit, money market
certificates, savings bonds (*Cont.*)

Institution	Type of Account	Owned (H, W, J)	Amount
————	———	———	———
————	———	———	———
————	———	———	———
————	———	———	———
————	———	———	———
————	———	———	———
————	———	———	———
————	———	———	———
————	———	———	———
————	———	———	———
————	———	———	———
————	———	———	———
————	———	———	———
————	———	———	———
————	———	———	———
————	———	———	———
————	———	———	———
		Total	$ ———

EXHIBIT I-1.   **Estate Planning Questionnaire** (*Cont.*)

PART 5:   Stocks and Bonds

Number of Shares (or Par Value)	Description (Name of Company, Municipality, etc.)	Market Value			
		Cost	Husband	Wife	Joint
_____	_____	$ _____	$ _____	$ _____	$ _____
_____	_____	_____	_____	_____	_____
_____	_____	_____	_____	_____	_____
_____	_____	_____	_____	_____	_____
_____	_____	_____	_____	_____	_____
_____	_____	_____	_____	_____	_____
_____	_____	_____	_____	_____	_____
_____	_____	_____	_____	_____	_____
_____	_____	_____	_____	_____	_____
_____	_____	_____	_____	_____	_____
_____	_____	_____	_____	_____	_____
_____	_____	_____	_____	_____	_____
_____	_____	_____	_____	_____	_____
_____	_____	_____	_____	_____	_____
_____	_____	_____	_____	$ _____	_____
_____	_____	_____	_____	_____	_____
_____	_____	_____	_____	_____	_____
_____	_____	_____	_____	_____	_____
	Totals	$ _____	$ _____	$ _____	$ _____

EXHIBIT I-1. **Estate Planning Questionnaire** (*Cont.*)

PART 6:   Life Insurance

1. Policies Owned By You On Your Life (Company & Policy Number)	Face Value	Type of Policy	Annual Premium	Cash Surrender Value	Designated Beneficiary	Settle- ment Option
No. _____ _____	$ _____	_____	$ _____	$ _____	_____	_____
No. _____ _____	_____	_____	_____	_____	_____	_____
No. _____ _____	_____	_____	_____	_____	_____	_____

2.   **Policies Owned By Others On Your Life (Company & Policy Number)**

No. _____ _____	$ _____	_____	$ _____	$ _____	_____	_____
No. _____ _____	_____	_____	_____	_____	_____	_____
No. _____ _____	_____	_____	_____	_____	_____	_____

3.   **Policies Owned By You On Lives Of Others (Company & Policy Number)**

No. _____ _____	$ _____	_____	$ _____	$ _____	_____	_____
No. _____ _____	_____	_____	_____	_____	_____	_____
No. _____ _____	_____	_____	_____	_____	_____	_____

EXHIBIT I-1. **Estate Planning Questionnaire (*Cont.*)**

PART 7: Miscellaneous Assets (At Current Fair Market Value)

1. Personal Effects	Husband	Wife	Joint
a. Clothing	\$ _____	\$ _____	\$ _____
b. Furs	_____	_____	_____
c. Jewelry	_____	_____	_____
d. Home furnishings	_____	_____	_____
e. Other (please list)			
_____	_____	_____	_____
_____	_____	_____	_____

2. Other Tangible Personal Property
    a. Collections (e.g., art, books, stamps, coins, guns). *Describe:*

_____	_____	_____	_____
_____	_____	_____	_____

    b. Automobiles

_____	_____	_____	_____
_____	_____	_____	_____

    c. Other (e.g., boats, aircraft, office contents). *Describe:*

_____	_____	_____	_____
_____	_____	_____	_____

3. Retirement Plans*

a. Company pension plan	_____	_____	_____
b. Company profit sharing plan	_____	_____	_____
c. IRA account	_____	_____	_____
d. Keogh Plan	_____	_____	_____
e. Social Security	_____	_____	_____
f. Veterans' benefits	_____	_____	_____

*In the case of each plan, show separately: name of company and/or fiscal agent, retirement benefits, amount currently vested, beneficiaries, your contributions to date, number of years of participation.

EXHIBIT I-1.   **Estate Planning Questionnaire (*Cont.*)**

PART 7:   Miscellaneous Assets (At Current Fair Market Value) (*Cont.*)

1. Personal Effects	Husband	Wife	Joint
g. Government pension	——	——	——
h. Other (railroad, teachers, etc.)			
	——	——	——
	——	——	——

4. Contract Rights
a. Patent, trademark, copyright ownership or royalty arrangements. *Describe:*

	$ ——	$ ——	$ ——
	——	——	——

b. Other (please list):

	——	——	——
	——	——	——

5. Mineral Interests
a. Oil and gas

	——	——	——

b. Other (please list:

	——	——	——
	——	——	——

6. Estates and Trusts
a. Anticipated benefits under estates and trusts

	——	——	——

b. Powers of appointment (general or limited)

	——	——	——
	——	——	——
	——	——	——

9. Any Others

	——	——	——
	——	——	——

EXHIBIT I-1.   **Estate Planning Questionnaire (Cont.)**

PART 8:   Personal Liabilities

Payable to (Secured by)	Amount Owed	Interest Rate (%)	When Due (Mo./Yr.)	Periodic Payments	
				When Paid (Monthly, Annually, etc.)	Amount

1. Real Estate Mortgages

_____ $ _____   _____   ___/___   _____ $ _____

_____

_____   _____   _____   ___/___   _____   _____

_____

_____   _____   _____   ___/___   _____   _____

_____

2. Notes to Banks or Other Financial Institutions

_____ $ _____   _____   ___/___   _____ $ _____

_____

_____   _____   _____   ___/___   _____   _____

_____

_____   _____   _____   ___/___   _____   _____

_____

3. Loans on Insurance Policies

_____ $ _____   _____   ___/___   _____ $ _____

_____

_____   _____   _____   ___/___   _____   _____

_____

_____   _____   _____   ___/___   _____   _____

_____

EXHIBIT I-1. **Estate Planning Questionnaire (*Cont.*)**

PART 8:   Personal Liabilities (Cont.)

Payable to (Secured by)	Amount Owed	Interest Rate (%)	When Due (Mo./Yr.)	Periodic Payments When Paid (Monthly, Annually, etc.)	Amount
4. Other Obligations					
_____	$ ____	____	__/__	____	$ ____
_____					
_____	____	____	__/__	____	____
_____					
_____	____	____	__/__	____	____
_____					
5. Charitable Pledges					
_____	$ ____	____	__/__	____	$ ____
_____	____	____	__/__	____	____
_____					
_____	____	____	__/__	____	____
_____					
6. Tax Liabilities					
_____	$ ____	____	__/__	____	$ ____
_____					
_____	____	____	__/__	____	____
_____	____	____	__/__	____	____
_____					

EXHIBIT I-1.   **Estate Planning Questionnaire** (*Cont.*)

PART 8:   Personal Liabilities (*Cont.*)

Payable to (Secured by)	Amount Owed	Interest Rate (%)	When Due (Mo./Yr.)	Periodic Payments When Paid (Monthly, Annually, etc.)	Amount
7. Contingent Liabilities					
_____	$ ____	____	___/___	____	$ ____
_____					
_____	____	____	___/___	____	____
_____					
_____	____	____	___/___	____	____
_____					

PART 9:   Business Interests (Use Similar Schedule for Each Business)

Name of business: _____Telephone number: _____

Address: _____

_____

Form of business: _____ State of incorporation: _____

Type of business: _____ Date of incorporation: _____

Ownership

Name	Address	Age	Percentage
_____	_____	____	____
_____	_____	____	____
_____	_____	____	____
_____	_____	____	____

EXHIBIT I-1. **Estate Planning Questionnaire (*Cont.*)**

PART 9:   Business Interests (Use Similar Schedule for Each Business) (*Cont.*)

Key Employees:

Name	Address	Position	Current Salary
_____	_____	_____	$ _____
_____	_____	_____	_____
_____	_____	_____	_____
_____	_____	_____	_____

Personal Guaranty of Company Debt:

_____

_____

Business Agreements *(Such as buy-sell, stock redemption, key person insurance, etc.):*

Type _____ Funding _____

Valuation method _____

Date of last review _____

Capitalization (for corporation) :

	Par	Total Authorized	Total Issued	Callable
Common stock	_____	_____	_____	_____
Preferred stock	_____	_____	_____	_____
Debentures	_____	_____	_____	_____

Retirement Plans *(Describe any revision or profit sharing plans; be sure to include your portion in Part 5)*

_____

_____

_____

EXHIBIT I-1. **Estate Planning Questionnaire** *Cont.*

PART 9: **Business Interests (Use Similar Schedule for Each Business) (***Cont.***)**

Stock Options *(Describe any stock option plans, with particular details on options availabale to you)*

_____

_____

_____

Value of Business:

Book value _____ Market value _____

Liquidation value _____ Goodwill _____

Gross annual revenues _____ Annual net income _____
Recent transfers of interest (date, amount transferred and price)

_____

_____

Plans for Ultimate Disposition *(Transfer to family, sale to co-owner, sale to key employees, acquisition, etc.)*

_____

_____

EXHIBIT I-2. Procedures in Estate Planning

	Responsibility of					Date
	CPA	Attorney	Executor	Trust Officer	Other	Completed

1. INVENTORY

 a. Inventory and value *all* assets

 b. List *all* liabilities

 c. Relate liabilities to respective assets

2. CLOSELY HELD BUSINESS(ES)

 a. Develop valuation

 b. Support with documentation

3. LIQUIDITY

 a. Estimate estate taxes

 b. Administrative and probate costs

 c. Need to repay immediately maturing debts

 d. Current needs of family (and other heirs)

4. INSURANCE CARRIED

 a. Schedule all insurance policies

 b. List the following for each:

  (1) Type of insurance

  (2) Face amount

  (3) Cash surrender value

  (4) Premium cost

  (5) Loans against policy

  (6) Owner of policy

  (7) Options for settlements

  (8) Special provisions (double indemnity, guaranteed renewable, etc.)

   c. Consider cost of carrying insurance versus alternative procedure

   d. Is insurance adequate for needs?

5. DOMICILE

   a. Was will prepared in present state of domicile?

   b. Are there assets located in other states (or countries)?

6. PRIOR GIFTS

   a. Determine dates and amounts of prior gifts of cash or property

   b. Obtain copies of gift tax returns of husband and wife

7. BASIS

   Determine cost and tax basis of all assets (for gift and estate tax calculations)

8. OWNERSHIP

   Determine ownership of all assets—husband, wife, or joint (in common, joint tenancy, etc.)

9. REVIEW ALL DOCUMENTS

   a. Wills and codicils thereto

   b. Buy-sell agreements in closely held businesses

   c. Pension and profit sharing plans

   d. Divorce decrees

   e. Trust agreements

   f. Other pertinent contracts and agreements

10. CHARITIES

   a. Are there any family charitable foundations or trusts?

   b. Will there be any bequests to charity?

11. GOALS

   Assist in the determination and defining of the goals of the estate plan

12. CALCULATIONS

   Compute the estimated amount of the estate, using various alternatives

EXHIBIT I-2. Procedures in Estate Planning (*Cont.*)

13. **PREPARE NEW DOCUMENTS RESULTING FROM PLAN**

    a. Wills and codicils _____

    b. Trust instruments testamentary or inter-vivos _____

    c. Pension and Profit Sharing plans _____

    d. Buy-sell agreement _____

    e. Recapitalization Plan _____

    f. ESOP documents _____

    g. Other pertinent contract and agreement _____

    Notes: _____

    _____

    _____

    _____

EXHIBIT I-3. **Projected Cash Requirements and Sources: (a)**
Worksheet for Projected Cash Requirements for the
Heirs (b) Worksheet of Sources to Meet Cash
Requirements

(a) Worksheet for Projected Cash Requirements for the Heirs (Based on Present Standard of Living)

Items Entered in Columns (1) (2) (3) Are to Be Multiplied by Applicable Factor and Extended to Column (4)	(1) Weekly Amount (× 52)	(2) Monthly Amount (× 12)	(3) Quarterly Amount (× 4)	(4) Annual Amount
1. Household				
Mortgage payment (or rent)	$ _____	$ _____	$ _____	$ _____
Electric, water, gas	_____	_____	_____	_____
Maid	_____	_____	_____	_____
Lawn	_____	_____	_____	_____
Exterminator	_____	_____	_____	_____
Telephone	_____	_____	_____	_____
Repairs and maintenance	_____	_____	_____	_____
Pool maintenance	_____	_____	_____	_____
Property taxes	_____	_____	_____	_____
Other	_____	_____	_____	_____
Total	$ _____	$ _____	$ _____	$ _____
2. Insurance				
Homeowners	$ _____	$ _____	$ _____	$ _____
Disability	_____	_____	_____	_____
Life	_____	_____	_____	_____
Medical	_____	_____	_____	_____
Auto	_____	_____	_____	_____
Other	_____	_____	_____	_____
Total	$ _____	$ _____	$ _____	$ _____
3. Loan payments				
Autos	$ _____	$ _____	$ _____	$ _____

EXHIBIT I-3. **Projected Cash Requirements and Sources: (a) Worksheet for Projected Cash Requirements for the Heirs (b) Worksheet of Sources to Meet Cash Requirements (Cont.)**

(a) Worksheet for Projected Cash Requirements for the Heirs (Based on Present Standard of Living) (Cont.)

Items Entered in Columns (1) (2) (3) Are to Be Multiplied by Applicable Factor and Extended to Column (4)	(1) Weekly Amount (× 52)	(2) Monthly Amount (× 12)	(3) Quarterly Amount (× 4)	(4) Annual Amount
Boat				
Charge accounts				
Bank				
Other				
Total	$	$	$	$
4. Investments				
Mortgage payments	$	$	$	$
Securities				
Other				
Total	$	$	$	$
5. Regular commitments				
Food	$	$	$	$
Auto (gas, oil, repairs)				
Clothing				
Entertainment				
Medical, dental				
Cash spending				
Religious contributions				
Gifts				
Miscellaneous				
Total	$	$	$	$
6. Special commitments				
Furniture purchases	$	$	$	$

(a) Worksheet for Projected Cash Requirements for the Heirs (Based on Present Standard of Living) (Cont.)

Items Entered in Columns (1) (2) (3) Are to Be Multiplied by Applicable Factor and Extended to Column (4)	(1) Weekly Amount (× 52)	(2) Monthly Amount (× 12)	(3) Quarterly Amount (× 4)	(4) Annual Amount
6. **Special commitments** (*Cont.*)				
Weddings, parties, etc.	_____	_____	_____	_____
Other	_____	_____	_____	_____
Total	$ _____	$ _____	$ _____	$ _____
7. **Income taxes**	$ _____	$ _____	$ _____	$ _____

Summary of Projected Cash Requirements for the Heirs

	(1) Weekly Amount (× 52)	(2) Monthly Amount (× 12)	(3) Quarterly Amount (× 4)	(4) Annual Amount
1. Household	$ _____	$ _____	$ _____	$ _____
2. Insurance	_____	_____	_____	_____
3. Loan payments	_____	_____	_____	_____
4. Investments	_____	_____	_____	_____
5. Regular commitments	_____	_____	_____	_____
6. Special commitments	_____	_____	_____	_____
7. Income taxes	_____	_____	_____	_____
Total cash requirements	$ _____	$ _____	$ _____	$ _____

Add projected cash requirements of the estate:

Estate taxes				$ _____
Estate liabilities (see Schedule H)				_____
Estate bequests				_____
Estate expenses				_____
Total				$ _____
Combined total				$ _____

EXHIBIT I-3. **Projected Cash Requirements and Sources: (a) Worksheet for Projected Cash Requirements for the Heirs (b) Worksheet of Sources to Meet Cash Requirements (Cont.)**

(b) Worksheet of Sources to Meet Cash Requirements

From Estate Planning Section		Per Annum
A. Present annual income	1. Salary (if continued)	
	2. Bonus (if any)	
	3. Interest	
	4. Dividends	
	5. Rents *(Schedule D)*	
	6. Partnerships	
	7. Capital gains	
	8. Other	
		_____
	Total	$ _____
B. Cash accounts	1. Checking	
	2. Savings	
	3. Certificates of deposit	_____
	Total	$ _____
C. Other personal property	1. Collection on notes (principal)	
	2. Collection on mortgages (principal)	
	3. Profit-sharing plan	
	4. Pension plan	
	5. IRA account	
	6. Keogh Plan	
	7. Other	_____
	Total	$ _____
D. Expectancies	1. _____	
	2. _____	_____
	Total	$ _____
E. Business interests	1. Partnership(s)	
	2. Joint venture(s)	
	3. Subchapter-S corporation(s)	
	4. Gift (widow) from corporation	
	5. Key-individual insurance	
	6. Stock redemption plan	
	7. Corporate distributions	
	8. Other	_____
	Total	$ _____

(b) Worksheet of Sources to Meet Cash Requirements (*Cont.*)

From Estate Planning Section		Per Annum
F. Life insurance	List *each* policy, including accumulated dividends, etc. (subtract amounts for policy loans):	

    1. _____

    2. _____

    3. _____

    4. _____

    5. _____

    6. _____

    7. _____   _____

            Total $ _____

G.   Other sources anticipated

    1.   Sales of any assets (detail)
    2.   Borrowing (detail)
    3.   Mortgaging of property
    4.   Other borrowing
    5. _____   _____

            Total $ _____

Total $ _____

(Use separate sheets to detail additional information. Cross reference to listed section and item number.)

Summary of Sources to Meet Cash Requirements

Section	Description	Amount
A	Present annual income	$ _____
B	Cash accounts	_____
C	Other personal property	_____
D	Expectancies	_____
E	Business interests	_____
F	Life insurance	_____
G	Other	_____

EXHIBIT I-4. **The Will Quiz**

Is your estate in order? Take this easy quiz and see. A **Yes** answer to any of the following could be a danger signal.

		Yes	No
1.	Do either you or your spouse *not* have a will?	☐	☐
2.	Have any beneficiaries named in your will died since the will was drawn?	☐	☐
3.	Have any beneficiaries become (since the will was drawn) more capable—or less capable—of managing their money and investments?	☐	☐
4.	Have children or grandchildren been born since your will was drawn?	☐	☐
5.	Does your will make gifts of specific property that you no longer own, or which has changed in character?	☐	☐
6.	Have any of the beneficiaries named in your will married since your will was drawn?	☐	☐
7.	Have you moved from one state to another since your will was drawn?	☐	☐
8.	Has the total value of your assets changed substantially since your will was drawn?	☐	☐
9.	Have you taken out more life insurance since your will was drawn?	☐	☐
10.	Have you become a participant in retirement plans or other fringe benefit programs provided by your employer company?	☐	☐
11.	Have you and another person put any property in your names jointly, with right of survivorship?	☐	☐
12.	Was your will drawn a long time ago, before certain important changes were made in the Federal estate and income tax laws?	☐	☐
13.	Did you fail this quiz?	☐	☐
14.	**Do you refuse to do something about it . . . *now*?**	☐	☐

Forms for Acceptance and Continuance of Clients[1]

Exhibit	Title	Usage
J-1	Office Control Checklist for New Clients	Prepared for all new clients. It incorporates controls (client numbers, engagement letter), practice development (welcome letter, thank you letter) and quality control procedures.
J-2	Client Continuation Decision	Clients are reviewed annually to determine continuation.
J-3	Client Acceptance Checklist	If a client reaches the threshold requiring committee approval for acceptance or continuation (Exhibits J-1 and J-2), this checklist is to be completed.

[1]See STEP 8.

OFFICE CONTROL
CHECKLIST FOR NEW CLIENTS
(ALL APPLICABLE ITEMS <u>MUST</u> BE COMPLETED)

*OBTAIN CLIENT NUMBER FROM <u>OFFICE MANAGER</u> FIRST   OFFICE: _____

PREPARED BY: _____ DATE: _____

SOURCE OF BUSINESS: _____ ESTIMATED ANNUAL BILLING: $ _____

NATURE OF CLIENT'S BUSINESS: _____ SIC # _____

CLIENT'S ATTORNEY: _____ BANK: _____

CHECK AS APPLICABLE:
- ☐ WRITTEN CONFIRMATION FROM CLIENT AS TO TERMINATION OF FORMER ACCOUNTANT, (Rule 21A - 6.01)
- ☐ CONTACT PREDECESSOR AUDITOR IF AUDIT ENGAGEMENT
- ☐ ENGAGEMENT LETTER PREPARED   ☐ THANK YOU LETTER, TO_____
- ☐ DO <u>NOT</u> SEND WELCOMING LETTER FROM MANAGING PARTNER (IF NOT CHECKED, GOES AUTOMATICALLY)

*NO. ASSIGNED

F.Y.E. _____
FORM _____
ID NO. _____
SSN NUMBERS:
  HUSBAND _____
  WIFE _____
☐ NO FISCAL YEAR

NAME(S) _____

ADDRESS _____

_____ ZIP CODE

PHONE(S) _____

AREA CODE (   )

MAILING ADDRESS (IF DIFFERENT) _____

NAMES OF PRINCIPALS _____

CHIEF ACCOUNTING PERSON _____

OTHER KEY PERSONNEL _____

RELATED COMPANIES _____

FEE ARRANGEMENT _____

SERVICES RENDERED ☐ MONTHLY, ☐ QUARTERLY, ☐ ANNUALLY, ☐ OTHER (SPECIFY) _____

DESCRIPTION OF SERVICES _____

REGULATORY AGENCIES TO WHICH SUBJECT _____

SPECIAL EXPERTISE REQUIRED _____

ASSIGNED TO ENGAGEMENT: SUPERVISOR _____ OTHER _____

NEW CLIENT ACCEPTED (SEE BELOW FOR ACCEPTANCE COMMITTEE CHECKLIST):

_____   _____
PARTNER IN CHARGE (AFTER REVIEW OF AVAILABLE   MANAGING PARTNER (PINK COPY)
FINANCIAL INFORMATION AND INQUIRIES ABOUT CLIENT)

APPROVAL BY ACCEPTANCE COMMITTEE

THE ACCEPTANCE COMMITTEE CHECKLIST MUST BE COMPLETED FOR ALL PROSPECTIVE CLIENTS WHO MEET ONE OR MORE OF THE FOLLOW-ING DESCRIPTIONS. (ALL OTHER PROSPECTIVE CLIENTS ARE ACCEPTED BY THE APPROVAL OF THE PIC AND THE MANAGING PARTNER.) SUBMIT THE COMPLETED CHECKLIST TO THE MANAGING PARTNER. PROSPECTIVE CLIENTS REQUIRE COMMITTEE REVIEW IF:

- ☐ PUBLICLY HELD COMPANY OR BROKER/DEALER
- ☐ ANNUAL FEE EXPECTED TO EXCEED $10,000 OR TOTAL HOURS TO EXCEED 300
- ☐ FIRM OPERATES IN HIGH RISK INDUSTRY (DIFFICULT TO ESTABLISH ADEQUATE INTERNAL CONTROLS, ESPECIALLY SENSITIVE TO GENERAL ECONOMIC CONDITIONS, ETC.)
- ☐ COMPANY IS IN DEVELOPMENT STAGE
- ☐ COMPANY IS IN SERIOUS FINANCIAL DIFFICULTY

- ☐ THERE HAS BEEN A RECENT SIGNIFICANT CHANGE IN:
  - ☐ MANAGEMENT   ☐ DIRECTORS
  - ☐ OWNERSHIP   ☐ LEGAL COUNSEL
  - ☐ FINANCIAL CONDITION   ☐ LITIGATION STATUS
  - ☐ NATURE OF BUSINESS   ☐ SCOPE OF AUDIT
- ☐ YOU ARE AWARE OF ANY OTHER REASON FOR COMMITTEE REVIEW

☐ **FILES TO BE OPENED**

STANDARD FIRM FILES WILL BE OPENED UNLESS NOTED TO THE CONTRARY:

CLIENT CONTINUATION DECISION
(AND INFORMATION UPDATE)

PART 1. CLIENT INFORMATION

NO.
NAME: _____

ADDRESS: _____   TELEPHONE: _____ _____

_____   _____ _____

_____   SIC # _____

_____   FYE _____

PRINCIPALS: _____

BANK AFFILIATION: _____ ATTORNEY: _____

PARTNER IN CHARGE: _____ CLIENT SINCE: _____

STAFF: SUPERVISORY _____ OTHER: _____

GENERAL DESCRIPTION OF SERVICE: _____

OTHER INFORMATION: _____

PARTNER IN CHARGE TO CORRECT OR COMPLETE ABOVE INFORMATION.

PART 2. FINANCIAL INFORMATION

ANNUAL FEES:

ACCUMULATED AT STANDARD RATES $ _____

BILLED TO CLIENT $ _____

PRESENT ACCOUNTS RECEIVABLE BALANCE $ _____

☐ CHECK HERE IF POTENTIAL INDEPENDENCE PROBLEM (PARA. 4d, INDEPENDENCE, PAGE 10 OF QUALITY CONTROL DOCUMENT) AND REFER TO ACCEPTANCE COMMITTEE. ATTACH SUPPLEMENTAL INFORMATION RELATING TO SATISFACTION OF OUTSTANDING BALANCES.

PART 3. SPECIAL CONSIDERATIONS

THE FOLLOWING TYPES OF ENGAGEMENTS ARE CONSIDERED TO BE OF A SPECIAL NATURE REQUIRING REVIEW ANNUALLY, OR WHEN THERE IS A SIGNIFICANT CHANGE (AS ENUMERATED). PLEASE CHECK APPLICABLE DESCRIPTIVE ITEMS.

☐ PUBLICLY HELD COMPANY OR BROKER/DEALER

☐ ANNUAL FEE EXPECTED TO EXCEED $10,000 OR TOTAL HOURS
   TO EXCEED 300

☐ FIRM OPERATES IN HIGH RISK INDUSTRY
   (DIFFICULT TO ESTABLISH ADEQUATE INTERNAL CONTROLS,
   ESPECIALLY SENSITIVE TO GENERAL ECONOMIC
   CONDITIONS, ETC.)

☐ COMPANY IS IN DEVELOPMENT STAGE

☐ COMPANY IS IN SERIOUS FINANCIAL DIFFICULTY

☐ THERE HAS BEEN A RECENT **SIGNIFICANT CHANGE** IN:
   ☐ MANAGEMENT   ☐ DIRECTORS
   ☐ OWNERSHIP   ☐ LEGAL COUNSEL
   ☐ FINANCIAL CONDITION ☐ LITIGATION STATUS
   ☐ NATURE OF BUSINESS ☐ SCOPE OF AUDIT

☐ YOU ARE AWARE OF ANY OTHER REASON FOR COMMITTEE
   REVIEW

(Partner In Charge To Check One Of The Two Boxes)   **PART 4. CONCLUSIONS**

1. ☐ THERE IS NO REASON INDICATED TO CONSIDER DISCONTINUANCE OF SERVICE, NOR AM I AWARE OF ANY OTHER FACTOR WHICH SHOULD PROMPT US TO CONSIDER DISCONTINUANCE. I THEREFORE RECOMMEND SERVICE BE CONTINUED.

APPROVED: Partner _____   Date _____

Managing Partner _____   Date _____

2. ☐ REFERRED TO ACCEPTANCE COMMITTEE FOR FOLLOWING REASONS:
   ☐ SEE PART 2   ☐ SEE PART 3
   ☐ OTHER _____

_____

(SUBMIT PERTINENT INFORMATION FOR GUIDANCE OF COMMITTEE)

ACTION BY ACCEPTANCE COMMITTEE: _____

SIGNATURES: _____   Date: _____

_____

PROCEDURES AND DISTRIBUTION OF COPIES

1. Accounting and Auditing Department alerts Bookkeeping Dept. to prepare form approximately 60 days prior to end of fiscal year.
2. Bookkeeping Dept. completes Part 1 and $ amounts of Part 2. **GOLD** copy goes back to Accounting and Auditing as a **Control Copy**. The other **three** copies go to Partner in Charge.
3. Partner in Charge completes the form and retains **PINK** copy for his records. **WHITE** and **CANARY** go to Managing Partner for the Acceptance Committee.
4. After conclusion by Acceptance Committee, the **WHITE** copy is retained by them, and the **CANARY** is returned to Partner in Charge for appropriate action and ultimate filing in Permanent File of client.

Client Acceptance Check List

1. This checklist is to be completed, in conjunction with an Office Control Checklist for New Clients (for those clients meeting the criteria as listed on the next page), by the Practice Partner, Principal or Manager having the initial contact with a prospective client. All material used to complete this checklist, (such as prior financial statements, tax returns, etc.) should be attached. Any questions which are not applicable should be marked N/A.

2. The completed checklists should be forwarded, along with any pertinent attachments, to the Chairman, Quality Control Committee. The Chairman will then convene a meeting of the Quality Control Committee.

3. When the process has been completed, this checklist should be filed in the client's permanent file and an engagement letter may then be sent to the client.

* * * * * * * * * *

NAME OF PROSPECTIVE CLIENT _____

ADDRESS: _____

_____

PHONE NUMBER: _____

CHECKLIST PREPARED BY:

_____	_____
Name	Date

* * * * * * * * * *

DECISION AS TO ACCEPTANCE (From Page 5):

Accept Client ☐

Do Not Accept Client ☐

CLIENT NOTIFIED BY:

_____	_____
Name	Date

A. CRITERIA FOR SUBMITTING ACCEPTANCE INFORMATION TO COMMITTEE

This form is required to be completed for the following:
(See Quality Control Document, Acceptance and Continuance of Clients)

Check if
Applicable

1. Publicly-held corporation (or broker/dealers) or where financial information will be submitted to potential investors. ☐

2. Where the annual fees is expected to exceed $10,000 or where the expected man-hour requirement exceeds 300 hours. ☐

3. Firms operating in high-risk industries, such as those industries where it is difficult to establish adequate systems of internal control or those industries whose operations are especially sensitive to general economic conditions. ☐

4. Firms in the development stage. ☐

5. Firms in financial difficulty. ☐

6. If there is a recent significant change, including a major change in one or more of the following:

   ● Management ☐

   ● Directors ☐

   ● Ownership ☐

   ● Legal counsel ☐

   ● Financial condition ☐

   ● Litigation status ☐

   ● Nature of the client's business ☐

   ● Scope of the auditor's work ☐

COMMENTS, IF ANY:

_____

_____

_____

B. VERIFICATION AND REVIEW PROCEDURES

1. Results of contact with predecessor accountants:

Firm Name
_____

Telephone Number
_____

Person Contacted (Name and Title)
_____

Results of Contact (including their opinion as to reasons for replacement)
_____
_____

2. Results of review of available financial information, including such items as latest available year-end and interim financial statements, tax returns, reports to regulatory agencies, registration statements, 10-K's, 10-Q's, 8-K's, etc.

ITEM REVIEWED	AS OF	FINDINGS
_____	_____	_____
_____	_____	_____
_____	_____	_____
_____	_____	_____

3. Results of contact with:

NAME (Firm and Individual Contacted)	TELEPHONE	RESULTS
Regular Attorney	_____	_____
		_____
SEC Attorney	_____	_____
		_____
Banker		_____
		_____
Underwriter	_____	_____
		_____
Other (Describe)	_____	_____
		_____
_____	_____	_____

4. Have the Company or its principals ever been charged with violations of any Federal, State or Local laws (such as securities, tax or anti-trust laws)? ☐ Yes ☐ No   If yes, give details and findings:

_____

_____

_____

5. Is there any pending litigation against the Company or its principals? ☐ Yes ☐ No   If yes, give details and potential outcome:

_____

_____

_____

6. Our opinion as to our ability to service the prospective client, taking into consideration such items as:

   a. Technical Skills Required _____

   _____

   b. Knowledge of Industry _____

   _____

   c. Availability of Qualified Personnel _____

   _____

   d. Other _____

   _____

7. Are there any potential unique accounting or auditing problems, such as in:

   ☐ Inventories

   ☐ Receivables

   ☐ Cutoffs

   ☐ Foreign Operations

   ☐ Dealings with Affiliates or Related Parties

   ☐ Consistency of Accounting Policies

   ☐ Internal Control

   ☐ Differences Between Financial Statement and Tax Return Reporting

   ☐ Other (or Explanations):

   _____

   _____

8. Details of any contemplated public offering:

Type: Primary   Secondary   Estimated Date of Filing: _____

Security: _____

Amount: _____

9. Purposes for which financial statements, with which Rachlin & Cohen will be associated, are to be used:

    _____

    _____

    _____

10. Who will prepare Form 8-K for replacement of auditors of record, if entity is publicly held? (Attach prior auditor's and company's letters as to reasons.)

    _____

    _____

    _____

11. Other Items or Comments:

    _____

    _____

    _____

C. SUMMARY

1. DECISION AS TO ACCEPTANCE:

		APPROVE	DISAPPROVE	REFER TO PARTNERS MEETING
Managing Partner	Date	☐	☐	☐
Director of Accounting & Auditing	Date	☐	☐	☐
Deputy Director of Accounting & Auditing	Date	☐	☐	☐

Note: Approval by the Managing Partner and the Director and Deputy Director of Accounting & Auditing must be unanimous. Any one of those three (who together comprise the Quality Control Committee) may request that the potential engagement be submitted to a partners' meeting for consideration. Acceptance at such a meeting shall require approval by at least two-thirds of the partners in attendance.

===

2. RESULTS AT PARTNERS' MEETING (if applicable):

Date of Partners' Meeting _____

Number of Partners:

	AMOUNT	%
Approving Acceptance		
Disapproving Acceptance		
Abstaining	——————	———
Total in Attendance	══════	═══

APPENDIX K

Long-Range Planning[1]

Exhibit	Title	Usage
K-1	Pro Forma Income Statement of Jefferson and Kaminski	An evaluation of whether this practice is worth purchasing for $275,000—or is there some way the firm can be helped?
K-2	Questions to Consider	Basis for stimulating discussions at planning session.
K-3	Growth Chart	Quantifying the past and future of the firm.
K-4	Agenda	A sample agenda for a partners' planning session in a resort area.
K-5	Checklist of Subjects	A list of subjects which can be considered for a firm's planning session.

[1]See STEP 10 for a discussion of long-range planning.

EXHIBIT K-1   Jefferson and Kaminski Pro Forma Income Statement (For Management Use Only)

Income:	Hours	Hourly Rate	
George W. Jefferson	2,800	$ 35	$ 98,000
Stanley L. Kaminski	3,000	30	90,000
Senior Accountant	2,000	25	50,000
	2,000	15	30,000
Total income	9,800	27	$268,000

Expenses:			
Senior accountant			$ 25,000
Junior accountant			15,000
Secretary			10,000
Rent			6,000
Telephone and utilities			4,000
Professional development			500
Practice development			500
Supplies and miscellaneous			2,000
Total expenses			63,000
Balance remaining for partners			$205,000

1. Clients
   a. Which clients are the most enthusiastic about us?
   b. Which clients have received the best service? Why?
   c. What clients did we lose and who got the worst service? Why?
   d. What kind of clients should we seek?
   e. What kind of clients should we discourage or get rid of?

   What to do: Define who our clients should be, where they are, and how we reach them.
2. Kinds of service
   a. What is the best kind of work we do?
   b. What is the worst kind of work we do?
   c. What are we known for?
   d. What is the most profitable work we do? Why?
   e. What is the least profitable work we do? Why?
   f. What kind of work should we add or expand?

   What to do: Define the services we should be rendering and how we should concentrate on them.
3. Present conditions
   a. What is the current status of the profession?
   b. How will litigation change the profession?
   c. How do you feel about peer group reviews?
   d. What is the present status of the community in which we operate?
   e. What is the present status of the economy and how will it affect us?
   f. What are our clients looking for under today's conditions?
   g. What are our prospective employees looking for?

   What do do: Analyze what is going on around us.
4. Future conditions
   a. What will our locality, state and country be like in the next five years?
   b. What will international conditions be like in the next five years ?
   c. What will accounting practice be like in the next five years?
   d. What services will clients be needing and how will we be able to satisfy these requirements?

   What to do: Project what we can expect in the future.

EXHIBIT K-3. **Growth Chart**

	History			Projection				
	1980	**1981**	**1982**	**1983**	**1984**	**1985**	**1986**	**1987**
Number of offices								
Number of partners								
Professional personnel								
Administrative personnel								
Annual billing (in thousands)	$	$	$	$	$	$	$	$
Income before partners' salaries	$	$	$	$	$	$	$	$

History: Where have you been?

Projection: Where are you going? How long will it take you to get there?

Agenda

Friday, 10 a.m.
Call to order; appoint secretary
Opening remarks by managing partner and program chairman
Progress and status of the firm
Major objectives of planning session
Review agenda for additions or changes

Long-range plan
   Review and update
   Appoint partners to update
   Distribute to all personnel
       Coffee break

Quality control document
   Status report
   Explanation of effect on firm

Practice development
   Proposed program
       Lunch

Newsletter
   Current effectiveness
   Proposed redesign

Disability insurance
   Partners
   Employees
Review agenda for Saturday
Adjourn at 3 p.m.

Saturday, 9 a.m.
Review of office opened last year
Consideration of new offices, short range and long range
Association affiliations
       Coffee break

Develop specific departmental objectives for 19X3–19X4
   Audit and review
   Small business services
   Tax
   Management consulting services
   Industry specialization
   Data processing services
   Internal administration

Review of clients gained and lost
       Lunch

Personnel
   Needs
   Development
   Firm party, annual picnic, personnel policies

Organization structure 19X3–19X4
Adjourn at 3 p.m.

Sunday, 9 a.m.
Budget for 19X3–19X4
  Billing rates
  Develop time budget
    Each employee
    Each partner
  Review revenues
  Review and project expenses

      Coffee break

Open floor for discussion
Summarize and finalize all conclusions, including timetables and responsibilities
Evaluate planning session
Adjourn at noon

EXHIBIT K-5. Checklist of Subjects for Your Partners' Planning Session[2]

Similar to the previous sample agenda, this is an extensive list of subjects which could be included on the agenda for your partners' planning session. It would probably be impossible to cover all these topics in one session, and many may not be currently applicable to your firm. But by reviewing this list, you will be able to select those subjects most relevant to the present operation of your firm and consider including these in your next planning session. (Or your first one!)

1. View of the practice
   a. Philosophical overview
   b. History of the firm
   c. Review of past years' operations
2. The environment in which we operate
   a. Status of the economy
   b. Politics—national and international
   c. Our state—past, present, future
   d. Our profession—what's happening:
      (1) The AICPA
      (2) FASB
      (3) SEC and other regulations
3. Financial administration
   a. Financial results of the past year
   b. Monitoring cash flow
   c. Establishing cash requirements and budget for next year
   d. Timekeeping—procedures and responsibilities
   e. Billing and collection—procedures and responsibilities
   f. Billing rates
   g. Financial controls—where new systems and procedures are needed
4. Client relations
   a. General expectations of the client
   b. Relationships with important clients
   c. Clients gained and referral sources
   d. Clients lost (why?)
   e. Type and size of new clients desired
   f. Client acceptance criteria
5. Firm management
   a. Effectiveness of partnership meetings
   b. Crisis management
   c. Areas where partner-staff relations need improvement
   d. Realignment of partner responsibilities?
   e. Review of systems, procedures, and decision-making approaches
      (1) Work selection
      (2) Client management
      (3) Billing procedures
      (4) Staff evaluation procedures
6. Partner compensation
7. Review of death, disability, and retirement benefits

8. Management of engagements
   a. Partner responsibilities
   b. Staff member responsibilities
   c. Administrative responsibilities
9. Staff management
   a. Hiring policies
   b. Promotion policies
   c. Remuneration policies
   d. Engagement assignments
   e. Junior supervision and evaluation
   f. Assessing partner potential
   g. Approaches to professional growth
10. Office administration
    a. Responsibilities of administrative manager
    b. Salary policy
    c. Work allocation priorities
    d. Problem areas that need special attention
    e. Future staff needs
    f. Telephone usage
    g. Copier usage
11. Paraprofessional training
12. Planning for the firm's growth
    a. Optimum client mix (how to achieve it)
    b. Size of firm desired
       (1) Number of partners
       (2) Number of staff
       (3) Number of paraprofessionals
    c. Admission of new partners
    d. Should firm consider mergers and acquisitions in next three to five years?
    e. Additional areas of practice
       (1) Management consultation
       (2) Computer services
       (3) Industry specialization
       (4) Governmental engagements
    f. Partner responsibilities in helping the firm grow
    g. Community involvement
    h. Locations for future offices
13. Follow-up plans
    a. Agenda for next partnership meeting at office
    b. Follow up on the plans made at planning session
       (1) Who is responsible for what?
       (2) By what date?
    c. Follow up implementation of policies formulated at session
       (1) Which partner responsible for which area?
       (2) Which staff members involved?
       (3) How should policies be communicated and executed?
       (4) How should partnership monitor the results?
14. Evaluation of the planning session and develop suggestions for future sessions

[2]Based on material from an article by Melvin Wallace, Ph.D., "How to Organize and Conduct an Annual Retreat" in *The Practical Accountant*, January–February 1978, p. 78.

INDEX

About the Author

Norman S. Rachlin opened his own CPA practice in Miami in 1955 with a handful of small clients, with his wife as a part-time assistant, and without capital. Through mergers and internal growth, that firm became one of the 100 largest CPA firms in America (based on 1979 AICPA memberships). It has three offices in South Florida, and its clients are spread throughout the country and overseas.

Mr. Rachlin has been the author or co-author of three courses offered by the American Institute of Certified Public Accountants (AICPA). He has written numerous articles for professional journals and has served as contributing editor for three of these journals. He has also been active on a number of national committees of the AICPA, and has served as chairman of the Management of an Accounting Practice Committee of the Florida Institute of CPAs. He is nationally known for his articles and for the seminars and speeches he has given before local, state, and national CPA organizations. His firm's newsletter is recognized throughout the United States.